The Extramercantile Economies of Greek and Roman Cities

Recent work on the ancient economy has tended to concentrate on market exchange, but other forces also caused goods to change hands. Such nonmarket transfers ranged from small private gifts to the wholesale confiscation of cities, lands, and their peoples. The papers presented in this volume examine aspects of this extramercantile economy, particularly benefaction and the role of associations, as well as their impact on the market economy.

This volume brings together ancient historians, New Testament scholars, and classicists to assess critically the New Institutional Economics framework. Combining theoretical approaches with detailed investigations of particular regions and topics, its chapters examine Greek economic thought, the benefits of membership in private associations, and the economic role of civic euergetism from classical Athens to the municipalities of Roman Spain.

The Extramercantile Economies of Greek and Roman Cities will be of use to those interested in the economic context of ancient religions, the role of associations in the economy, theoretical approaches to the study of the ancient economy, labor, and politics in the ancient city, as well as how Greek philosophers, from Xenophon to Philodemus, developed ethical ideas about economic behavior.

David B. Hollander is Associate Professor of History at Iowa State University, USA.

Thomas R. Blanton IV is Auxiliary Professor in New Testament Studies at the Lutheran School of Theology at Chicago, USA.

John T. Fitzgerald is Professor of New Testament and Early Christianity at the University of Notre Dame, USA.

Routledge Monographs in Classical Studies

Titles include:

Rethinking 'Authority' in Late Antiquity
Authorship, Law, and Transmission in Jewish and Christian Tradition
Edited by A.J. Berkovitz and Mark Letteney

Thinking the Greeks
A Volume in Honour of James M. Redfield
Edited by Bruce M. King and Lillian Doherty

Pushing the Boundaries of Historia
Edited by Mary C. English and Lee M. Fratantuono

Greek Myth and the Bible
Bruce Louden

Combined Warfare in Ancient Greece
From Homer to Alexander the Great and his Successors
Graham Wrightson

Power Couples in Antiquity
Transversal Perspectives
Edited by Anne Bielman Sánchez

The Bible, Homer, and the Search for Meaning in Ancient Myths
Why We Would Be Better Off With Homer's Gods
John Heath

The Extramercantile Economies of Greek and Roman Cities
New Perspectives on the Economic History of Classical Antiquity
Edited by David B. Hollander, Thomas R. Blanton IV, and John T. Fitzgerald

For more information on this series, visit: www.routledge.com/classicalstudies/series/RMCS

The Extramercantile Economies of Greek and Roman Cities

New Perspectives on the Economic History of Classical Antiquity

Edited by David B. Hollander, Thomas R. Blanton IV, and John T. Fitzgerald

Routledge
Taylor & Francis Group

LONDON AND NEW YORK

First published 2019
by Routledge
2 Park Square, Milton Park, Abingdon, Oxon OX14 4RN

and by Routledge
52 Vanderbilt Avenue, New York, NY 10017

Routledge is an imprint of the Taylor & Francis Group, an informa business

First issued in paperback 2021

British Library Cataloguing-in-Publication Data
A catalogue record for this book is available from the British Library

Library of Congress Cataloging-in-Publication Data
Names: Hollander, David B. (David Bruce), editor. | Blanton, Thomas R., 1968– editor. | Fitzgerald, John T., 1948– editor.
Title: The extramercantile economies of Greek and Roman cities : new perspectives on the economic history of classical antiquity / edited by David B. Hollander, Thomas R. Blanton IV, and John T. Fitzgerald.
Description: Abingdon, Oxon ; New York, NY : Routledge, 2109. | Series: Routledge monographs in classical studies | Includes bibliographical references and index.
Identifiers: LCCN 2018058187 (print) | LCCN 2018061758 (ebook) | ISBN 9781351004824 (ebook) | ISBN 9781351004817 (web pdf) | ISBN 9781351004794 (mobi/kindle) | ISBN 9781351004800 (epub) | ISBN 9781138544253 (hardback : alk. paper)
Subjects: LCSH: Economic history—To 500. | Greece—Economic conditions—To 146 B.C. | Rome—Economic conditions—510–30 B.C. | Rome—Economic conditions—30 B.C.–476 A.D. | Civilization, Ancient.
Classification: LCC HC31 (ebook) | LCC HC31 .E97 2019 (print) | DDC 330.938—dc23
LC record available at https://lccn.loc.gov/2018058187

ISBN: 978-1-138-54425-3 (hbk)
ISBN: 978-1-03-209308-6 (pbk)
ISBN: 978-1-351-00482-4 (ebk)

Typeset in Times New Roman
by Apex CoVantage, LLC

Contents

Contributors

Thomas R. Blanton IV is Auxiliary Professor in New Testament Studies at the Lutheran School of Theology at Chicago, USA. He is the author of *A Spiritual Economy: Gift Exchange in the Letters of Paul of Tarsus* (2017) and *Constructing a New Covenant: Discursive Strategies in the Damascus Document and Second Corinthians* (2007), and co-editor (with Raymond Pickett) of *Paul and Economics: A Handbook* (2017); his articles include "Economics and Early Christianity," in *Religious Studies Review* 43 (2017). Blanton is currently co-chair of the SBL Early Christianity and the Ancient Economy program unit.

John T. Fitzgerald is Professor of New Testament and Early Christianity at the University of Notre Dame, USA, and the author of numerous works dealing with Paul, including "Paul, Wine in the Ancient Mediterranean World, and the Problem of Intoxication," in *Paul's Graeco-Roman Context* (ed. Cilliers Breytenbach [2015]), *The Writings of St. Paul: Annotated Texts, Reception, and Criticism* (with Wayne A. Meeks, 2007), and *Cracks in an Earthen Vessel: An Examination of the Catalogues of Hardships in the Corinthian Correspondence* (1988). His edited volume *Passions and Moral Progress in Greco-Roman Thought* appears in the Routledge Monographs in Classical Studies series (Routledge, 2008). He is currently preparing a commentary on the Pastoral Epistles for the Hermeneia series.

Marc Domingo Gygax is Professor of Classics at Princeton University, USA. He is the author of *Untersuchungen zu den lykischen Gemeinwesen in klassischer und hellenistischer Zeit* (2001) and *Benefaction and Rewards in the Ancient Greek City: The Origins of Euergetism* (2016). His articles include "Gift-giving and Power-Relationships in Greek Social Praxis and Public Discourse," in *The Gift in Antiquity* (ed. Michael Satlow [2013]).

David B. Hollander is Associate Professor of History at Iowa State University, USA. He is the author of *Money in the Late Roman Republic* (2007) and *Farmers and Agriculture in the Roman Economy* (Routledge, 2018). He is an editor of *The Encyclopedia of Ancient History* and the co-editor with Tim Howe of the forthcoming *A Companion to Ancient Agriculture*.

John S. Kloppenborg is University Professor and Professor and Chair of the Department for the Study of Religion at the University of Toronto, Canada.

He has published widely in the field of synoptic studies, social history of Mediterranean antiquity, and the letter of James. His most recent publications are *Early Christians and Their Associations* (forthcoming 2019), *Luke on Jesus, Paul, and Earliest Christianity: What Did He Really Know?* (with J. Verheyden, 2017), *James, 1 & 2 Peter, and the Early Jesus Tradition* (with A. Batten, 2014), *Associations in the Greco-Roman World: A Sourcebook* (with P. Harland and R. Ascough, 2012), *Attica, Central Greece, Macedonia, Thrace*, vol. 1 of *Greco-Roman Associations: Texts, Translations, and Commentary* (with R. Ascough, 2011), and *The Tenants in the Vineyard: Ideology, Economics, and Agrarian Conflict in Jewish Palestine* (2006).

Rachel Meyers is Assistant Professor of Classical Studies at Iowa State University, USA. Her work on Roman portrait statues, architecture, cultural identity, and the practice of civic benefaction appears in numerous journals including the *American Journal of Archaeology*, the *Journal of Ancient History*, *Classical World*, and *L'Antiquité Classique*.

Nicolas Tran is Professor of Roman History at the University of Poitiers, France. He is the author of *Les membres des associations romaines* (2006), *Dominus tabernae: Le statut de travail des artisans et des commerçants de l'Occident romain* (2013), and *Rome, cité universelle, de César à Caracalla* (with P. Faure and C. Virlouvet, 2018). He is the editor of the *Cahiers du Centre Gustave Glotz* and coordinates the database project *Epigraphica Romana*.

Arjan Zuiderhoek is Associate Professor of Ancient History at the Department of History of Ghent University, Belgium. He is author of *The Politics of Munificence in the Roman Empire: Citizens, Elites and Benefactors in Asia Minor* (2009) and of *The Ancient City* (2017), and co-editor (with Paul Erdkamp and Koenraad Verboven) of *Ownership and Exploitation of Land and Natural Resources in the Roman World* (2015) and of *Capital, Investment, and Innovation in the Roman World* (forthcoming) and (with Wouter Vanacker) of *Imperial Identities in the Roman World* (Routledge, 2017).

Acknowledgements

The editors wish to thank our contributors for their papers, Amy Davis-Poynter at Routledge for accepting our volume for publication, as well as Elizabeth Risch and the editorial staff at Routledge for their help along the way. They also appreciate the input of Agnes Choi, Jinyu Liu, and Michelle Christian, all members of the Early Christianity and the Ancient Economy steering committee, as well as William Metcalf and Joseph Manning who, along with Jinyu Liu, shared with us numerous insights into the extramercantile economy. At Iowa State University, David Hollander would like to thank Simon Cordery, chair of the History Department, for his support, and Michael D. Bailey for advice on editorial matters. He is also grateful to William V. Harris and Dan Tompkins for sharing work on various topics. John T. Fitzgerald wishes to thank the Institute for Scholarship in the Liberal Arts (ISLA) at the University of Notre Dame for financial support of his scholarship in international contexts. Tom Blanton would like to thank Claudia D. Bergmann, Jörg Rüpke, and Benedikt Kranemann, the directors of the Research Center "Dynamics of Jewish Ritual Practices in Pluralistic Contexts from Antiquity to the Present" at the Max-Weber-Kolleg für kultur- und sozialwissenschaftliche Studien of the University of Erfurt, for their warm hospitality and collegiality during his term as a research fellow from July to December 2018, when – among other projects – the editing of the present volume took place.

Abbreviations and acronyms

Technical symbols, abbreviations, and eras

[]	brackets indicate a spurious work
BCE	Before Common Era
c.	century
ca.	circa
CE	Common Era
col(s).	column(s)
dem.	Demotic
ed(s).	editor(s), edited by, edition
e.g.	*exempli gratia*, for example
esp.	especially
i.e.	*id est*, that is
l(l).	line(s)
n(n).	note(s)
n.s.	new series
par(r).	parallel(s)
p(p).	page(s)
repr.	reprinted
rev.	revised
schol.	scholia (on)
suppl.	supplement
trans.	translator, translated by

Ancient texts

Alc.	Plutarch, *Alcibiades*
Ant.	Josephus, *Jewish Antiquities*
[Ath.]	Pseudo-Aristotle, *Athēnaiōn Politeia*; Pseudo-Xenophon, *Respublica atheniensium*
Ben.	Seneca, *On Benefits*
Bib. hist.	Diodorus of Sicily, *Library of History*
Cim.	Plutarch, *Cimon*

Cor.	Demosthenes, *On the Crown*
Dig.	Justinian, *Digest*
Ep.	Pliny the Younger, *Epistles*
Eth. eud.	Aristotle, *Eudemian Ethics*
Eth. nic.	Aristotle, *Nicomachean Ethics*
Flor.	Stobaeus, *Anthology*
Geogr.	Strabo, *Geography*
Hell.	*Hellenica*
Il.	Homer, *Iliad*
Lept.	Demosthenes, *Against Leptines*
Matt	Gospel of Matthew
Mem.	Xenophon, *Memorabilia*
Mor.	Plutarch, *Moralia*
Nat.	Pliny the Elder, *Natural History*
Nic.	Plutarch, *Nicias*
Nub.	Aristophanes, *Clouds*
Od.	Homer, *Odyssey*
Oec.	Xenophon, *Oeconomicus*; Theophrastus, *Oeconomica*
[Oec.]	Pseudo-Aristotle, *Oeconomica*
Oik.	Bryson, *Management of the Estate*
Op.	Hesiod, *Works and Days*
Or.	Dio Chrysostom, *Orations*
Per.	Plutarch, *Pericles*
Pol.	Aristotle, *Politics*
[Rhet. Alex.]	Pseudo-Aristotle, *Rhetoric to Alexander*
Top.	Aristotle, *Topics*
Vect.	Xenophon, *On Revenues* (or, *Ways and Means*)
Vesp.	Suetonius, *Vespasian*
Vit. phil.	Diogenes Laertius, *Lives of Eminent Philosophers*
VP	Iamblichus, *On the Pythagorean Way of Life*

Modern editions and other abbreviations

AE	*Année épigraphique*
AGJU	Arbeiten zur Geschichte des antiken Judentums und des Urchristentums
Agora	*The Athenian Agora*. Princeton: American School of Classical Studies at Athens, 1953 – .
BGU	*Aegyptische Urkunden aus den Königlichen* (later, *Staatlichen*) *Museen zu Berlin, Griechische Urkunden*. Berlin: Weidmann, 1895 – .
BSGRT	Bibliotheca Scriptorum Graecorum et Romanorum Teubneriana
BZNW	Beihefte zur Zeitschrift für die neutestamentliche Wissenschaft

CIL	*Corpus Inscriptionum Latinarum*. Berlin, 1862 – .
CILA	*Corpus de Inscripciones Latinas de Andalucía*. Edited by Julián González Fernández. Seville: Consejería de Cultura de la Junta de Andalucía, 1989 – .
CIMRM	*Corpus Inscriptionum et Monumentorum Religionis Mithriacae*. Edited by Maarten J. Vermaseren. Hagae Comitis: Nijhoff, 1956–1960.
EAH	*Encyclopedia of Ancient History*. 13 vols. Edited by Roger Bagnall, Kai Brodersen, Craige B. Champion, Andrew Erskine, and Sabine R. Huebner. Malden, MA: Wiley-Blackwell, 2013.
ECAE	Early Christianity and the Ancient Economy
FGrHist	*Die Fragmente der griechischen Historiker*. 2 vols. Edited by Felix Jacoby. Leiden: Brill, 1968.
FHSG	*Theophrastus of Eresus: Sources for His Life, Writings, Thought and Influence*. 2 vols. Edited by W.W. Fortenbaugh, P.M. Huby, R.W. Sharples, and D. Gutas. Leiden: Brill, 1992.
GDP	gross domestic product
GRA	*Greco-Roman Associations: Texts, Translations, and Commentary*. Edited by John S. Kloppenborg, Philip A. Harland, and Richard S. Ascough. 2 vols. Berlin: de Gruyter, 2011–2014.
HEp	*Hispania Epigraphica*. Madrid: Ministerio de Cultura, 1989 – .
IBeroia	*Inscriptiones Beroiae* [Greek]. Vol. 1 of *Inscriptiones Macedoniae Inferioris*. Edited by L. Gounaropoulou and M.B. Hatzopoulos. Athens: Hypourgeio Politismou, 1998.
IBulg.	*Spätgriechische und spätlateinische Inschriften aus Bulgarien*. Edited by Veselin Beševliev. Berlin: Akademie-Verlag, 1964.
IDelos	*Inscriptions de Délos*. 7 vols. Paris: Champion, 1926–1972.
IEph	*Die Inschriften von Ephesos*. Edited by Helmut Engelmann, Hermann Wankel, and Reinhold Merkelbach. 8 vols. Inschriften griechischer Stadte aus Kleinasien 11–17. Bonn: Habelt, 1979–1984.
IG	*Inscriptiones Graecae. Editio Minor*. Berlin: de Gruyter, 1924 – .
IGLAM	*Voyage archéologique en Grèce et en Asie Mineure, Tome III: Inscriptions grecques et latines recueillies en Asie Mineure*. Edited by Philippe Le Bas and William Henry Waddington. Paris: Didot, 1870.
IGRR	*Inscriptiones Graecae ad res Romanas Pertinentes*. Edited by René Cagnat et al. 3 vols. Paris: Leroux, 1906–1927.
ILER	*Inscripciones latinas de la España romana*. Edited by José Vives. Barcelona: Universidad de Barcelona, 1971–1972.

ILS	*Inscriptiones Latinae Selectae*. Edited by Hermann Dessau. Berlin: Weidmann, 1892–1916.
IRAl	*Inscripciones romanas de Almería*. Edited by Rafael Lazaro Perez. Almería: Cajal, 1980.
IRC	*Inscriptions romaines de Catalogne*. 5 vols. Edited by Georges Fabre, Marc Mayer, and Isabel Rodà. Paris: de Boccard, 1984–2002.
ISmyrna	*Die Inschriften von Smyrna*. Edited by Georg Petzl. Bonn: Habelt, 1982–1990.
JSNTSup	Journal for the Study of the New Testament, Supplement series
LCL	Loeb Classical Library
LNTS	Library of New Testament Studies
LSAM	*Lois sacrées de l'Asie Mineure*. Edited by Franciszek Sokolowski. Travaux et mémoires 9 (École française d'Athènes). Paris: de Boccard, 1955.
MnemosyneSup	Mnemosyne Supplement Series
NIE	New Institutional Economics
NovTSup	Supplements to Novum Testamentum
OGIS	*Orientis Graeci Inscriptiones Selectae*. Edited by Wilhelm Dittenberger. 2 vols. Leipzig: Hirzel, 1903–1905.
OIE	Original Institutional Economics
P.Assoc.	*Les associations religieuses en Égypte d'après les documents démotiques*. Edited by Françoise de Cenival. Cairo: Institut français d'archéologie orientale, 1972.
P.Bagnall	*Papyrological Texts in Honor of Roger S. Bagnall*. Edited by Rodney Ast, Hélène Cuvigny, Todd Michael Hickey, and Julia Lougovaya. Durham, NC: American Society of Papyrologists, 2013.
P.Berl.Spieg.	*Demotische Papyrus aus den königlichen Museen zu Berlin*. Edited by Wilhelm Spiegelberg. Leipzig: Giesecke & Devrient, 1902.
P.Bremen	*Die Bremer Papyri*. Edited by Ulrich Wilcken. Berlin: de Gruyter, 1936.
P.Cair.	*Service des Antiquités de l'Égypte, Catalogue Général des Antiquités égyptiennes du Musée du Caire: Die demotischen Denkmäler*. 3 vols. Edited by Wilhelm Spiegelberg. Leipzig: Drugulin, 1904–1932.
P.Hamb.	*Griechische Papyrusurkunden der Hamburger Staats- und Universitätsbibliothek*. 4 vols. Edited by Paul M. Meyer. Leipzig: Teubner, 1911–1924.
P.Hercul.	See *Catalogo dei papiri ercolanesi*. Edited by Marcello Gigante. Naples: Bibliopolis, 1979. See also *Manuale di papirologia ercolanese*. Edited by Mario Capasso. [Lecce]: Congedo, 1991.

PIR[2]	*Prosopographia Imperii Romani Saeculi I, II, III*. 2nd ed. Berlin: de Gruyter, 1933 – .
P.LilleDem	*Papyrus démotiques de Lille*. 3 vols. Edited by H. Sottas and Françoise de Cenival. Paris: Geuthner, 1921–1984.
P.Lond.	*Greek Papyri in the British Museum*. 7 vols. London: British Museum; Milan: Cisalpino-Goliardica, 1893–1974.
P.LouvreEisenlohr	Donker van Heel, Koenraad. *Abnormal Hieratic and Early Demotic Texts collected by the Theban Choachytes in the Reign of Amasis: Papyri from the Louvre Eisenlohr Lot*. PhD diss., Rijksuniversiteit te Leiden, 1996.
P.Mich.	*Michigan Papyri*. Ann Arbor: University of Michigan Press, 1931 – .
P.Mich.Zen.	*Zenon Papyri*. Vol. 1 of *Michigan Papyri*. Edited by C.C. Edgar. Ann Arbor: University of Michigan Press, 1931.
P.Mil.Vogl.	*Papiri della R. Università di Milano*. Edited by Achille Vogliano. Milan: Hoepli, 1937 – .
P.Oslo	*Papyri Osloenses*. Edited by Sam Eitrem and Leiv Amundsen. 3 vols. Oslo: Dybwad, 1925–1936.
P.Oxy.	*The Oxyrhynchus Papyri*. Edited by Bernard P. Grenfell and Arthur S. Hunt. London: Egypt Exploration Society, 1898 – .
P.Prag.	*Papyri Graecae Wessely Pragenses*. Edited by Rosario Pintaudi. 3 vols. Firenze: Gonnelli, 1988–2011.
P.Rain.Cent.	*Papyrus Erzherzog Rainer (P. Rainer Cent.): Festschrift zum 100-jährigen Bestehen der Papyrussammlung der Österreichischen Nationalbibliothek, Papyrus Erzherzog Rainer*. Vienna: Hollinek, 1983.
P.Sijpesteijn	*Papyri in Memory of P. J. Sijpesteijn*. Edited by A.J.B. Sirks and K.A. Worp. Oakville, Conn.: American Society of Papyrologists, 2007.
P.StanGreenDem	Demotic papyrus text. Stanford University Green Library Rare Books and Manuscripts collection.
P.Strasb.	*Griechische Papyrus der Kaiserlichen Universitäts- und Landes-bibliothek zu Strassburg*. Edited by Friedrich Preisigke. Leipzig: J.H. Hinrichs, 1912 – .
P.Tebt.	*The Tebtunis Papyri*. 5 vols. Edited by B.P. Grenfell, A.S. Hunt, and J.G. Smyly. London: Oxford University Press, 1902–2005.
P.Würzb.	*Mitteilungen aus der Würzburger Papyrussammlung*. Edited by Ulrich Wilcken. Berlin: de Gruyter, 1934.
RE	*Real-Encyclopädie der klassischen Altertumwissenschaft*. Edited by August F. Pauly, Georg Wissowa, and Wilhelm Kroll. Stuttgart: Metzler, 1894 – .
REG	*Revue des études grecques*
RIT	*Die römischen Inschriften von Tarraco*. Edited by Géza Alföldy. Berlin: de Gruyter, 1975.

SB	*Sammelbuch griechischer Urkunden aus Aegypten.* Edited by Friedrich Preisigke et al. Wiesbaden: Harrassowitz, 1915 – .
SBL	Society of Biblical Literature
SEG	*Supplementum Epigraphicum Graecum.* Leiden: Brill, 1923 – .
SIG	*Sylloge Inscriptionum Graecarum.* Edited by Wilhelm Dittenberger. 4 vols. 3rd ed. Leipzig: Hirzel, 1915–1924.
Stud.Pal.	*Studien zur Palaeographie und Papyruskunde.* Edited by Carl Wessely. Leipzig: Haessel, 1901–1924.
TAM	*Tituli Asiae Minoris.* Vienna: Hoelder-Pichler-Tempsky, 1901 – .
TM	*Trismegistos: An Interdisciplinary Portal of Papyrological and Epigraphical Resources.* Willy Clarysse et al., eds. Leuven: Katholieke Universiteit Leuven, 2005 – .
TSulp.	*Tabulae Pompeianae Sulpiciorum: edizione critica dell'archivio puteolano dei Sulpicii.* Edited by Giuseppe Camodeca. Rome: Quasar, 1999.
WGRW	Writings from the Greco-Roman World
WUNT	Wissenschaftliche Untersuchungen zum Neuen Testament

Introduction

John T. Fitzgerald, David B. Hollander, and
Thomas R. Blanton IV

The essays contained in this volume reflect the work of scholars associated with the Early Christianity and the Ancient Economy research project (henceforth ECAE). This project operates as a program unit of the Society of Biblical Literature (henceforth SBL), an international organization that fosters scholarship on the Bible and the ancient Mediterranean world. Since this volume is the first publication to appear fully under the auspices of the ECAE program unit, some description of its origins, activities, and goals seems appropriate. The reasons for the volume's focus specifically on what we have labeled the "extramercantile economy" are addressed in detail in Chapter 1 herein, by Thomas Blanton and David Hollander.

The ECAE project both builds on and contributes to contemporary research on the ancient economy. Modern scholarship on the ancient economy reflects the fact that history and the economy are so closely intertwined that it is impossible to study the history of any state without paying close attention to the vitality of its economy. Over time, the economies of all countries wax and wane, resulting in times of prosperity and adversity. The history of any people is, at least in part, the story of how they respond to this economic ebb and flow, a phenomenon that not only evokes creativity but also tests character. Given this dynamic relationship between history and the economy, historians of the ancient world have paid due attention to the economic aspects and conditions of the countries they have studied. This is especially true for both Greece and Rome,[1] with some historians giving particular attention to how ancient governments responded to economic crisis (e.g., Haskell, 1939; Marsh, 1943; MacMullen, 1976; Garnsey, 1988). Other historians have emphasized the extractive character of the economies of Greece and Rome (Bang, 2007, 2012; Boer and Petterson, 2017). Such approaches place theories of economic cycles in a different light: the economic "ebb" created in various provinces through the enforced extraction of goods and monies by plunder, tribute, and taxation contribute directly to the "flow" of economic prosperity in the imperial state. In our view, more research needs to be conducted on the complex interrelations between imperial states and their provinces.

Religion, though often neglected in studies of the economy, plays a role in all countries and inevitably in their economies. Sometimes religion's role is substantial, as in the temple-states of the ancient world or in the modern state of Israel, and sometimes it is peripheral, particularly in countries where the practice of religion (or of a specific religion) is proscribed. Religion contributes to the general economy at both the institutional and the personal level. At the institutional level, for example, religious groups may operate hospitals, medical clinics, orphanages, homes for the elderly, and youth camps, and they may also provide countless other social services. At the personal level, the members of various religious bodies, like other residents in a country, contribute to the economy in countless ways, not only by the goods that they produce and consume but also by the funds that they give to charities, political campaigns, professional organizations, and by the way they respond to economic challenges and the like.

Like all nations, all religions have economic aspects and face financial challenges. Many of the issues with which they deal have economic as well as ethical components, and many theological doctrines have considerable social, political, and economic ramifications. Although most scholars of religion readily acknowledge the role that religion plays in the economy and the economic aspects of religion itself, they have until recently paid substantially less attention to the issue of "religion and the economy" than historians and economists have to the issue of "history and the economy."

Symptomatic of this neglect is the absence of "unemployment" from most classics and Bible dictionaries.[2] It must be pointed out that the problem of unemployment, taken by contemporary economists as a key indicator of economic performance, is largely a by-product of urbanization; it is less an issue in economies characterized by subsistence production on land from which the laborers may retain and consume the produce.[3] Yet the issue of unemployment and what to do about it is certainly present in ancient texts commenting on economic conditions of particular cities. Josephus, for example, notes that when work on the so-called Herodian temple in Jerusalem was completed in the early 60s of the first century CE, more than eighteen thousand workers were faced with the prospect of unemployment, and a proposal was made to raise the height of the temple's east portico in order to keep the workers employed (*Ant.* 20.219). Agrippa II rejected that proposal as too costly and time-consuming, and he commissioned a much quicker and less expensive alternative project, thus postponing the problem of unemployment rather than dealing with it. Whether unemployment was a factor that contributed to the outbreak of the war against Rome in 66 is debated, but if true, it means that Agrippa II's solution was shortsighted.

The Roman emperor Vespasian had a different perspective. According to Suetonius,

> An engineer offered to haul some huge columns up to the Capitol at moderate expense by a simple mechanical contrivance, but Vespasian declined his services; "I must always ensure," he said, "that the working classes earn enough money to buy themselves food." Nevertheless, he paid the engineer a very handsome fee.
>
> (*Vesp.* 18, trans. R. Graves)

That Vespasian elected to spend more money in order to keep people at work rather than keep his expenses as low as possible says something about the emperor's understanding of the economy and of the government's role within it. But what was the understanding of the Christians in regard to the issue of unemployment, both before they came to power and after the time of Theodosius I? Was their attitude more akin to that of Agrippa II or to that of Vespasian, and how common were the perspectives of those two rulers? As yet, there are no clear answers to these questions.

Because early Christianity usually has been thought of simply as a religious movement (as opposed to a country or state), scholars have paid scant attention to many of its economic aspects and to the role that it played in the ancient economy. Consequently, the economic history of early Christianity has not yet been written. Nor is there even a commentary on the New Testament that focuses on the economic aspects of various passages. That is certainly not because economic issues were foreign to the first Christians. Indeed, one cannot even read through the first document in the canonical ordering of the New Testament, the Gospel of Matthew, without finding numerous references to various economic problems, issues, and conditions.[4] The same is true for every book of the New Testament.

Both demographically and geographically, early Christianity went through an incredible metamorphosis. It began as a Jewish sect centered in Jerusalem, yet by the end of the first century, its adherents were largely non-Jews drawn from the large urban centers of the Greco-Roman world. At that point, it was still a small and statistically insignificant religion, but by the end of the fourth century, it had become the official religion of the Roman Empire.[5] Throughout this period, it dealt with different economic issues, though the role that it played in the overall Roman economy was constantly changing and becoming more substantial. Furthermore, the economic life of Rome was by no means static during this period, as any number of studies vividly demonstrate.[6]

In the twentieth century, various scholars made important contributions to some of the economic issues in the New Testament and to the history of early Christianity and the ancient economy, but these treatments tended to be isolated studies focused on particular questions.[7] Furthermore, very few of these investigations were undertaken from the standpoint of the economic histories of Greece and Rome or informed by economic theory in the Greco-Roman world. In short, the economies and economic theories of antiquity had never been related to the history of early Christianity in any kind of comprehensive, systematic way.

In 2007, John T. Fitzgerald and Fika J. van Rensburg established an ongoing international, interdisciplinary project to address these questions and issues. The project seeks to delineate the relationship between early Christianity and the ancient economy in the period from Jesus to Justinian, demonstrating both similarities and differences in attitudes, approaches to problems, and attempted solutions. The chronological scope of this research project was intentionally left broad and explicitly designed to appeal to classicists and ancient historians as well as biblical and patristic scholars. Fitzgerald and van Rensburg were convinced that this kind of project was best pursued as a multidisciplinary endeavor, and thus sought to involve scholars with vastly different areas of expertise. To prevent the project from becoming too unwieldy, it was divided into three programs (or research areas), each with a specific focus. The first program involves a study of all the major aspects of the economy in the ancient world, especially the Roman Empire but also Classical and Hellenistic Greece. This volume is thus a product mainly of the first program.[8] The second program examines first-century Christianity both in relation to the ancient economy and in regard to its own economic aspects. The third program does the same for Christianity in the second to the fifth centuries.

Although the ECAE project officially began operating as a "consultation" at the 2008 annual meeting of the SBL in Boston, we held a preliminary, introductory session at the 2007 annual meeting in San Diego. Walter Scheidel was kind enough to deliver an inaugural presentation on "The Ancient Economy since Moses Finley." In the following decade, we organized more than twenty-five sessions at the annual and international meetings of the SBL, with participants coming from at least sixteen countries and representing the fields of New Testament studies, ancient history, patristics, archaeology, ancient Judaism, numismatics, and art history. Although it is difficult to track perfectly what becomes of particular papers after they are presented at meetings, at least two dozen papers have subsequently been published in some form.[9] At least six completed dissertations contain material first presented in our sessions. Furthermore, the program unit has served an important role in facilitating networking among scholars interested in economic aspects of early Christianity. The onset of the global financial crisis of 2007–2009 also seems to have stimulated interest in ancient economic history among both biblical scholars and classicists. In addition to a growing number of published and forthcoming studies on the subject,[10] recent years have seen the addition of two program units pertaining to the ancient economy in the SBL Annual Meeting (Economics in the Biblical World, Poverty in the Biblical World). These new units reflect biblical scholars' enhanced recognition of the importance of treating economic factors in dealing with ancient texts and their contexts.

The ECAE program unit also holds considerable significance for its contribution to the methods used to study biblical literature, Greek economic thought and practice, the culture of ancient Rome, and religion more broadly. In the history of theology and religious studies, religion has frequently been treated as a system of ideas or beliefs to which individual adherents cognitively assent. On the basis of this idealist approach, the material contexts and aspects of religion – including its economic aspects – are treated as secondary concerns, if they are addressed at all. As a corrective to this overemphasis on the ideational aspects of religion, the academy is now experiencing what some have called a "material turn."[11] Renewed attention is now being paid to the material components of religion: ritual objects; architectural spaces; the production, use, and consumption of food, clothing, housing, and other resources; and the physical bodies that produce and reproduce religiosocial systems. As the production, transmission, and consumption of material products are definitive aspects of all economies, the ECAE research project hopes to contribute to this "material turn" in the study of religion by examining the economic aspects of early Christianity and imperial Rome, while at the same time maintaining its focus on the ideas and ideals that served to structure material exchanges.

The ECAE program unit plans to continue its examination of the extramercantile economy in future sessions and publications. In the next phase of our work, we intend to assess the economic effects of Roman imperialism on the regional economies of Galilee and Judea. Specific issues that we plan to address include refugeeism, taxation, the state of the Galilean economy before and after the Roman invasion of 67 CE, banditry, and the claiming of the balsam plantations at En Gedi as a territory of the Roman fiscus. We anticipate that these future studies will be published in the near future as a complement to the present volume.

Notes

1 See discussion in Chapter 1 of this volume.
2 The term does, however, appear as an entry in the *Encyclopedia of Ancient History*. See Mac Mahon (2013).
3 On subsistence production, see Boer and Petterson (2017: xi–xii, 131–3).
4 For example, the command to give to beggars and not refuse to loan money (Matt 5:42) and a discussion of taxation (Matt 17:24).
5 On the demographic, geographic, theological, and political changes involved in the metamorphosis of early Christianity, see Fitzgerald and Green (2011: 368–71).
6 Indeed, much current work on the Roman economy focuses on quantifying the economic changes Rome experienced during the Republic and empire. See, for example, Bowman and Wilson (2009).
7 The most important contribution is probably that of Grant (1977), who treats both the New Testament and the early church, offering treatments of "Taxation and Exemption" (44–65), "Work and Occupations" (66–95), "Private Property" (96–123), "The Organization of Alms" (124–45), and "Temples, Churches, and Endowments" (146–64). See also Bassler (1991), Gnuse (1985), Hengel (1974), and Johnson (1977).
8 David Hollander joined the project in 2007, while Tom Blanton joined in 2014. Jinyu Liu, Michelle Christian, and Agnes Choi also now serve on the steering committee.
9 These publications include Adams (2013), Aviam (2013), Batten (2009, 2014), Brookins (2013, 2014), De Wet (2015), Downs (2008), Fiensy (2012, 2013), Fuhrmann (2012), Goodrich (2012a, 2012b), Hays (2010, 2011), Howes (2015), Ogereau (2014a, 2014b, 2014c), Rhee (2012), Standhartinger (2013), and Welborn (2013).
10 For example, Blanton and Pickett (2017), Brown (2012, 2015), Longenecker (2010), Rhee (2017), and Downs (2016); see also the review article of Blanton (2017) for an overview of works on early Christianity and the ancient economy published between 2012 and 2016.
11 This phrase appears to have been introduced by Hazard (2013).

Bibliography

Adams, Edward. *The Earliest Christian Meeting Places: Almost Exclusively Houses?* London: Bloomsbury T&T Clark, 2013.

Aviam, Mordechai. "People, Land, Economy and Belief in First-Century Galilee and Its Origins: A Comprehensive Archaeological Synthesis." Pages 5–48 in *The Galilean Economy in the Time of Jesus*. Edited by David A. Fiensy and Ralph A. Hawkins. Atlanta: Society of Biblical Literature, 2013.

Bang, Peter Fibiger. "Predation." Pages 197–217 in *The Cambridge Companion to the Roman Economy*. Edited by Walter Scheidel. Cambridge: Cambridge University Press, 2012.

———. "Trade and Empire: In Search of Organizing Concepts for the Roman Economy." *Past and Present* 195 (2007): 3–54.

Bassler, Jouette M. *God and Mammon: Asking for Money in the New Testament*. Nashville: Abingdon, 1991.

Batten, Alicia J. "Neither Gold Nor Braided Hair (1 Timothy 2:9; 1 Peter 3:3): Adornment, Gender, and Honour in Antiquity." *New Testament Studies* 55 (2009): 484–501.

———. "The Paradoxical Pearl: Signifying the Pearl East and West." Pages 233–50 in *Dressing Judeans in Antiquity*. Edited by K. Upson-Saia, C. Daniel-Hughes, and Alicia J. Batten. Burlington: Ashgate, 2014.

Blanton, Thomas R., IV. "Economics and Early Christianity." *Religious Studies Review* 43 (2017): 93–100.

Blanton, Thomas R., IV, and Raymond Pickett, eds. *Paul and Economics: A Handbook*. Minneapolis: Fortress, 2017.

Boer, Roland, and Christina Petterson. *Time of Troubles: A New Economic Framework for Early Christianity*. Minneapolis: Fortress, 2017.

Bowman, Alan K., and A.J.N. Wilson, eds. *Quantifying the Roman Economy: Methods and Problems*. Oxford: Oxford University Press, 2009.

Brookins, Timothy. *Corinthian Wisdom, Stoic Philosophy, and the Ancient Economy*. Cambridge: Cambridge University Press, 2014.

———. "The (In)frequency of the Name 'Erastus' in Antiquity: A Literary, Papyrological, and Epigraphical Catalog." *New Testament Studies* 59 (2013): 496–516.

Brown, Peter. *The Ransom of the Soul: Afterlife and Wealth in Early Western Christianity*. Cambridge: Harvard University Press, 2015.

———. *Through the Eye of a Needle: Wealth, the Fall of Rome, and the Making of Christianity in the West, 350–550 AD*. Princeton: Princeton University Press, 2012.

De Wet, Chris. *Preaching Bondage: John Chrysostom and the Discourse of Slavery in Early Christianity*. Oakland: University of California Press, 2015.

Downs, David J. *Alms: Charity, Reward, and Atonement in Early Christianity*. Waco: Baylor University Press, 2016.

———. *The Offering of the Gentiles: Paul's Collection for Jerusalem in its Chronological, Cultural, and Cultic Contexts*. Tübingen: Mohr Siebeck, 2008.

Fiensy, David A. "Assessing the Economy of Galilee in the Late Second Temple Period: Five Considerations." Pages 165–86 in *The Galilean Economy in the Time of Jesus*. Edited by David A. Fiensy and Ralph A. Hawkins. Atlanta: Society of Biblical Literature, 2013.

———. "Did Large Estates Exist in Lower Galilee in the First Half of the First Century CE?" *Journal for the Study of the Historical Jesus* 10 (2012): 133–53.

Fitzgerald, John T., and William Scott Green. "Conclusions, Observations, and Limitations: Reflections on the Visions of the Social Order Collaborative Project." Pages 363–76 in *Judaic and Christian Visions of the Social Order: Describing, Analyzing, and Comparing Systems of the Formative Age*. Edited by Jacob Neusner, Bruce D. Chilton, and Alan J. Avery-Peck. Lanham: University Press of America, 2011.

Fuhrmann, Sebastian. "Leben verlieren und Leben finden: Nachfolge und Martyrium in den Evangelien." Pages 167–89 in *Martyriumsvorstellungen in Antike und Mittelalter: Leben oder Sterben für Gott*. Edited by Sebastian Fuhrmann and R. Grundmann. Leiden: Brill, 2012.

Garnsey, Peter. *Famine and Food Supply in the Graeco-Roman World: Responses to Risk and Crisis*. Cambridge, UK and New York: Cambridge University Press, 1988.

Gnuse, Robert K. *You Shall Not Steal: Community and Property in the Biblical Tradition*. Mayknoll: Orbis, 1985.

Goodrich, John. *Paul as an Administrator of Good in 1 Corinthians*. Cambridge: Cambridge University Press, 2012. (2012b).

———. "Voluntary Debt Remission and the Parable of the Unjust Steward (Luke 16:1–13)." *Journal of Biblical Literature* 131 (2012): 547–66. (2012a).

Grant, Robert M. *Early Christianity and Society: Seven Studies*. San Francisco: Harper & Row, 1977.

Haskell, Henry J. *The New Deal in Old Rome: How Government in the Ancient World Tried to Deal with Modern Problems*. New York: Knopf, 1939.

Hays, Christopher M. *Luke's Wealth Ethics: A Study in Their Coherence and Character*. Tübingen: Mohr Siebeck, 2010.

———. "Resumptions of Radicalism: Christian Wealth Ethics in the Second and Third Centuries." *Zeitschrift für die neutestamentliche Wissenschaft und die Kunde der älteren Kirche* 102 (2011): 261–82.

Hazard, Sonia. "The Material Turn in the Study of Religion." *Religion and Society: Advances in Research* 4 (2013): 58–78.

Hengel, Martin. *Property and Riches in the Early Church: Aspects of a Social History of Early Christianity*. Philadelphia: Fortress, 1974.

Howes, Llewellyn. "Agricultural Slavery and the Parable of the Loyal and Wise Slave in Q 12:42–46." *Acta Classica* 58 (2015): 70–110.

Johnson, Luke Timothy. *The Literary Function of Possessions in Luke-Acts*. Society of Biblical Literature Dissertation Series 39. Missoula: Scholars Press, 1977.

Longenecker, Bruce W. *Remember the Poor: Paul, Poverty, and the Greco-Roman World*. Grand Rapids, MI: Eerdmans, 2010.

Mac Mahon, Ardle. "Unemployment." *EAH* (2013): 6915–16.

MacMullen, Ramsay. *Roman Government's Response to Crisis, AD 235–337*. New Haven: Yale University Press, 1976.

Marsh, Frank B. *Modern Problems in the Ancient World*. Austin: The University of Texas Press, 1943.

Ogereau, Julien M. "The Earliest Piece of Evidence of Christian Accounting: The Significance of the Phrase εἰς λόγον δόσεως καὶ λήμψεως (Phil 4:15)." *Comptabilité(S): Revue d'histoire des comptabilités* 6 (2014): 1–16. (2014b).

———. *Paul's Koinonia with the Philippians: A Socio-Historical Investigation of a Pauline Economic Partnership*. Tübingen: Mohr Siebeck, 2014. (2014c).

———. "Paul's Κοινωνία with the Philippians: Societas as a Missionary Funding Strategy." *New Testament Studies* 60.3 (2014): 360–78. (2014a).

Rhee, Helen. *Loving the Poor, Saving the Rich: Wealth, Poverty, and Early Christian Formation*. Grand Rapids: Baker Academic, 2012.

———, ed. *Wealth and Poverty in Early Christianity*. Ad Fontes: Early Christian Sources. Minneapolis: Fortress, 2017.

Standhartinger, Angela. "'Und alle aßen und wurden satt' (Mk 6,42 par.): Die Speisungserzählungen im Kontext römisch-hellenistischer Festkulturen." *Biblische Zeitschrift* 57.1 (2013): 60–81.

Welborn, Laurence. "'That There May Be Equality': The Contexts and Consequences of a Pauline Ideal." *New Testament Studies* 59 (2013): 73–90.

1 The extramercantile economy

An assessment of the New Institutional
Economics paradigm in relation
to recent studies of ancient Greece
and Rome*

Thomas R. Blanton IV and David B. Hollander

As the area of economic theory known as New Institutional Economics, or NIE, has been utilized in recent studies of the economies of Greece and Rome – most notably in the *Cambridge Economic History of the Greco-Roman World* – some critical reflection on the origins, main themes, and assumptions built into the theoretical model is desirable. In this chapter, we seek to identify some of the strengths, weaknesses, and limitations inherent in the model. This chapter proceeds in three major steps: (1) it briefly describes the historical process by which "economics" was increasingly restricted to the market economy, (2) it describes the emergence of NIE within the field of economics and its subsequent adoption in studies of Greek and Roman economies, and (3) it provides reasons why economic historians of ancient Greece and Rome should consider the significant role of extramercantile transmissions of goods and services – that is, transmissions that occur outside of the marketplace – as they develop and elaborate theoretical models of "the ancient economy."

The reduction of "economy" to "market" in classical and neoclassical economic theory

The field of economics has a long history of restricting its purview to encompass only exchanges that occur within the context of the marketplace – a restriction that is incompletely overcome by NIE. We note here only two illustrative examples within the history of classical (mid- to late 1800s) and neoclassical (late 1800s to present) economic thought that indicate this trend. During a formative stage of what later would become the discipline of economics proper, John Stuart Mill wrote the following in his *Essays on Some Unsettled Questions of Political Economy*, first published in 1844:

> What is now commonly understood by the term "Political Economy" is not the science of speculative politics, but a branch of that science. It does not treat of the whole of man's nature as modified by the social state, nor of the whole conduct of man in society. It is concerned with him solely as a being who desires to possess wealth, and who is capable of judging of the

comparative efficacy of means for obtaining that end. It predicts only such of the phenomena of the social state as take place in consequence of the pursuit of wealth. It makes entire abstraction of every other human passion or motive. . . . Political Economy considers mankind as occupied solely in acquiring and consuming wealth; and aims at showing what is the course of action into which mankind, living in a state of society, would be impelled, if that motive . . . were absolute ruler of all their actions.

(Mill, 1874: Essay 5)

Mill hastens to add: "Not that any political economist was ever so absurd as to suppose that mankind are really thus constituted, but because this is the mode in which science must necessarily proceed" (Mill, 1874: Essay 5). Mill's restriction of the purview of "political economy" – the forerunner of what later would be termed simply "economics" – to "only such of the phenomena of the social state as take place in consequence of the pursuit of wealth" through mercantile exchange occurs in the context of a larger argument in which he attempts to establish "political economy" as a "science" that aims to uncover the putative "laws" governing wealth production. Mill's eagerness to validate economics as a "science" is coupled with a frank admission that the study of the "political economy" is predicated on a methodological reduction of human motive and action to the creation of wealth through mercantile production, exchange, and consumption. This reduction Mill takes to be the precondition necessary to define economics as a science: economics is to wealth production as the theory of projectiles is to the art of gunnery, or as trigonometry is to land surveying (Mill, 1874: Essay 5).

The same methodological reduction is evident in Alfred Marshall's *Principles of Economics*. First published in 1890, the influential work was printed in its eighth edition in 1920, and that was reprinted by Palgrave Macmillan as recently as 2013. Marshall writes:

Political economy or economics is a study of mankind in the ordinary business of life; it examines that part of individual and social action which is most closely connected with the attainment and with the use of the material requisites of well-being. Thus it is on one side a study of wealth; and on the other, and more important side, a part of the study of man. For man's character has been moulded by his every-day work, and the material resources which he thereby procures, more than by any other influence unless it be that of his religious ideals.

(Quoted in Medema and Samuels, 2003: 504)

Again, we see the same methodological reduction: economics "examines that part of individual and social action" connected with well-being – wealth, work, and material resources. Like Mill before him, Marshall recognizes that human behavior is not reducible to activities within the marketplace, as the quote continues: "The two great forming agencies of the world's history have been the religious and the economic" (quoted in Medema and Samuels, 2003: 504). That said, Marshall also follows Mill when he constricts the purview of economics to include those aspects of human behavior most directly related to the marketplace.[1] Economics does not, for example, include what Marshall construes as the second "great forming agency of the world's history," religion, within its purview.

Closely connected to the tendency of classical economists, such as Smith, and neoclassical theorists, such as Marshall, to restrict the purview of "economics" to the activities of the marketplace was a second tendency: to describe economic activity in mathematical terms. The mathematization of economics constituted an attempt to establish economics as a "science," on par with the other sciences that were gaining prominence during the nineteenth century, and effectively isolated those aspects of market activity that were in theory quantifiable from extramercantile aspects of human society. William Stanley Jevons was an early exponent of this view. In his *Theory of Political Economy* (1871), he wrote:

> It is clear that Economics, if it is to be a science at all, must be a mathematical science. There exists much prejudice against attempts to introduce the methods and language of mathematics into any branch of the moral sciences. . . . My theory of Economics, however, is purely mathematical in character. . . . The theory consists in applying the differential calculus to the familiar notions of wealth, utility, value, demand, supply, capital, interest, labour, and all the other quantitative notions belonging to the daily operations of industry. As the complete theory of almost every other science involves the use of that calculus, so we cannot have a true theory of Economics without its aid.
>
> (Quoted in Medema and Samuels, 2003: 415–16)

Jevons has a clear idea of the purview of economics, which is limited to the examination of "wealth, utility, value, demand, supply, capital, interest, labour, and all the other quantitative notions belonging to the daily operations of industry."

The mathematization of (neoclassical) economics evident already in Jevons's work would later blossom into what Mark Blaug identifies as the "formalist revolution" of the late 1940s and 1950s:

> The metamorphosis of economics in the late 1940s and 1950s is aptly called a "formalist revolution" because it was marked, not just by a preference, but by an absolute preference for the form of an economic argument over its content. This frequently, but not necessarily, implied reliance on mathematical modeling because its ultimate objective was to emulate the notorious turn-of-the-century Hilbert program in mathematics by achieving the complete axiomatization of economic theories.
>
> (Blaug, 2003: 145)

Just as mathematician David Hilbert attempted theoretically to ground the foundations of mathematics in a finite number of axioms that could be shown to be internally consistent, Blaug argues, economists turned to formal and mathematical models based on axioms that, while internally consistent, did not necessarily reflect "real world" conditions. The result is that economic theory has become increasingly self-referential and has lost its grounding in the observable economic activity that takes place in markets. Blaug's argument implies that since the 1950s, neoclassical economic discourse has distanced itself not only from extramercantile factors that structure exchange but even from the observable functioning of "real-world" market activity.[2]

Thomas Piketty offers a colorful critique of the state of the field of neoclassical economics that echoes some of the criticisms identified by Blaug. In his analysis of the global distribution of income in the early decades of the twenty-first century, Piketty describes the reasons for his departure from an academic post in the United States to return to his native France, where, in his view, economists are less insulated from social scientists in other fields. He offers the following critique of the state of his field, particularly as it is practiced in the United States:

> To put it bluntly, the discipline of economics has yet to get over its childish passion for mathematics and for purely theoretical and often highly ideological speculation, at the expense of historical research and collaboration with other social sciences. Economists are all too often preoccupied with petty mathematical problems of interest only to themselves. This obsession with mathematics is an easy way of acquiring the appearance of scientificity without having to answer the far more complex questions posed by the world we live in.
>
> (Piketty, 2014: 41)

Piketty's comments ought not be taken to imply that he does not make use of mathematics in his work. On the contrary, he uses mathematical analyses to show that in periods when the rate of return on capital exceeds overall economic growth, the result is the concentration of capital in fewer hands over time (as described in the formula $\beta = s/g$, where β indicates the capital/income ratio, s = savings, and g = national economic growth) (Piketty, 2014: 166). But for Piketty, purely mathematical reasoning or deduction from axioms provides only a "first approximation" that must be adjusted in light of additional "real world" data (e.g., Piketty, 2014: 136, 191–4, 396–7, 453).

Although Piketty is not classified as an institutional economist, institutional economics in its various forms shares his conviction that economics ought not be content to elaborate mathematical models that bear a dubious relationship to real-world transactions, but ought instead to address "the . . . complex questions posed by the world we live in." The methods and perspectives used to understand complex, real-world transactions, however, are diverse, as the following brief survey of the field of institutional economics indicates.

The rise of institutional economics

The origins of institutional economics are frequently traced to Thorstein Veblen, who linked his emphasis on the institutional context of economic activity with an evolutionary approach derived from Charles Darwin – an approach that Veblen took as the hallmark of science in his day (Chavance, 2009: 10–11). Veblen's emphasis "on the process of economic change above all else" remains a central component of Douglass North's formulations almost exactly one century later, as we will see (Chavance, 2009: 10). John R. Commons is also seen as a founder of institutional economics; Commons pointed to the role of law in settling "conflicts between interest groups" and guiding "individual behavior in such a way that a better outcome results for the whole of society": law is thus viewed as a key building block of the institutional framework of the capitalist economy (Groenewegen, Spithoven, and van den Berg, 2010: 87).

More recent iterations of institutional economics are sometimes labeled "Original Institutional Economics" (OIE) to distinguish them from NIE. Unlike NIE, they do not necessarily grant the construct of the market pride of place in their formulations. Institutional economists Marc Tool and Warren Samuels, for example, instead take as central the postulate that "the economy is a system of power," with power defined as "the capacity and opportunity to exercise discretion over the rules that organize social life" (Tool and Samuels, 1989: vii–viii). Power, however, is a notoriously vague and abstract construct, and can be taken only as an entrée to a more detailed examination of institutions and social relations. Wallace Peterson understands power as operating through the agency of families, social groups, firms, corporations, trade unions, and other institutions, while William Dugger emphasizes the roles of economic, educational, military, kinship, political, and religious institutions in mediating power (Peterson, 1989; Dugger, 1989). Dugger notes that power does not operate autonomously, but is "literally and figuratively incorporated into an institutional structure of corporate hegemony" (Dugger, 1989: 137). Whereas OIE tends to position itself in opposition to neoclassical tenets (e.g., methodological individualism), NIE tends to position itself more firmly within the tradition of neoclassical economics, even though it rejects or modifies several neoclassical assumptions.[3]

New Institutional Economics refers to that branch of economic theory most closely associated with the work of Oliver Williamson, Ronald Coase, and Douglass North, who together founded the International Society for New Institutional Economics in 1997 (Ménard and Shirley, 2014: 19). New Institutional Economics does not represent a single, internally consistent theoretical construct, but rather is an evolving "conceptual framework" that incorporates significant internal diversity, as the following brief overview suggests.[4]

Ronald Coase contributed to the development of NIE by emphasizing the ineffectiveness of neoclassical assumptions to explain why firms arose: if resources are allocated solely on the basis of the "automatic" adjustment of supply in response to demand, then it should be equally as cost-effective for entrepreneurs to conduct transactions independently as to coordinate their actions within a firm. By what incentive do firms arise? The answer is that firms reduce *transaction costs* – costs associated with searching for materials and finding the best price for them, and drawing up and enforcing contracts – and spread the risk associated with price fluctuations.[5] Transaction costs are not considered in abstract supply and demand functions, but they have a direct bearing on "real-world" business dealings.

Oliver Williamson, who refers to his work as "transaction cost economics," elaborated Coase's insights by detailing the conditions under which "vertical integration," or the formation of a hierarchically ordered firm, is more efficient than exchange on the open market. These include situations in which protracted bargaining between independent parties is foreseen, when intraorganizational conflict resolution is less costly than interorganizational resolution, and when the technical complexity of a product favors incorporating various stages of production rather than supplying them through the open market (Williamson, 1971, 2010).

Unlike Coase and Williamson, Douglass North has applied the tools of economic analysis to the study of economic history. For that reason, North's work has had a greater influence in fields that, like classical studies, involve the study of ancient economic history. However, significant shifts took place within North's work over time as he progressively rejected several neoclassical economic assumptions, as Bernard Chavance has noted.[6] In what follows, we consider only a few of North's notable contributions to the field of economic history and briefly note developments in his thought.

In a salient passage that was utilized as a point of departure in the *Cambridge Economic History of the Greco-Roman World*, North describes a research agenda that applies the concepts of NIE to the study of economic history:

> I take it as the task of economic history to explain the structure and performance of economies through time. By "performance" I have in mind the typical concerns of economists – for example, how much is produced, the distribution of costs and benefits, or the stability of production. The primary emphasis in explaining production is on total output, output per capita, and the distribution of income of the society. By "structure" I mean those characteristics of a society which we believe to be the basic determinants of performance. Here I include the political and economic institutions, technology, demography, and ideology of a society. "Through time" means that economic history should explain temporal changes in structure and performance. Finally, "explanation" means explicit theorizing and the potential of refutability.[7]
>
> (North, 1981: 3)

Although North makes some important criticisms of neoclassical economic assumptions, including the assumption of instrumental rationality, the construct of the wealth-maximizing individual, the notion of fully informed parties who calculate costs and benefits correctly, the understanding of price as a sufficient allocative mechanism, and the convenient fiction of costless transactions, the focus of his work clearly remains on the construct of the market.[8] This is indicated first by his use of the key term *performance* – by which North refers to "the typical concerns of economists," including production costs, output per capita, and income distribution – and second by identifying factors such as institutions, technology, demography, and ideology, all of which are understood to play significant roles as the "basic determinants" of performance. The market is the central construct in this framework: the institutionalized "basic determinants" are discussed only to the extent that they either facilitate or hinder the functioning of the marketplace and thus either promote or hinder economic growth. In short, in the 1980s and 1990s, North's work took a decisive step beyond neoclassical economics in that it took both ideology and institutions specifically into account, but it remained hampered by its neoclassical roots in that it analyzed institutions only to the extent that they were understood either to promote or to hinder the development of markets. Since neoclassical assumptions alone proved inadequate to explain historical data, institutional analysis assumed an increasing role as an aid to understanding the primary object of study, market performance.

More recently, with John Joseph Wallis and Barry R. Weingast, North co-wrote *Violence and Social Orders*, ambitiously subtitled *A Conceptual Framework for Interpreting Recorded Human History*. The book assumes the neoclassical notion that perfect competition improves the functioning of markets and applies that notion to the political sphere, arguing that, in an analogous fashion, ideologies and practices that facilitate unfettered, egalitarian participation in representative democracy improve the functioning of societies by creating conditions conducive to the formation of "open access orders." Such societies place limits on economically and socially destructive patterns of violence by imposing a monopoly on its legitimate use: the right to use violence is monopolized by the representative government. In this work, markets and sociopolitical systems are viewed as existing in an interactive and symbiotic relation. The book clearly stands in the trajectory of North's earlier work in that it focuses on market activity and emphasizes the role that institutions play in shaping that activity. In *Violence and Social Orders*, however, the market does not retain the same place of preeminence within the theoretical model that it had assumed during the 1980s and 1990s; it rather takes its place *alongside* institutional structures as the twin poles with respect to which the model is oriented.[9]

The adoption of NIE in classical studies

Despite its considerable influence elsewhere, ancient historians were slow to embrace NIE. There are many reasons for this, but the main ones are no doubt that, of the two major schools of thought within classical studies, one simply denied the applicability of modern economics to the ancient economy, whereas the other seems to have been largely unaware or uninterested in how the field of economics was developing.

The debate over the nature of the ancient economy goes back at least to the nineteenth century, and there are many accounts of its earlier stages.[10] Thus we will be brief. The debate begins with the works of Karl Bücher (1893) and Eduard Meyer (1895). Bücher saw the ancient economy as primarily based on the *oikos* and thus at an early stage of economic development, that is, *not* a market economy. This is sometimes referred to as the primitivist position. By contrast,

Eduard Meyer saw many similarities between the ancient economy and his own. This "modernist" position, at least in its initial form, would strike most scholars today as highly anachronistic. Tenney Frank and Mikhail Rostovtzeff are usually considered (perhaps unjustly) as the leading exponents of the modernist perspective in the first half of the twentieth century. A related debate, that between formalists and substantivists, owes its inception to Karl Polanyi. As Willem Jongman describes it, the substantivist position "represents a cultural explanation of economic behavior (the economy is 'embedded')," while "formal economics only applies if the economy has a system of price-making markets" (which, Polanyi argued, was a relatively recent development).[11] Polanyi was, of course, a major influence on Moses Finley, to whose work we must now turn.

Finley's *The Ancient Economy*, first published in 1973, came to dominate debate over the nature of the ancient economy from the 1970s through at least the 1990s. Finley's position is usually characterized as primitivist, although some have called it substantivist or minimalist, or a combination of primitivism, substantivism, and minimalism. Ian Morris noted in his 1999 foreword to an updated edition of *The Ancient Economy* that "it is notoriously difficult to find a sentence or two in Finley's articles and books that serve to sum up his whole argument" (Morris, 1999: xix). That being said, central to Finley's view of the ancient economy was that it was underdeveloped, and was dominated by subsistence agriculture and consumer cities; furthermore, it had little technological innovation, economic rationality, long-distance trade, capital investment in productivity, or economic growth, and, fundamentally, was embedded in societies where status was of paramount concern.[12]

Finley's critics have attacked many aspects of his position and, despite dominating discussions of the nature of the ancient economy for decades, Morris is surely right in saying that Finley "never commanded majority support among classicists" (Morris, 2002: 27). Both his methodology and conclusions came under sustained criticism. Jean Andreau, for example, noted Finley's distrust of archaeology, while David J. Mattingly and others have argued that there was considerably more long-distance trade than Finley "was prepared to admit" (Andreau, 2002: 38; Mattingly, 1996: 239–40). Mitchell and Katsari pointed out that his perspective "was a normative one," based on the writings of the intellectual elite (Mitchell and Katsari, 2005: xv). Jeremy Paterson, furthermore, noted that Finley "spent a lot of time seeking to demonstrate what the ancient economy was *not*, rather than what it was" (Paterson, 2011: 171). Kevin Greene has shown that his views on technology were unfounded; Morris and others reject Finley's dismissal of the usefulness of economic models (Greene, 2000: 30; Morris, 2002: 41). Several scholars have shown that Finley was unduly pessimistic about transport capabilities and their impact on trade (e.g., Laurence, 1999: 95). Others have argued against Finley's claims that "money was essentially coined metal and nothing else," that there were no ancient statistics, and no "economic system which was an enormous conglomeration of interdependent markets."[13] A significant argument against Finley, ironically, was that his approach was anachronistic. As Andrea Carandini put it, he "passes a negative judgement on the Roman economy because the Romans were not English, and did not live in the eighteenth century" (Carandini, 1983: 179). Pieter Willem de Neeve, arguing against Finley's views on economic rationality in ancient agriculture, observed that what Finley and those in his camp "have done is to choose a model which does not even apply to present day agriculture as a whole, measure the ancient economy by it, establish that the ancient economy does not answer to the model, and conclude that the ancient economy is primitive" (de Neeve, 1985: 91).

Nevertheless, Finley had and still has his defenders. Peter Bang has argued that Finley was "often . . . misunderstood," and Martin Millett, writing just a few years ago, stated that he was "more sympathetic to the views . . . developed by M. I. Finley."[14] He acknowledges that "there was more movement of goods than previously thought," but doubts whether this "does anything to undermine the view that ancient economic activity was both heavily socially constrained and probably conceptualized in a very different way than today" (Millett, 2012: 774). Similarly, Matthew Hobson (2013: 21) has argued that "the theoretical standpoint taken by Finley in *The Ancient Economy* was far more sophisticated than that currently being recommended by the Stanford School" (i.e., Scheidel, Morris, and Saller).

Other scholars have tried to stay above the fray. Martin W. Frederiksen, in a review of the original edition of *The Ancient Economy*, viewed the "old battle between primitivists and modernists" as "a small and rather unimportant duel," finding "neither thesis really acceptable without a good deal of emendation" (Frederiksen, 1975: 170). He believed the ancient economy – indeed all economies – lie "somewhere between the theoretical extremes, between the static traditional economy and the perfectly fluid market economy" (Frederiksen, 1975: 171). In his essay, "Between Archaic and Modern: Problems in Roman Economic History," William V. Harris suggested a similar approach (Harris, 1993). In 2002, Richard P. Saller rightly described the debate as in a "rut" and "increasingly sterile." Furthermore, in comparing the views of Finley and Rostovtzeff (as opposed to how those views were characterized in subsequent scholarship), he found that they were not as diametrically opposed as one would expect. In fact, he observed "considerable common ground" (Saller, 2002: 252).

The debate over the ancient economy was not, of course, as simple as a conflict between two different perspectives. First of all, as Peter Garnsey and Saller recently observed, "no one self-identifies as part of either camp."[15] Typically, however, ancient economic historians do situate their work in relation to these "camps," generally with Greek historians tending to be more sympathetic to Finley than Romanists. Second, there were other perspectives, most notably the Marxist or neo-Marxist one (e.g., de Ste. Croix, 1981; Giardina and Schiavone, 1981).

Though once a student of Finley, Keith Hopkins is sometimes credited with creating his own school, applying modern economic methods such as the Fisher Price Equation to the Roman economy by means of rough estimates of things like the money supply. While it might be an exaggeration to speak of a Hopkins "school," his 1980 *Journal of Roman Studies* article, "Taxes and Trade in the Roman Empire" (along with his several revisions and expansions of its argument), continue to receive much attention (Hopkins, 1980, 1995/1996, 2000). In terms of citation frequency, at least among Roman economic historians, it probably rivals Finley's *Ancient Economy*. Not implausibly, Hobson (2013: 17) ascribes to Hopkins the start of a "new trajectory, angled more towards the ideological outlook of development economics," leading ultimately to ancient economic historians' embrace of the NIE approach.

By the early 2000s, the study of the ancient economy was moving clearly in the direction of NIE. Although some scholars had begun to employ the NIE approach earlier,[16] the 2007 publication of the *Cambridge Economic History of the Greco-Roman World* marked its definitive arrival in ancient history. Edited by Walter Scheidel, Ian Morris, and Richard Saller, this nearly thousand-page-long book consists of twenty-eight chapters that apply NIE to the classical world. Chapters 2 through 6 discuss ecology, demography, household and gender, law and economic institutions, and technology as "Determinants of Economic Performance." The following twenty-two chapters cover regions and periods of the Classical world in roughly chronological order, beginning with the Aegean Bronze Age and ending with "the transition to late antiquity."[17]

The clearest application of NIE to the ancient economy has probably been achieved by Dennis Kehoe, both in the Cambridge volume and in his book *Law and the Rural Economy in the Roman Empire*, which also came out in 2007. Kehoe used NIE "to examine how law and legal institutions affected the economic interests and relative bargaining power of Roman landowners and tenants" (2007: 11). He argues that Roman legal institutions helped smallholders and promoted some "investment and cooperation that could lead to economic growth" (2007: 194) at least in the early empire.

The reviews of the *Cambridge Economic History* were extremely positive. It was called a "landmark," an "extraordinary book," a "remarkable achievement," and even a "mighty and awe-inspiring tome."[18] While all reviewers had some criticisms, these mainly concerned omissions and underdeveloped issues rather than arguments against the overall approach or conclusions. There was, for example, insufficient coverage of slavery, the Achaemenids, Phoenicians, and Carthaginians, ideology, religion, and the later Roman Empire.[19] Christianity, it must be noted, makes few appearances. Several reviewers also complained about the lack of a consistent "theoretical standpoint" between chapters, with David Tandy even speaking of "rogue chapters."[20] We would highlight two observations made by Bang in his review of the volume. The first offers some redemption for Finley, since Bang observes that "according to North, in order to work, traditional economic theory had to be modified substantially by taking account of culture and ideology, precisely the linchpins of the anthropologically informed analyses of *The Ancient Economy*" (Bang, 2009: 197). The second is Bang's suggestion that we need to give greater consideration to "the effect of war and violence on the economy" (Bang, 2009: 203). This forms part of our extramercantile project. There are certainly studies of Roman ravaging and plundering, but there is more work to be done on its economic implications.[21]

The situation is similar for many other aspects of what we call the extramercantile economy. There has been a lot of work on benefaction, euergetism, gift giving, reciprocity, public goods (such as water supplies), the grain supply, and so forth. This work should be integrated into a view of the Roman economy, ideally one that does not privilege the market.

As many of the ancient historians using it freely admit, NIE is just one perspective. It does not pretend to answer all questions about the economy, nor does it demand to be employed exclusively. In the more than ten years since the publication of the *Cambridge Economic History of the Greco-Roman World*, many other approaches to the ancient economy and ancient economic behavior have started to garner more attention. These include behavioral economics, economic anthropology, *régulation* theory, and others. The editors of the *Cambridge* volume themselves recommended that ancient historians engage more with fields like development economics, human capital theory, and economic sociology (Scheidel, Morris, and Saller, 2007: 7). There is not the space, nor is it our purpose, to review all these various perspectives here, but we would like to highlight a few important contributions. To begin with, Koenraad Verboven (2015) has produced an excellent assessment of NIE, coupled with a discussion of development economics and behavioral economics. Development economics, employed by a number of scholars in recent years, examines capabilities and entitlements in order to get at questions of quality of life (since per capita GDP is viewed with increasing skepticism). Behavioral economics has its roots in the mid-twentieth century but has grown in prominence recently, thanks in part to mainstream accounts of its development and ideas (Thaler, 2015; Lewis, 2017). According to Weber and Dawes (2010: 91), the "main goal of behavioral economists is to change the way that economics is done by replacing behaviorally unrealistic assumptions of economic theory and analysis, while keeping the approach of economic research that has proved valuable." Such economists argue that "many of the basic assumptions in standard economic models (e.g., self-interest, optimization) are not based on how people actually make economic decisions." Thaler (2015), for example, notes the importance of loss aversion behavior that runs counter to self-interest, the problem of self-control, mental accounting practices, and how perceptions of fairness change people's attitudes towards potential transactions. It is too early to tell how the insights of behavioral economics will affect ancient economic history, but this is clearly an approach with considerable potential. How, for example, did loss aversion manifest itself in the decisions of Roman farmers? Cato the Elder advised them to store their crops and wait for high prices. Would they sell too soon when prices went up but hold on to their surpluses for too long when prices dropped?[22] What economic decisions challenged the self-control of the average Roman consumer? To what extent did associations promote altruistic behavior among members?

The contributions of economic anthropology and *régulation* theory

In contrast to New Institutional Economics, which tends to privilege the construct of the market and focuses on institutions only to the extent that they influence the performance of markets, economic anthropology has a long and rich history of viewing the economy holistically. In a work that has shaped research agendas in the fields of sociology and anthropology for almost a century, and that falls into the category of what today would be termed economic anthropology, Marcel Mauss outlines a view of society in which social, economic, legal, and moral elements together constitute features of an indivisible *system of total services*:

> In the economic and legal systems that have preceded our own ["modern," Western systems], one hardly ever finds a simple exchange of goods, wealth, and products in transactions concluded by individuals [in contrast to the methodological individualism assumed by neoclassical economic theories in Mauss's day]. First, it is not individuals but collectivities that impose obligations of exchange and contract upon each other. The contracting parties are legal entities: clans, tribes, and families who confront and oppose one another either in groups who meet face to face in one spot, or through their chiefs, or in both these ways at once. Moreover, what they exchange is not solely property and wealth, moveable and immovable goods, and things economically useful. In particular, such exchanges are acts of politeness: banquets, rituals, military services, women, children, dances, festivals, and fairs, in which economic transaction is only one element, and in which the passing on of wealth is only one feature of a much more general and enduring contract. Finally, these total services and counter-services are committed to in a somewhat voluntary form by presents and gifts, although in the final analysis they are strictly compulsory, on pain of private or public warfare. We propose to call this the *system of total services.*[23]

(Mauss, 2000: 5–6)

Mauss finds that "primitive" systems of total services are significantly altered by the introduction of "modern" forms of contract and sale, as well as coinage minted and inscribed by "Semitic, Hellenic, Hellenistic, and Roman" peoples; nevertheless, he opines that even "modern," Western societies "are still permeated with this same atmosphere of the gift" and of reciprocity: "Everything is still not wholly categorized in terms of buying and selling" (Mauss, 2000: 65). Although one rightly balks at the culturally imperialistic view implied by Mauss's characterization of Western, European societies as "modern" and contemporary Polynesian, Inuit, and other social orders as "primitive," his basic insight that the transmission and consumption of goods and services take place in interactions occurring both within and without the marketplace has proven remarkably durable: "economy" cannot be reduced to "market." This insight remains fundamental to economic anthropology today (e.g., Godbout and Caillé, 1998; Hart, 1986; Hann and Hart, 2011; Gudeman, 2001, 2008). The social and institutional aspects of the economy that the field of New Institutional Economics only "discovered" as recently as the 1980s have been understood as well-established areas of research for almost a century in cognate fields such as sociology and economic anthropology: such is the effect of disciplinary siloing, and the legacy of neoclassical economics' attempts to reduce "economics" to the "scientific" analysis of market transactions.

A second area of research that holds promise is *régulation* theory, which, like economic anthropology, tends to view the economy as entailing a system of social relations rather than a system of abstracted or "disembedded" markets.[24] Combining an analysis of institutions with a focus on historical change, Marxist-inspired *régulation* theory examines the ways in which systems of resource distribution are normalized and perpetuated. Economic theorists operating from within this framework prefer to denominate it using the French term *régulation*, which concerns the interaction among social relations, institutionalized economic forms, and sociopolitical structures; rather than the English term *regulation*, which connotes very different processes of governmental regulation of the economy and, conversely, neoliberal policies of deregulation (Boyer and Saillard, 2002: 1; Boer and Petterson, 2017: 40).

Régulation theorist Michel Aglietta's definition of economics is instructive in that it places social relations rather than abstract markets at the center of analysis:

> The definition of economic science does not derive from a universal principle that founds a pure economy. It is solely a methodological demarcation within the field of social relations, one perpetually probed and shifted by the development of theoretical analysis itself. The study of capitalist regulation, therefore, cannot be the investigation of abstract economic laws. It is the study of the transformation of social relations as it creates new forms that are both economic and non-economic, that are organized in [sociopolitical] structures and themselves reproduce a determinant structure, the mode of production.
>
> (Aglietta, 1979: 16)

Roland Boer and Christina Petterson have applied *régulation* theory to the study of ancient economic history, specifically the histories of ancient Israel and of early Christianity in its Roman context (Boer, 2007, 2015; Boer and Petterson, 2017). Boer and Petterson argue that Greco-Roman economies were based largely on resource extraction from subject regions, and view market exchange as nothing more than a by-product of military conquest. Understanding market exchange as a derivative of conquest, they invert the high priority placed on the market both by neoclassical economics and by New Institutional Economics practitioners such as North.

Perhaps the greatest strength of *régulation* theory is its recognition that economies are constituted by a number of coinciding, institutionalized forms of economic production, including (in the Roman context) subsistence production; the urban-rural relationship, in which rural areas produce food for consumption in cities (and in which markets play a role); land tenure, referring to the "conditions under which land is used and the obligations of labor related to such usage"; slavery; and tribute-exchange, or "variations on plunder, which involves the expropriation of goods from the labor and resources one does not possess or control" (Boer and Petterson, 2017: 75 and *passim*; Boer, 2015: 146). All of this renders moot the old primitivist-modernist debate about whether Greece or Rome, for example, could be characterized as a "market economy": markets were present, but they existed alongside and were likely subordinate to other forms of economic activity.[25]

Conclusions

The profusion of available theoretical approaches hints at exciting new insights into the ancient economy, but the vast literature associated with each of these theories present an immense challenge. Indeed, it is not entirely clear how to apply some of these approaches to antiquity. That said, a few conclusions may be drawn from the various approaches surveyed in this chapter.

1   The utilization of the NIE paradigm by recent studies such as the *Cambridge Economic History of the Greco-Roman World* has had a positive effect inasmuch as it has provided a theoretical framework that has helped to usher scholarship into a post-Finleyan period in which the older debates between primitivism and modernism, and substantivism and formalism, have largely been supplanted by a concern to understand the "structure and performance of economies through time."[26]

2   It must be borne in mind, however, that NIE is an offshoot of neoclassical economic theory, and as such retains a heavy emphasis on mercantile transactions, even though that emphasis is tempered by the recognition that institutions play a significant role in shaping markets. New institutional economic theory typically does not account adequately for extramercantile aspects of the economy, including plunder, theft, property destruction (as in war), patronage and euergetism, associative practices, and gift exchange, for example. The mercantile focus of NIE is to be attributed to the fact that its theoretical framework was developed through reflection on modern, capitalist economies, rather than premodern, precapitalist economies such as are known from Mediterranean antiquity. To state that these economies were premodern does not imply that they had no markets, but serves as an invitation to understand markets within the context of broader economic systems in which several institutionalized forms of economic production existed simultaneously.

3   When NIE is applied to the study of the ancient economy, an inevitable distortion of the data occurs, as extramercantile aspects of the economy tend to be elided. Three remedies to this methodological shortcoming may be envisioned: the NIE framework may be extended to consider additional extramercantile aspects of the economy not typically encountered in contemporary, capitalist economics (e.g., plunder, associative practices, major public works funded by euergetism); new models may be developed; or extant, competing models may be elaborated. These three remedies need not be understood as mutually exclusive, as there is considerable overlap between various theoretical models (e.g., unlike neoclassical economics, NIE, *régulation* theory, and economic anthropology all take cultural and ideological factors into

account). Care must be taken, however, to identify the inconsistencies and contradictions that arise when various perspectives are juxtaposed, particularly as those concern problematic neoclassical assumptions that tend to be retained in NIE (e.g., methodological individualism).

4   It must be recognized that any theoretical model originally developed to facilitate the study of contemporary, capitalist societies will need to be refined and elaborated to render it more useful for the study of ancient economies in which extramercantile aspects played a significant role; we must, therefore, constantly probe our theoretical models by testing them against such "real-world" data as are available.[27] For that reason, the formulation and reformulation of theoretical models is an open-ended and dialogical process. It is not our intention here to advocate for or against any particular model, but to point to the benefits and shortcomings entailed in one influential model, NIE, and to suggest ways in which the model could be improved, or other models considered, either alongside or in place of it. As David Lewis has recently suggested (2018: 21–2), there is much to be gained from "methodological pluralism."

We believe the challenges posed by the study of ancient economies require interdisciplinary collaboration and realistic objectives. Hence, our current project of looking at extramercantile exchanges and transfers is intended as a corrective to the overemphasis on the market characteristic of studies that adopt the theoretical framework of NIE.

Notes

* The authors would like to thank Roland Boer and Koenraad Verboven for reading a draft of this article and offering helpful suggestions.
1 Marshall goes on to treat the themes of land, labor, capital, and supply and demand equilibria.
2 For additional critiques of the mathematization of neoclassical economics, see Beed and Kane (1991).
3 Methodological individualism: the idea that the self-governing individual represents the basic unit of analysis in economics and the social sciences, and that social phenomena are constituted by the aggregate decisions of rational, individual actors. Ben Fine and Dimitris Milonakis (2003) offer a critique of what they perceive to be Douglass North's methodological individualism. However, because the phrase "methodological individualism" is defined in different ways, it is not entirely clear that North should be characterized as a methodological individualist. Geoffrey M. Hodgson notes that, strictly speaking, the phrase should be confined to the notion that "social phenomena should be explained entirely in terms of individuals *alone*" (emphasis in original). North's work would better be described by the statement "social phenomena should be explained in terms of individuals *plus* relations between individuals" – a view that, as Hodgson argues, ought not be characterized as methodological individualism (Hodgson, 2007: 220). That said, Fine and Milonakis have nonetheless identified a problematic aspect of North's work.
4 In Douglass C. North, John Joseph Wallis, and Barry R. Weingast, *Violence and Social Orders: A Conceptual Framework for Interpreting Recorded Human History*,

the authors write: "We develop a conceptual framework, not a formal or analytical theory. . . . We do not present a formal model that generates empirical tests or deterministic predictions about social change. Instead, we propose a conceptual framework that incorporates explicitly endogenous patterns of social, economic, political, military, religious, and educational behavior. The challenge is to explain how durable and predictable social institutions deal with an ever-changing, unpredictable, and novel world within a framework consistent with the dynamic forces of social change" (North, Wallis, and Weingast, 2012: xviii). Note that North himself registers disagreement with some of Williamson's positions; see North (1990: 54–5 n. 1).

5 The seminal essay is that of Coase (1937).

6 Chavance (2009: 48) writes: "[North's] work as an economic historian has evolved from a fairly radical neo-classical position . . . to a discovery of the importance of institutions and a gradual distancing from, and even criticism of, the limitations of the neo-classical tradition." Fine and Milonakis (2003: 548) write: "Thus, despite or even because of his intellectual foundations within neoclassical economics, North has recognized and emphasized its limitations. As the irrational has become rational, the exogenous rendered endogenous, so he has embraced, retained, and strengthened his commitment to such dualities. This has had two important effects. First, it has led some to be confused about whether North's institutionalism is neoclassical or not, and whether it can or cannot be wedded to older institutional traditions." In the view of Fine and Milonakis, North's commitment to rational choice (even though rationality is for North both "bounded" and shaped by ideology) and methodological individualism vitiate his utility for economic history.

7 The passage is quoted in Scheidel, Morris, and Saller (2007: 1–2). According to Fine and Milonakis (2003: 561 n. 14), North later abandoned the idea that ideology could be subsumed under the category of structure.

8 North (1990): critique of instrumental rationality (108), the wealth-maximizing individual (15, 20), fully informed parties who calculate costs and benefits correctly (23), price as a sufficient allocative mechanism (30), the convenient fiction of costless transactions (28, 108, 131–2).

9 Peter Bang (2012) has put *Violence and Social Orders* to good use by engaging the work in an essay on Roman predation.

10 See, for example, Morris (1999), Morris and Manning (2010), or Andreau (2010). Hobson (2013) discusses developments in the study of the Roman economy since the 1970s.

11 Jongman (2013: 2717). Another common way of describing the formalist position is that it assumes "the existence of an economic sphere separate from social relations" (Scheidel and Von Reden, 2002: 2).

12 For some attempts to summarize Finley's position: Mattingly and Salmon (2001: 3), Andreau (2002), Morris and Manning (2005: 13–14), and Mattingly (2006: 283).

13 Finley (1985: 196, 26, 22); for examples of objections, see Hollander (2007) on money; Nicolet (1996: 23–4) on statistics; and Temin (2001: 181) on markets.

14 Bang (2007: 7); Millett (2012: 774); see also Meikle (2002: 235).

15 Garnsey and Saller (2015: 89).

16 E.g., Scheidel and Von Reden (2002: 1), who quote North on the first page of their *The Ancient Economy*; Morris, 2002; and Christesen (2003: 31), who mentions him in the second sentence of his article about economic rationalism in fourth-century Athens. Morris and Manning (2005: 2) described ancient economic history as "radically undertheorized and methodologically impoverished" and sought to "increase the diversity of approaches" (34), mentioning game theory, development economics, economic sociology, and NIE.

17 One of the first sessions organized by the Early Christianity and the Ancient Economy program unit (see the introduction to this volume for a description) was a

discussion of the volume, held at the Society of Biblical Literature Annual Meeting in Boston in 2008.
18 Osgood (2010: 370), Paterson (2011: 171), Katsari (2009), Verboven (2010: 617), and Bang (2009: 194).
19 On the treatment of slavery, see Paterson (2011) and Verboven (2010); Silver (2011) for the Achaemenids; Osgood (2010) and Tandy (2009) for the Phoenicians and Carthaginians; Osgood (2010) and Verboven (2010) for lack of discussion of ideology; Silver (2011) for lack of discussion of religion and the later empire.
20 Paterson (2011: 172) and Tandy (2009: 302).
21 Harris (e.g., 1971) has long been aware of this issue and its importance.
22 See chapter 4 of Thaler (2015) on Value Theory.
23 Italics in original. The phrase "total services" renders the French *prestations*. Keith Hart (2014: 40) writes: "Mauss's key term for the range of archaic contracts he intends to investigate is untranslatable into English and something of a feudal relic in French. *Prestation* is a service performed out of obligation, something like 'community service' as an alternative to imprisonment."
24 Karl Polanyi argued that markets in antiquity were always "embedded" within sociocultural contexts from which they could not be extricated. Some theorists object to the use of this terminology; Roland Boer and Christina Petterson (2017: 43) write: "The Polanyi-derived terminology of 'embedded' economic practices is misleading since it may give the false impression that such practices can be undertaken and understood outside the 'bed' [of social networks and cultural expectations] independently before being 'put to bed.'"
25 Temin (2001: 180), who argues for a Roman market economy, nonetheless acknowledges that "even full-blown modern market economies do not channel all transactions through markets."
26 For a similar assessment, see Morris, Saller, and Scheidel (2008: 11–12).
27 Compare Boer (2015: 9–10) and Verboven (2015).

Bibliography

Aglietta, Michel. *A Theory of Capitalist Regulation: The US Experience*. Translated by David Fernbach. London: NLB, 1979.

Andreau, Jean. *L'économie du monde romain*. Paris: Ellipses, 2010.

———. "Twenty Years after Moses I. Finley's *The Ancient Economy*." Pages 33–49 in *The Ancient Economy*. Edited by Walter Scheidel and Sitta Von Reden. New York: Routledge, 2002.

Bang, Peter Fibiger. "The Ancient Economy and New Institutional Economics." *Journal of Roman Studies* 99 (2009): 194–206.

———. "Predation." Pages 197–217 in *The Cambridge Companion to the Roman Economy*. Edited by Walter Scheidel. Cambridge: Cambridge University Press, 2012.

———. "Trade and Empire: In Search of Organizing Concepts for the Roman Economy." *Past and Present* 195 (2007): 3–54.

Beed, Clive, and Owen Kane. "What Is the Critique of the Mathematization of Economics?" *Kyklos* 44.4 (1991): 581–612.

Blaug, Mark. "The Formalist Revolution of the 1950s." *Journal of the History of Economic Thought* 25.2 (2003): 145–56.

Boer, Roland. *The Sacred Economy of Ancient Israel*. Library of Ancient Israel. Louisville: Westminster John Knox, 2015.

———. "The Sacred Economy of Ancient 'Israel'." *Scandinavian Journal of the Old Testament* 21.1 (2007): 29–48.

Boer, Roland, and Christina Petterson. *Time of Troubles: A New Economic Framework for Early Christianity*. Minneapolis: Fortress, 2017.

Boyer, Robert, and Yves Saillard, eds. *Régulation Theory: The State of the Art*. London: Routledge, 2002.

Bücher, Karl. *Die Entstehung der Volkswirtschaft*. Tübingen: Laupp, 1893.

Carandini, Andrea. "Columella's Vineyard and the Rationality of the Roman Economy." *Opus* 2 (1983): 177–204.

Chavance, Bernard. *Institutional Economics*. Translated by Francis Wells. Routledge Frontiers in Political Economy. London: Routledge, 2009.

Christesen, Paul. "Economic Rationalism in Fourth-Century BCE Athens." *Greece and Rome* 50.1 (2003): 31–56.

Coase, Ronald H. "The Nature of the Firm." *Economica* n.s. 4.16 (1937): 386–405.

de Ste. Croix, G.E.M. *The Class Struggle in the Ancient Greek World from the Archaic Age to the Arab Conquests*. London: Duckworth, 1981.

Dugger, William M. "Power: An Institutional Framework of Analysis." Pages 133–43 in *The Economy as a System of Power*. 2nd ed. Edited by Marc R. Tool and Warren J. Samuels. New Brunswick, NJ: Transaction, 1989.

Fine, Ben, and Dimitris Milonakis. "From Principle of Pricing to Pricing of Principle: Rationality and Irrationality in the Economic History of Douglass North." *Comparative Studies in Society and History* 45.3 (2003): 546–70.

Finley, M.I. *The Ancient Economy*. Berkeley: University of California Press, 1985.

Frederiksen, Martin W. "Theory, Evidence, and the Ancient Economy." *Journal of Roman Studies* 65 (1975): 164–71.

Frier, Bruce W., and Dennis P. Kehoe. "Law and Economic Institutions." Pages 113–43 in *The Cambridge Economic History of the Greco-Roman World*. Edited by Walter Scheidel, Ian Morris, and Richard P. Saller. Cambridge: Cambridge University Press, 2007.

Garnsey, Peter, and Richard P. Saller. *The Roman Empire: Economy, Society and Culture*. 2nd ed. Oakland: University of California Press, 2015.

Giardina, Andrea, and Aldo Schiavone, eds. *Società Romana e Produzione Schiavistica*. Rome: Laterza, 1981.

Godbout, Jacques T., and Alain Caillé. *The World of the Gift*. Translated by Donald Winkler. Montreal: McGill-Queen's University Press, 1998.

Greene, Kevin. "Technological Innovation and Economic Progress in the Ancient World: M. I. Finley Reconsidered." *Economic History Review* 53 (2000): 29–59.

Groenewegen, John, Antoon Spithoven, and Annette van den Berg, eds. *Institutional Economics: An Introduction*. New York: Palgrave Macmillan, 2010.

Gudeman, Stephen. *The Anthropology of Economy: Community, Market, and Culture*. Oxford: Blackwell, 2001.

———. *Economy's Tension: The Dialectics of Community and Market*. New York: Berghahn Books, 2008.

Hann, Chris, and Keith Hart. *Economic Anthropology: History, Ethnography, Critique*. Cambridge: Polity, 2011.

Harris, William V. "Between Archaic and Modern: Problems in Roman Economic History." Pages 11–29 in *The Inscribed Economy: Production and Distribution in the Roman Empire in the Light of* Instrumentum Domesticum: *The Proceedings of a Conference Held at the American Academy in Rome on 10–11 January, 1992*. Edited by William V. Harris. Ann Arbor: University of Michigan, 1993.

———. "On War and Greed in the Second Century B.C." *American Historical Review* 76 (1971): 1371–85.

Hart, Keith. "Heads or Tails? Two Sides of the Coin." *Man* n.s. 21.4 (1986): 637–56.
———. "Marcel Mauss's Economic Vision, 1920–1925: Anthropology, Politics, Journalism." *Journal of Classical Sociology* 14.1 (2014): 34–44.
Hobson, Matthew S. "A Historiography of the Study of the Roman Economy: Economic Growth, Development, and Neoliberalism." Pages 11–26 in *TRAC 2013: Proceedings of the Twenty-Third Annual Theoretical Roman Archaeology Conference, London 2013*. Edited by Hannah Platts, Caroline Barron, Jason Lundock, John Pearce, and Justin Yoo. Oxford: Oxbow, 2014.
Hodgson, Geoffrey M. "Meanings of Methodological Individualism." *Journal of Economic Methodology* 14 (2007): 211–26.
Hollander, David B. *Money in the Late Roman Republic*. Leiden: Brill, 2007.
Hopkins, Keith. "Rents, Taxes, Trade and the City of Rome." Pages 253–67 in *Mercati permanenti e mercati periodici nel mondo romano: atti degli Incontri capresi di storia dell' economia antica (Capri 13–15 ottobre 1997)*. Edited by Elio Lo Cascio. Bari: Edipuglia, 2000.
———. "Rome, Taxes, Rents and Trade." *Kodai* 6/7 (1995/1996): 41–75.
———. "Taxes and Trade in the Roman Empire (200 B.C.-A.D. 400)." *Journal of Roman Studies* 70 (1980): 101–25.
Jongman, Willem. "Formalism-Substantivism Debate." Pages 2715–18 in *The Encyclopedia of Ancient History*. Edited by Roger Bagnall, et al. Malden, MA: Blackwell, 2013.
Katsari, Constantina. Review of *The Cambridge Economic History of the Greco-Roman World*. Edited by Walter Scheidel, Ian Morris, and Richard P. Saller. *Bryn Mawr Classical Review* 2009.04.74. http://bmcr.brynmawr.edu/2009/2009-04-74.html.
Kehoe, Dennis P. "The Early Roman Empire: Production." Pages 543–69 in *The Cambridge Economic History of the Greco-Roman World*. Edited by Walter Scheidel, Ian Morris, and Richard P. Saller. Cambridge: Cambridge University Press, 2007.
———. *Law and the Rural Economy in the Roman Empire*. Ann Arbor: University of Michigan Press, 2007.
Laurence, Ray. *The Roads of Roman Italy: Mobility and Cultural Change*. London: Routledge, 1999.
Lewis, David. "Behavioural Economics and Economic Behaviour in Classical Athens." Pages 15–46 in *Ancient Greek History and Contemporary Social Science*. Edited by M. Canevaro, Andrew Erskine, B. Gray, and J. Ober. Edinburgh: Edinburgh University Press, 2018.
Lewis, Michael. *The Undoing Project: A Friendship that Changed Our Minds*. New York: Norton & Co., 2017.
Marshall, Alfred. *Principles of Economics*. 8th ed. London: Palgrave Macmillan, 1920. Repr., Palgrave Classics in Economics. New York: Palgrave Macmillan, 2013.
Mattingly, David J. "First Fruit? The Olive in the Roman World." Pages 213–53 in *Human Landscapes in Classical Antiquity: Environment and Culture*. Edited by John Salmon and Graham Shipley. London: Routledge, 1996.
———. "The Imperial Economy." Pages 283–97 in *A Companion to the Roman Empire*. Edited by David S. Potter. Malden, MA: Blackwell, 2006.
Mattingly, David J., and John Salmon. "The Productive Past: Economies Beyond Agriculture." Pages 3–14 in *Economies beyond Agriculture in the Classical World*. Edited by David J. Mattingly and John Salmon. London: Routledge, 2001.
Mauss, Marcel. *The Gift: The Form and Reason for Exchange in Archaic Societies*. Translated by W.D. Halls. New York: Norton, 2000.

Medema, Steven G., and Warren J. Samuels, eds. *The History of Economic Thought: A Reader*. London: Routledge, 2003.

Meikle, Scott. "Modernism, Economics, and the Ancient Economy." Pages 233–50 in *The Ancient Economy*. Edited by Walter Scheidel and Sitta Von Reden. New York: Routledge, 2002.

Ménard, Claude, and Mary M. Shirley. "The Contribution of Douglass North to New Institutional Economics." Pages 11–29 in *Institutions, Property Rights, and Economic Growth: The Legacy of Douglass North*. Edited by Sebastian Galiani and Itai Sened. New York: Cambridge University Press, 2014.

Meyer, Eduard. *Die wirtschaftliche Entwicklung des Altertums*. Jena: Fischer, 1895.

Mill, John Stuart. "On the Definition of Political Economy; and on the Method of Investigation Proper to It." Essay 5 in Mill, *Essays on Some Unsettled Questions of Political Economy*. 2nd ed. London: Longmans, Green, Reader, and Dyer, 1874. Library of Economics and Liberty. www.econlib.org/library/Mill/mlUQP5.html.

Millett, Martin. "Perceptions of the Imperial Landscape." *Journal of Roman Archaeology* 25 (2012): 772–5.

Mitchell, Stephen, and Constantina Katsari, eds. *Patterns in the Economy of Roman Asia Minor*. Swansea: Classical Press of Wales, 2005.

Morris, Ian. "Foreword to Updated Edition." Pages ix–xxxvi in *The Ancient Economy*, by M.I. Finley. Berkeley: University of California Press, 1999.

———. "Hard Surfaces." Pages 8–43 in *Money, Labour and Land: Approaches to the Economies of Ancient Greece*. Edited by P.A. Cartledge, Edward E. Cohen, and Lin Foxhall. London: Routledge, 2002.

Morris, Ian, and J.G. Manning. "The Economic Sociology of the Ancient Mediterranean World." Pages 131–59 in *The Handbook of Economic Sociology*. 2nd ed. Edited by Neil J. Smelser and Richard Swedberg. Princeton, NJ: Princeton University Press, 2010.

———, eds. *The Ancient Economy: Evidence and Models*. Stanford: Stanford University Press, 2005.

Morris, Ian, Richard J. Saller, and Walter Scheidel. Introduction to *The Cambridge Economic History of the Greco-Roman World*. Edited by Walter Scheidel, Ian Morris, and Richard P. Saller. Cambridge: Cambridge University Press, 2008.

Neeve, P.W. de. "The Price of Agricultural Land in Roman Italy and the Problem of Economic Rationalism." *Opus* 4 (1985): 77–109.

Nicolet, Claude. *Financial Documents and Geographical Knowledge in the Roman World*. Oxford: Leopard's Head, 1996.

North, Douglass C. *Institutions, Institutional Change and Economic Performance*. Cambridge: Cambridge University Press, 1990.

———. *Structure and Change in Economic History*. New York: Norton & Co., 1981.

North, Douglass C., John Joseph Wallis, and Barry R. Weingast. *Violence and Social Orders: A Conceptual Framework for Interpreting Recorded Human History*. Cambridge: Cambridge University Press, 2012.

Osgood, Josiah. Review of *The Cambridge Economic History of the Greco-Roman World*. Edited by Walter Scheidel, Ian Morris, and Richard P. Saller. *Classical Journal* 105.4 (2010): 370–4.

Paterson, Jeremy. "An Economic History." *Classical Review* 61.1 (2011): 171–4.

Peterson, Wallace C. "Power and Economic Performance." Pages 89–131 in *The Economy as a System of Power*. 2nd ed. Edited by Marc R. Tool and Warren J. Samuels. New Brunswick, NJ: Transaction, 1989.

Piketty, Thomas. *Capital in the Twenty-First Century*. Translated by Arthur Goldhammer. Cambridge: Harvard University Press, 2014.

Saller, Richard P. "Framing the Debate over Growth in the Ancient Economy." Pages 251–69 in *The Ancient Economy*. Edited by Walter Scheidel and Sitta Von Reden. New York: Routledge, 2002.

Scheidel, Walter, Ian Morris, and Richard P. Saller, eds. *The Cambridge Economic History of the Greco-Roman World*. Cambridge: Cambridge University Press, 2007.

Scheidel, Walter, and Sitta Von Reden, eds. *The Ancient Economy*. New York: Routledge, 2002.

Silver, Morris. Review of *The Cambridge Economic History of the Greco-Roman World*. Edited by Walter Scheidel, Ian Morris, and Richard P. Saller. *Journal of Economic History* 71.1 (2011): 260–7.

Tandy, David W. Review of *The Cambridge Economic History of the Greco-Roman World*. Edited by Walter Scheidel, Ian Morris, and Richard P. Saller. *American Journal of Philology* 130.2 (2009): 299–303.

Temin, Peter. "A Market Economy in the Early Roman Empire." *Journal of Roman Studies* 91 (2001): 169–81.

Thaler, Richard H. *Misbehaving: The Making of Behavioral Economics*. New York: Norton & Co., 2015.

Tool, Marc R., and Warren J. Samuels. Introduction to *The Economy as a System of Power*. 2nd ed. New Brunswick, NJ: Transaction, 1989.

Verboven, Koenraad. "The Knights Who Say NIE: Can Neo-Institutional Economics Live Up to Its Expectation in Ancient History Research?" Pages 33–57 in *Structure and Performance in the Roman Economy: Models, Methods and Case Studies*. Edited by Paul Erdkamp and Koenraad Verboven. Collection Latomus 350. Brussels: Latomus, 2015.

———. Review of *The Cambridge Economic History of the Greco-Roman World*. Edited by Walter Scheidel, Ian Morris, and Richard P. Saller. *L'Antiquité Classique* 79 (2010): 616–18.

Weber, Roberto, and Robyn Dawes. "Behavioral Economics." Pages 90–108 in *The Handbook of Economic Sociology*. 2nd ed. Edited by Neil Smelser and Richard Swedberg. Princeton: Princeton University Press, 2010.

Williamson, Oliver E. "Transaction Cost Economics: The Natural Progression." *American Economic Review* 100.3 (2010): 673–90.

———. "The Vertical Integration of Production: Market Failure Considerations." *American Economic Review* 61.2 (1971): 112–23.

2   Early Greek economic thought

John T. Fitzgerald

The ancient Greeks engaged in economic activity long before they wrote about it. Nevertheless, various references to the economy, to economic practices, and the economic status of individuals and cities begin already with Homer and continue throughout Greek antiquity. In the survey that follows, we shall begin with a brief discussion of Homer and Hesiod, and then give attention to the earliest Greek economic theorists, who were concerned primarily with the management of the people and property that comprised a private household (*oikos*), though they occasionally also gave attention to the economy of the polis.

Homer and Hesiod

Although Homer was not an economist, he tells us important things about the ancient economy. Just how much can be learned from Homer was demonstrated by Moses Finley, the scholar whose work on the ancient economy as a whole has proved so pivotal for later research.[1] In his seminal work *The World of Odysseus* (1954), Finley followed the lead of Karl Polanyi (1944) in arguing that the ancient economy, in contrast to the modern one, was not a separate sphere of society for archaic Greeks.[2] Homeric economy was instead embedded in social relations and because of this embeddedness, social rather than economic concerns were the primary motivators of economic actions. Finley emphasized that reciprocity was central to social relationships in aristocratic Homeric society, with an exchange of gifts constituting the most conspicuous manifestation of the Homeric economy. "The act of giving was, therefore, in an essential sense always the first half of a reciprocal action, the other half of which was a counter-gift" (2002: 61). Gift giving was pervasive. "There was scarcely a limit to the situations in which gift-giving was operative" (2002: 62). Indeed, the word *gift* was a comprehensive term that covered what later generations would call financial transactions, fees, loans, services, payments, and other things:

> More precisely, the word "gift" was a cover-all for a great variety of actions and transactions which later became differentiated and acquired their own appellations. There were payments for services rendered, desired or antici-pated; what we would call fees, rewards, prizes, and sometimes bribes. . . .

Then there were taxes and other dues to lords and kings, amends with a penal overtone . . ., and even ordinary loans – and again the Homeric word is always "gift."

(2002: 62–3)

Because of the importance of gift exchange in the Homeric world, Walter Donlan (among others) subsequently called the Homeric economy a gift economy (1989) and argued that it had an important ethical component:

The moral foundation of a gift economy is that every act of giving, whether of things or of services, incurs a debt which carries a strong obligation to repay. Inherent in this construction of give and receive is a powerful ethical bias toward fair-play.

(Donlan, 1997: 649)

More than a half-century after Polanyi and Finley wrote, the ancient practice of gift giving, the existence of gift economies, and the idea of embedded economies in the ancient world continue to be the subject of scholarly research (Carlà and Gori, 2014).

Although much about Homer and the ancient economy remains debated, it is certain that the household *(oikos)* was foundational, forming the primary economic and social unit of Homeric society, and that is true for Hesiodic society and the subsequent Greek and Roman worlds as well. Finley (2002: 57–8) emphasized the centrality of the household, and subsequent scholarship has confirmed this emphasis (e.g., Donlan, 1997: 650). It was "the basic unit of consumption as well as production" (Saller, 2007: 87). As Raaflaub (1997: 632) notes in regard to Homeric society, "Undoubtedly, then, the oikos is centrally important and a primary focus of loyalty and identification. This remained true for centuries to come." Furthermore, these archaic households appear to have been largely self-sufficient in practice (Raaflaub, 1997: 636), so that "individual *oikoi* produced what they ate, including wine and olive oil, and did their own grinding, baking, spinning, and weaving" (Donlan, 1997: 650). "Hesiod's account of Ascra sets up domestic self-sufficiency as a goal, and the archaeological finds suggest that EIA [Early Iron Age] households achieved this in many respects" (Morris, 2007: 233).

At the same time, these households were not completely isolated from one another, so that "there was undoubtedly some economic interdependence among the villages of a region" (Donlan, 1997: 650). Ideally, therefore, the *oikos* was mostly self-reliant, and its members were expected to take care of themselves in regard to food, clothes, tools, and so forth.[3] But if the members of the *oikos* needed or wanted assistance with certain aspects of everyday life, or if they had bigger or more complicated tasks to perform (such as building a house), they could avail themselves of the services of specialized craftsmen, especially potters, metalworkers, and carpenters. Some of these specialists were undoubtedly localized (such as blacksmiths and other metalworkers), whereas others were transients, such as the skilled carpenter, whose skills were used mostly in building ships, temples, large houses, and various civic projects. As Morris (2007: 234) suggests:

> Families would take care of simple needs themselves . . .; would go to a village specialist for others . . .; and would rely on traveling experts, or perhaps specialists based in the few large towns, for major tasks.[4]

As both the *Iliad* and the *Odyssey* amply attest, it was possible to amass wealth in the Homeric world, and this was true not only for individuals and their households but also for entire cities. Homer's favorite term to designate affluence is *aphneios*, "wealthy," a term that together with its cognates occurs some sixteen times in the *Iliad*, fifteen times in the *Odyssey*, and twice in the Homeric Hymns, thus a little more than thirty times altogether in the Homeric corpus. As far as individuals are concerned, it is used, as one might expect, especially of kings. As Telemachus says in book 1 of the *Odyssey*, "It's really not so bad to be a king. All at once your palace grows in wealth, and your honors grow as well" (*Od.* 1.393).[5] This association of kingship with wealth and honor will remain a fixture in ancient thought, with the apostle Paul invoking that same triad of associated concepts when he writes 1 Cor 4:8–10 centuries later.

Agamemnon is doubtless the most conspicuous Homeric example of a wealthy king, yet it is not Agamemnon, Odysseus, or one of the other major Homeric kings who is designated "the richest man in all the world" (*Il.* 20.220). That distinction is reserved for King Erichthonius, with Homer quantifying one aspect of his wealth by saying that "he owned 3000 mares, grazing the marshes, brood-mares in their prime, proud of their leaping foals" (*Il.* 20.221–2). He also gives the basis of his wealth – namely, that he had inherited both the kingdom of his father and that of his maternal grandfather.

Homer's designation of people as wealthy occurs several times in the *Iliad* in conjunction with his narration of their death. By noting that the victim or his father is wealthy (*Il.* 5.709; 16.594–6; 17. 575–6, 584), he is using that motif to heighten the pathos of death. Their death ends the luxurious way of life that wealth makes possible, and that luxury appears especially in references to feasting. In book 11 of the *Odyssey*, for example, the shade of the dead Agamemnon compares his death and that of his men to the slaughter of "white-tusked boars butchered in some rich lord of power's halls for a wedding, banquet, or groaning public feast" (*Od.* 11.414–15).

But what is particularly interesting about Homer's usage of the word "wealthy" is that whereas *aphneios* is frequently used of individuals or residents of a particular locale, it is used once and only once of a place, and that place is Corinth (*Il.* 2.570). Unfortunately, when Homer says that Corinth is wealthy, he does not provide any indication of why Corinth was rich, much less quantify it. Nevertheless, we will probably not be too far from the truth if we suggest that the basis for ancient Corinth's wealth was the land. That is already suggested by several Homeric texts that associate wealth with the land. Of particular interest in this regard is book 14 of the *Iliad*, where Diomedes tells how his father "married one of Adrastus' daughters, settled down in a fine, wealthy house, with plenty of grainland, ringed with row on row of blooming orchards and pastures full of sheep, his own herds" (*Il.* 14.121–4). In this passage, three bases of wealth are indicated: (1) arable lands, yielding cereal crops; (2) orchards, full of such things as olive trees, fig trees, and vines; and (3) grazing land for animals, sufficient for many sheep. Again, Amphius is described as "rich in possessions, rich in rolling wheatland" (*Il.* 5.612), and the seven citadels offered to Achilles are inhabited by men who "are rich in sheep-flocks and rich in shambling cattle" (*Il.* 9.155). Elsewhere in Homer we find wealth closely associated with rivers and lakes, and thus with fertile lands (*Il.* 2.825, 854; 5.708).

This is exactly what we find when we look at the Corinthia. In his epitaph for the Corinthians who died at Salamis in 480 BCE, Simonides, the Greek lyric poet, refers to "the well-watered city of Corinth." And as far as land was concerned, the richness of the land between Corinth and Sicyon was well known. According to Diodorus of Sicily (*Bib. hist.* 8.21.3), the Partheniae of Sparta once consulted the Delphic oracle about the feasibility of settling in that location, with the Pythia denying that they would live there but confirming the desirability of the land by saying, "Good is the land between Corinth and Sicyon." J. D. Salmon (1984: 12) is thus right on target when he argues that "the basis of Corinth's evident prosperity lay in the natural resources of her territory, no doubt especially in the plenteous water-supply and in the agricultural potential of the coastal plain where the settlements [of the Corinthia] were concentrated." Consequently, whether one dates the Homeric Catalogue of Ships early or late, its reference to Corinth as wealthy precedes the period when commerce could have been a significant factor in making it so. That is an important conclusion, for it means that commerce did not create Corinth's famed wealth but only increased it in subsequent centuries. The Greek economy in general, and the ancient Corinthian economy in particular, was rooted in agriculture, and most ancient Greeks would have been involved in one way or another in the production of foodstuffs.

As this brief discussion of Homer and others indicates, the household was the primary economic and social unit of the ancient Greek economy, though at certain points the polis also comes into view. It is, therefore, not surprising that when Greeks begin to give literary attention to the ancient economy, the primary focus is on the household. Secondarily, however, attention is also given to the polis. Both are concerns of Xenophon of Athens, to whom we now turn.

Xenophon of Athens

Xenophon of Athens (ca. 430–after 355/354 BCE) was the son of a well-heeled Athenian who belonged to the second highest of the Athenian property-based social classes and who owned land in east Attica. Several of his works reflect an interest in the economy, but two are particularly important for the purposes of this survey. The first and better known of the two is his *Oeconomicus*, the first major extant work on household management. Antisthenes, the precursor of the Cynics and Xenophon's older contemporary, was the first person that we know of to write a work with this title, but it unfortunately did not survive (Diogenes Laertius, *Vit. phil.* 6.16). According to Diogenes Laertius (*Vit. phil.* 6.15), Xenophon held Antisthenes in esteem, calling him "the most agreeable of men in conversation and the most temperate in everything else" (trans. Hicks, LCL). Because of this esteem, some scholars assume that Antisthenes's work influenced that of Xenophon, but that assumption cannot be verified.

As is well known, the *Oeconomicus*, which was probably written after 362 BCE, has two major parts. In chapters 1–6, Xenophon reports a conversation that Socrates had with Critobulus regarding household management *(Oec.* 1.1: *peri oikonomias)*. This first conversation is followed in chapters 7–21 by Socrates's report of a conversation that he had with Ischomachus on the same subject. The treatise focuses on topics central to the successful management of a household and its property, such as agriculture, the land, and food production (which was a heightened concern in the years following the Peloponnesian War), the husband's training of the wife in the craft of managing the household, the duties of husband and wife, and the treatment of slaves (on the latter, see Fitzgerald, 2010). It not only survived but also was highly influential in the patriarchal societies of antiquity as well as in Renaissance Italy and England (Pomeroy, 1994). In terms of economic theory, perhaps the most innovative is the theory that he advances regarding the value of goods using a flute to make a distinction between their use value and their exchange value (*Oec.* 1.9–13; 2.13). According to Amemiya (2007: 118):

Xenophon develops a strikingly original theory of values through the mouth of Socrates. Goods have use values and exchange values. A flute does not have any use value to a person who does not play the flute, but because it can be exchanged for money at the market, it has an exchange value. If the person misused the money he obtained at the market, however, it would become worthless.

To this work we shall return later in the discussion of Theophrastus.

The second of Xenophon's works that is most relevant for the ancient economy is his *Poroi*, or *Ways and Means* (sometimes also referred to as *On Revenues* or, using the Latin name, *De vectigalibus*). Inasmuch as this work is much less known than the *Oeconomicus* and focuses on the polis rather than the household, I shall give more attention to it in this survey. It was written toward the end of his life, after Xenophon's ties to Athens and Attica had been severely strained owing to his pro-Spartan actions and sympathies, which had prompted the Athenians to exile him (Diogenes Laertius, *Vit. phil.* 2.51), doing so between 399 and 392 BCE. Most of his time in exile – more than twenty years – was spent in Scillus in the Peloponnese, where the Spartans had given him land (Diogenes Laertius, *Vit. phil.* 2.51), but he later moved to Corinth (Diogenes Laertius, *Vit. phil.* 2.53), where Demetrius of Magnesia, the first century BCE contemporary of Pomponius Atticus and Cicero, says he died (see Diogenes Laertius, *Vit. phil.* 2.56). That may be the case, but many modern scholars argue differently, asserting that he was recalled from exile and spent his final years in Athens (e.g., Gauthier, 1976: 64).

Whether Xenophon spent his final years in Athens or Corinth or somewhere else, three things are clear. First, for most of his adult life, Xenophon had a rather strained relationship with his native city of Athens. Second, at least by the time of his final years, Xenophon and the Athenians were officially reconciled, so much so that he can sing their praises, amend history in Athens's favor in the *Hellenika*, and offer them counsel. Furthermore, at the same time, as Ernst Badian (2004: 33) argued, throughout his life, Xenophon "regarded himself as, and indeed remained, a loyal Athenian, at least by his own lights." He may have opposed much of what happened in Athens, but he regarded himself as part of the loyal opposition. And, third, he was well informed about Athens's economic situation when he wrote his treatise on the political economy, and it is to that treatise that we now turn.

By "political economy," I mean a work that concerns the economy of the polis, not the domestic economy of the household, which was the focus of Xenophon's *Oeconomicus*.[6] The title of Xenophon's work on the political economy in Greek is *Poroi*, literally, "ways" or "means" to achieve something. In the work, Xenophon often refers to *poroi proshodōn*, or "ways of revenue," which is similar to the more common expression *poroi chrēmatōn*, "ways of getting or raising money." The emphasis in the title is thus not on revenue per se, but on the ways and means of creating or increasing it. Hence, the best English translation is probably *Ways and Means*, or perhaps more fully, *Sources of Revenue*.[7]

The traditional date for the *Poroi*, 355/354 BCE, remains the most persuasive proposal and thus is generally affirmed by modern scholars (e.g., Gauthier, 1976: 4–6, 210; Bloch, 2004), who view it as among his last works (e.g., Anderson, 1974: 193), if not his very last work (e.g., Dillery, 1995: 16).[8] This dating means that the historical context for the treatise is best seen as the Social War of 357–355 BCE. This conflict of Athens with its allies in the Second Athenian Confederacy had proved ruinous to the Athenian economy. "The high costs of the war and the loss of important parts of the confederacy's *syntaxeis* ('contributions') brought Athens into a precarious financial situation" (Dreher, 2013: 6303). This was the economic situation that elicited the economic proposals that Xenophon makes in the *Poroi* (Dreher, 2013: 6303).

As Xenophon puts it toward the beginning of *Poroi*, the Athenian masses were reduced to poverty, and the treatise is best seen with Jansen (2007) as an instance of deliberative rhetoric, aimed at a small group of Athenian politicians and finan-cial specialists responsible for the formation and implementation of policies that would address and resolve the fiscal crisis. What, then, was Xenophon trying to persuade them to do, and to dissuade them from doing? How were they to raise the necessary revenues to end the poverty of many Athenians?

One option that he vigorously rejects is the resumption of Athenian imperialism – the belief that Athenian hegemony and prosperity can be attained only by a resump-tion of war (*Vect.* 5.5, 11; see Dillery, 1993). The view that war is a highly lucrative form of acquisition was a cherished belief in Athens and elsewhere, and Aristotle, who recognized the need for states to raise revenues and to have statesmen to understand finance (*Pol.* 1.4.8, 1259a35–8), was later to endorse it as a natural means of acquisition (*Pol.* 1.3.8, 1256b23–6; Ambler, 1984: 493–4). But war as a means of generating revenue, counters Xenophon, entails injustice *(adikōteroi)* toward its allies (*Vect.* 1.1), and peace is far more conducive to prosperity than is war. By framing the issue in terms of justice (1.1: *to dikaion*), he not only acknowledges that Athens has been unjust toward its allied cities (see also 5.13) but also makes economic policy an exercise in applied ethics. The injustice implicit in an imperialistic economy raises for him the question that he tries to answer in the *Poroi*. As he says in 1.1:

> I therefore undertook to see if there was a way for the citizens of Athens to sustain themselves *from their own resources*, which would be the most just *[dikaiotaton]* system, because that would, in my opinion, not only provide them with a remedy for their poverty, but also alleviate the mistrust in which they are held in Greece.[9]

That is, a just domestic economic system enables a state to pursue a just foreign policy.

In the rest of the treatise, Xenophon offers numerous observations and suggestions that would enable Athens to establish a self-sufficient economy, no longer dependent on an imperialistic agenda. He begins by arguing that the natural properties of Attica are "naturally capable of providing a very good income" (*Vect.* 1.2), and these include the land, the weather, the sea, its marble and silver, and its location, all of which make a self-sufficient economy a viable option. In chapter 2, he argues that the resident aliens – the immigrants of antiquity – should be treated more fairly, which entailed relieving them of burdens, granting them more opportunities (such as serving in the cavalry), and giving them the right to own real estate and build houses. In chapter 3, he unfolds a vision of Athens as a commercial center, which would entail the development of the harbor, the expansion of imports and exports, the creation of both material and moral incentives for foreigners to do business in Athens (such as more hotels, business space, and special reserved seats in the theater for merchants and shipowners) and, significantly, the institution of a publicly financed merchant marine.

In chapter 4, Xenophon unfolds a detailed plan for the development of Athenian silver mines, with the plan including public investment in slaves to work in the mines. This public investment would be massive, so that eventually

> the state would imitate those private individuals who have arranged things so that their ownership of slaves is a permanent source of income for themselves, and would acquire state-owned slaves, up to the level of three for each Athenian citizen.
>
> (*Vect.* 4.17)

Of course, such investments could theoretically be done by private individuals, yet he argues that "public funding is a far more realistic proposition than raising that kind of money from private citizens" (*Vect.* 4.18). Here, Xenophon is challenging traditional and "entrenched Athenian notions of what it was proper for the state to do economically, and what should be left to private enterprise" (Cartledge, 1997: 224). Yet he is confident that "there is no reason to worry about either the state-run operation interfering with the private concerns or vice versa" (*Vect*. 4.32). He even suggests a way in which the financial risks of making cuts in rocks and mines to discover new veins of silver can be diminished. He proposes that each of the ten Athenian tribes be given an equal number of slaves, and that if one tribe's slaves discover a new vein of silver, all the tribes would share in the financial benefit (*Vect*. 4.30). Along with these proposals he also makes observations on supply and demand – for example, he notes that "when grain or wine is plentiful, the price of the crops falls, [and] working the land becomes unprofitable" (*Vect*. 4.6). The result is that "large numbers of farmers abandon their work and become traders or retailers or money-lenders" (*Vect*. 4.6). Conversely, when new silver ores are discovered, more people turn to mining (*Vect*. 4.6).

Xenophon recognizes that he is calling for what we today might call a huge economic stimulus plan, so he is cautious enough to argue that his entire plan does not need to be implemented overnight. It should be done gradually, he argues, confident that whatever is done will immediately begin to pay financial dividends (*Vect*. 4.35, 37), and that as part of the plan, "there will be sufficient money in the public treasury to pay every Athenian his allowance" (*Vect*. 4.33).

In chapter 5, he returns to the theme that peace is more conducive to fiscal prosperity than war, and argues that the Athenians, far from waging war, should seek "to reconcile *[diallatein]* warring states with one another and to make peace *[synallattein]* between the factions tearing various states apart" (*Vect*. 5.8). That is, instead of acting as warmonger, Athens should function as the peacemaker.[10] In chapter 6, he concludes by affirming that his plan would have two salutary benefits. The first is that the poor would be maintained in comfort, thanks to a daily three-obol payment that would be made to every Athenian, and the second is that the rich would be relieved of the burden of financing wars (*Vect*. 6.1).

In the *Poroi*, Xenophon offered an innovative plan to achieve the conventional goals of alleviating poverty and increasing revenues. Its details, and especially its idea of public maintenance, have been variously interpreted by scholars, and some (or sometimes all) of his various recommendations have been dismissed as ill-conceived or unrealistic.[11] Yet it seems undeniable that his economic plan was grounded in a vision of a just society and reflected his awareness that when the leaders of a state act unjustly, the citizens will do the same. "Leading politicians act unjustly and, in doing so, serve as a role model to Athenian citizens, with the result that they become (*gignesthai*, 1.1) unjust too" (Schorn, 2012: 694). In addition to advocating for greater equity, Xenophon was arguing for a much more substantial role by the Athenian polis in the economic life of the city. From a philosophical perspective, his aim may well have been "to put into practice in Athens the ideal of governance espoused by Socrates in the *Memorabilia* or demanded by Xenophon himself in the works on monarchic rule" (Schorn, 2012: 717). If Athens had heeded his moral exhortation (Figueira, 2012: 684) and adopted his plan, the result would have been not only a more just society but also a more inclusive one (Jansen, 2012). Yet the historical reality was that Athens did not adopt his plan; if it had, the economic history of Athens and other states would have been different, but whether that would have been better or worse than what happened depends on one's own economic view and values.

Pseudo-Aristotle and the *Oeconomica*

In the centuries following Xenophon, both the household and broader economy were discussed, with primary attention focused on the household and its management. The *Oeconomica* of Pseudo-Aristotle is illustrative of this phenomenon. It consists of three different books, almost certainly by three different authors. Books 1 and 2 are preserved in Greek, whereas book 3 is extant only in Latin. Book 1 deals with "economics" in its older, traditional sense of the principles and rules for the management of an *oikos*, which includes both people and property. Financial factors, such as the acquisition of wealth, are involved in what may be called the economy of the family, but only as they relate to the efficient running of a household. Book 3 is even narrower, and focuses on one aspect of the household, namely, the proper relationship of husband and wife. Book 2, however, moves far beyond the operation of a mere household and its members, and deals with various kinds of governments and their finances, and with issues such as city planning and municipal revenue. For the purposes of this survey, attention will be restricted to the authors who wrote on household management.

Pseudo-Aristotle, Theophrastus, and Philodemus

As for book 1 of Pseudo-Aristotle's *Oeconomica*, we have solid evidence that it was written by the first century BCE, for Philodemus of Gadara (ca. 110–ca. 40 BCE) quotes it in his own work on household management. In this work, he also explicitly names Theophrastus of Eresus as its author. Indeed, the name Theophrastus is mentioned three times in the work (col. VII.38, 44; XXVII.14),[12] and the Theophrastean authorship of the work is consistent with claims by Stobaeus and Eustathius that Theophrastus wrote about household management.[13] Philodemus never quotes Books 2 or 3, so we cannot be sure that he was aware of their existence or whether the three works had even been joined together by his time.[14] But it is a reasonable conjecture that Philodemus was aware of the work prior to its mistaken identification as one of Aristotle's treatises. In any case, Philodemus sets out to refute both Xenophon and Theophrastus, and this dual polemic is prompted in part by the fact that the author of the Aristotelian *Oeconomica* draws upon both Aristotle's *Politics* and Xenophon's *Oeconomicus* as sources for his thought.

Philodemus's treatise was one of the works discovered between 1752 and 1754 in the Villa of the Papyri at Herculaneum and probably unrolled in 1791. The first edition of this papyrus (P.Hercul. 1424) was done in 1824 by Thom Gaisford, and the text began to be studied and reedited during the course of the nineteenth century. Christian Jensen, who was one of the best papyrologists to edit the Herculaneum papyri, produced what has become the standard critical edition in

1906, and all subsequent discussions rely strongly on his text and entail various proposals to modify it. That is the case with the text of Philodemus printed in the Society of Biblical Literature's edition of this work by Voula Tsouna (2012). Although Tsouna offers some new readings and punctuates the text differently at some places, her text is essentially a modified version of Jensen's 1906 Teubner edition. Most important, Tsouna offers the first English translation of this work in her volume, which appeared in 2012.

With Philodemus's treatise, we thus have a copy of a text originally written in Greek. The original was written at some point in the first century BCE, and the copy was made by a scribe at some point prior to the eruption of Mt. Vesuvius in 79 CE, which covered Herculaneum with a pyroclastic surge. As with most papyri from Herculaneum, only the last part of the papyrus roll has been preserved, and in the case of the treatise on household management, only about one-third. Only thirty-three columns of the original ninety-eight are preserved, and to appreciate what that really means, P.Hercul. 1424 is "one of the best preserved of the Herculaneum papyri" (Janko, 2015: 329). The opening section is quite damaged, and Jensen relied heavily on works by Xenophon and Theophrastus (Pseudo-Aristotle) to arrange the fragments and edit the opening part of this text. His operating assumption as editor was that Philodemus began by giving a largely neutral exposition of what Xenophon and Theophrastus had to say about property management, and that our current text begins with the very end of this neutral exposition – that is, with his exposition of Theophrastus (columns A and B). This is what I shall call part 1 of the extant text. What follows next in part 2 is Philodemus's critique of Xenophon (frag. 1–col. VII.37) and of Theophrastus (col. VII.3–XII.1). Jensen estimated that some twelve columns of his critique of Xenophon is missing, and it is only at column VII.27 that the text of the treatise begins to become continuous and more coherent. Part 3, the final portion of the extant text, is devoted to an exposition of the Epicurean views about household and property management (col. XII.2–XXVIII.10).

Philodemus's discussion largely assumes the view, traditional by the time he wrote, that the economy of the household involved four key activities: the acquisition *(ktēsis)* of goods, the orderly arrangement *(diakosmēsis)* of those goods for use, the actual use *(krēsis)* of the goods, and the preservation *(tērēsis* or *phylakē)* of those goods for posterity (Tsouna, 2012: xiii). For his part, however, Philodemus argues that *oikonomia* is specifically concerned with the acquisition and preservation of wealth (XII.5–12), and he treats the arrangement of goods as the least important (X.45–XI.3).

It is the final section of the treatise that is often the point of most interest in the work, for it contains "the most extensive discussion of *oikonomia* . . . found in any Epicurean author" (Tsouna, 2012: xii). The chief debate among Epicurean specialists regarding this section is the extent to which Philodemus is presenting his own views about property management and how much he owes to Metrodorus of Lampsacus's work *On Wealth*. Siegfried Sudhaus (1906) argued that most of this section (XII.45–XX1.35) derives from Metrodorus, who was a member of Epicurus's inner circle and was thus one of the founding fathers of the school, and he is followed in this regard by Renato Laurenti (1973: 151–3), who also views XXII.17–XIII.36 as stemming from Metrodorus. Tsouna (Tsouna-McKirahan, 1996; Tsouna, 2012: 94), by contrast, attributes this section primarily to Philodemus himself. At stake here is an important issue: to what extent do the views found in the treatise reflect traditional Epicurean perspectives on property management, and to what extent may we see in them Philodemus's own adaptation of those views to the circumstances of elite Romans? Tsouna's basic position is strongly buttressed by the analysis and arguments of Elizabeth Asmis (2004), who argues persuasively that, though Philodemus is indebted to Metrodorus and the Epicurean ethical tradition, he is adapting that Greek tradition to the situation of Roman aristocrats.

However one comes down on the issue of tradition versus innovation and adaptation in Philodemus's work, this much is clear: Philodemus did not envision this treatise as one of his "stand alone" or single-volume essays, such as *The Good King according to Homer*. It was intended as a book, or chapter, if you will, in a massive, multivolume work on ethics, to which was given the fulsome title, *On Vices and Their Corresponding Virtues, and the People in Whom They Occur and the Situations in Which They Are Found*. The discussion of *oikonomia* was envisioned as book 9 of this massive work *On Vices*, with proper exercise of *oikonomia* almost certainly intended as the virtue set over the vice of greed and the love of money *(philargyria/philochrēmatia)*, vices that Philodemus discusses in a number of fragmentary pieces (P.Hercul. 253; see also P.Hercul. 465, 896, 1090, 1613, and fragments 8–10 and 12 of 1077).

Virtue is understood here as a kind of practical skill that enables individuals to live in such a way that they can realize life goals, such as imperturbability and the good life. Virtues are thus like crafts *(technai)*, such as medicine and shoe-making (O'Keefe, 2016: 37). Just as the knowledge of the cobbler's craft and skill in putting that expertise to use enable a shoemaker to make and repair shoes, so knowledge of household management and skill in applying that knowledge enable the householder to manage well the household's people and possessions. But this skill comes with an important caveat in the case of Philodemus. He does not believe that philosophers need to be professionals in order to be good household managers. His analogy involves food preparation and the production of bread. All of us need to know how to cook so as to be able to take sufficient care of our needs (col. XVII) and to live a healthy life. But we do not require the expertise of a professional chef working in a five-star restaurant to perform this task. His discussion of financial management is intended for those who wish to live the philosophic life, not for just anyone (col. XII), and certainly not for the manager of a hedge fund or mutual fund who has the goal of maximizing capital appreciation. That is the goal of the money-maker, not the household manager (col. XVII).

From a philosophical standpoint, the truly important point here is that Philodemus regards his discussion of *oikonomia* as fundamentally concerned with ethics (Tsouna, 2007: 163–94). Philodemus, like most ancient philosophers, views *economics as a branch of ethics*. As Tsouna has convincingly argued, Philodemus is indeed concerned especially with the acquisition, use, and preservation of material goods, and his chief concern is with how such necessary activities are compatible with a good life and to what extent they contribute to happiness. The good life – what it is and how to attain it – was, in fact, a central focus of ancient ethics, so it is not surprising that finances and financial planning should be major aspects of ancient discussions of the economy of the household.

One of his major problems with both Xenophon and Theophrastus is that, from his perspective, both presuppose that there is no limit to material acquisition or growth of capital, provided that the means of acquisition is legal. Both Xenophon and Theophrastus think that the man who maximizes his wealth is acting virtuously, especially if he personally supervises his agricultural property, and that those who either fail to maximize their profit or, worse, suffer losses, do so because of vice. For Philodemus, that is hardly the case, and he argues that "the wise property-manager will need to temper the need to maximize profit with other considerations" (Janko, 2015: 329), such as the ethical need to share with his friends. And he will also avoid certain means of profit-making that, though legal, are ethically dubious, such as augmenting income through the exploitation of slaves in mines. "His ideal source of income will be contributions gratefully received from friends to whom he imparts his wisdom" (Janko, 2015: 330).

As all of this suggests, Philodemus's concern with property and property management overlaps to a certain extent with the attention that he gives elsewhere to wealth and wealth management. Following Metrodorus's lead, Philodemus discussed this subject in a separate work titled *On Wealth*. He mentioned this other treatise in his work on property management (col. XII.21), and fragments from at least one book of *On Wealth* are found among the Herculaneum papyri.[15]

Two additional examples of criticisms that he levels against Xenophon and Theophrastus should be mentioned. The first concerns their instructions regarding slave management, which typically employed the carrot-versus-stick method of rewarding hardworking and obedient good slaves and punishing the less industrious and disobedient ones (Fitzgerald, 2010). One of these practices was to give a good male slave a woman with whom he could have sex and procreate, but deny sexual gratification and children to the bad slave. Thus, Xenophon argued, "House slaves may not breed without our consent. For honest slaves generally prove more loyal if they have a family, but wicked slaves, if they live together in wedlock, become all the more prone to mischief" (*Oec.* 9.5). Theophrastus, by contrast, declined to withhold procreation as a punishment for bad slaves, arguing that permitting it would foster loyalty (*Oec.* 1.5.6). Philodemus criticizes them both, saying, "To affirm, indiscriminately, that one should bind slaves to one's service by letting them have children seems worse than what is found in Xenophon, who recommends breeding children from the good slaves, not from the bad ones" (col. X.15–21).

Philodemus was similarly displeased with Theophrastus's counsel regarding slaves and wine, which was to deny them the pleasure of wine or give it to them rarely (*Oec.* 1.5.2). For Philodemus,

It is a harsh claim of his that a drink of wine in general, and not just too much wine, makes even free men insolent, . . . and to say that for these reasons it is obvious that one should distribute wine to the slaves either not at all or very seldom.

(col. IX.32–40)

For him, "the obvious thing is rather that a certain quantity of wine strengthens the spirit and is in ready supply among those who work most" (col. IX.40–4). In short, one should give even bad slaves some wine because doing so will strengthen their spirit, and one should give more wine to industrious slaves.

The second criticism concerns the suggestions that involve the owners and managers of the property. Philodemus rejects certain proposals on the grounds of hedonic calculus and the kind of life appropriate to the philosopher. For example, he discusses the idea of Theophrastus that the husband and wife should not only engage in the personal inspection of their property but also do so with utter vigilance, rising before the slaves, retiring after them, and even getting up in the middle of the night, confident that doing so was beneficial to their own health. For Philodemus, that is crazy. "To wake up before the servants and go to sleep after them is wretched and unfitting for the philosopher . . . and it is very bothersome to acquire the habit of getting up in the course of the night" (col. XI.30–8). As for the claim that doing so is beneficial for one's health and for the study of philosophy, he is at best dubious (col. XI.38–41).

In addition to these overt polemical remarks about his predecessors, there is a not-so-subtle difference in perspective regarding the household. This difference is not unique to Philodemus but rather one that he shares with other Epicureans. As Asmis (2004: 166) points out:

Traditionally the household was viewed as the basic unit from which society is built up. Aristotle developed this view in detail: the household, composed of father, mother, children and slaves, forms the smallest governing unit and is governed in turn by the city, which is composed of households. By contrast, the Epicureans did not privilege the household as the foundation of social or moral life. They rejected the family, just as they did political life. Epicurus held that the wise person will not marry or have children except in special circumstances. This is directly opposed to the Stoic view, which continues the Aristotelian tradition, that a person will marry and have children except under special circumstances.

This means that in Epicurean thought in general, and in that of Philodemus in particular, there is "a shift from taking the household as the basic social and economic unit to treating the individual as an autonomous member of society" (Asmis, 2004: 166). Philodemus may make repeated references to the household, but his operating assumptions are different. Whereas the wife was essential to the traditional household, its economy, and its happiness, Philodemus argues that the happy life does not require a wife (col. IX.1–3).

Finally, it should be noted in all of this that while Philodemus polemicizes against Xenophon and Theophrastus in particular, his argument has a broader relevance. Long before Philodemus was born, Aristotle noted without qualification in the *Nichomachean Ethics* that just as the goal of medicine was health, the *telos* of *oikonomia* was wealth (*Eth. nic.* 1.1.3, 1094a9). In the *Politics*, Aristotle notes that some people consider wealth acquisition through money-making *(chrēmatistikē)* as synonymous with *oikonomia*, whereas others view it as the most important part of household management (*Pol.* 1.2.2, 1253b12–14). So, in short, money-making and the accumulation of wealth were intimately and widely associated with household management, and it is over against this simple identification and association that Aristotle in book 1 of the *Politics* will endeavor to discern what role acquisition has in household management. Aristotle, for his part, defended the acquisitive part of household management as both natural and limited to goods that were necessary to sustain life, such as food. In addition, he emphasized that it was the function of household management to make use of the goods of the household (1.3.2, 1256a11–13).

Bryson

Bryson is the name of a putative Neopythagorean author who wrote a short treatise in Greek on household management titled *Oikonomikos Logos (Management of the Estate)*. Stobaeus (*Flor.* 4.28.15) preserves two extracts of this Greek treatise, which has been dated anywhere from the third century BCE to the mid-first century CE. The treatise remained almost entirely unknown to both classicists and New Testament scholars until Simon Swain (2013) translated it from the Arabic in which it is preserved.

The name Bryson is undoubtedly a pseudonym, not the real name of the treatise's author. Many later Hellenistic and Neopythagorean writings were penned under the name of an early Pythagorean figure, and Iamblichus informs us that "Bryson" was a member of the oldest generation of Pythagoreans, having been a young student when Pythagoras was old (*VP* 104). Furthermore, in keeping with the Hellenistic and Neopythagorean penchant for giving later writings an ancient form of expression, Bryson's treatise, like many other pseudo-Pythagorean writings, was written at least partly in the pseudo-Doric dialect. This linguistic preference was grounded in the conviction of Pythagoras and the earliest Pythagoreans that Doric was the best dialect (Iamblichus, *VP* 241–3). The use of this fake ancient language in composition was thus popular in later pseudo-Pythagorean circles and implied that the ideas were ancient as well. As Swain (2013: 105) notes, "The use of pseudo-Doric . . . is a claim to authority."

Although Bryson is putatively Pythagorean, there is little in his treatise that is distinctively Pythagorean. Aside from the well-known Pythagorean concern with communal life and its concomitant social rules and behaviors, "there is virtually no other sign of Pythagorean philosophy in" the treatise (Swain, 2013: 34). This lack of specific Pythagorean content is, in fact, a common feature of pseudo-Pythagorean writings; as Zhmud (2018: 15) has observed, there is "not a single authentic quotation . . . of any . . . ancient Pythagorean" in "the whole corpus of *Pseudopythagorica*." In view of this characteristic feature, most scholars believe that the philosophy reflected in pseudo-Pythagorean writings should be seen within the general framework of Middle Platonism (Centrone, 2014: 320), which incorporated elements of both Peripatetic and Stoic thought. Zhmud (2018: 3, 20) opines that "most of the authors of [these pseudo-Doric] pseudepigrapha . . . were Platonists" whose "principal aim . . . was to present Pythagoras and his school as the most important predecessors" of Plato.

In any event, Bryson divides his treatment of household management into four parts. The first part deals with property, the second with servants and slaves, the third with the woman (that is, the wife), and the fourth with the child (with the focus on male children). In what follows, I shall limit my focus to part 1.

Part 1, the discussion of property, has four sections. The first deals with the human body and innate human faculties, the nourishment of the body through plants and animals, crafts, urbanization, and barter and the exchange of goods. The second section treats the acquisition of property (that is, the creation of wealth), the third section concerns the preservation of wealth, and the fourth section deals with the expenditure of wealth.

The opening section is the longest. In it, Bryson essentially explains human interconnectivity and our need for one another. We are neither immortal nor intrinsically self-sustaining but must consume food in order for our bodies to grow and develop. Our foodstuffs consist of plants and animals. Indeed, "all (foodstuffs) come from plants and animals because food for each thing comes from what is closest to it, and there is nothing closer to the nature of man's body than animals and plants" (*Oik.* 7).[16]

But plants and animals by themselves are insufficient for our bodily needs. "Plants and animals need various types of crafts in order to come into existence and reach completion" (*Oik.* 8). A garden does not just appear – "plants need sowing or planting, then watering and cultivating" (*Oik.* 8) in order to produce food for humans to eat. Similarly, "animals need feeding, protecting, [and] sheltering" (*Oik.* 9). Food production thus requires crafts, and although we humans have the capacity to discover and learn every craft, the brevity of life means that no one person can learn and master all the crafts (*Oik.* 10). The problem is that knowledge of some crafts is insufficient; "for the management of his life, a man needs all the crafts" (*Oik.* 11).

Furthermore, the crafts are closely interconnected. The builder needs the carpenter, who needs the blacksmith, who needs the miner, who in turn is dependent on the builder (*Oik.* 12). Consequently, "since each man needed for managing the affairs (of his life) a variety of things to feed himself with and to cover himself with," the ultimate result was that "all people needed one another for managing their lives." Given this chain of human interconnectivity and dependence on one another, cities arose. "For this reason," Bryson says, "people needed to form cities and live together in them to help each other with the crafts" (*Oik.* 14).

But urbanization and the physical proximity of craftsmen did not solve two problems involving human need: the amount of need and the occasion of need.

What one person needed and *when* he needed it did not always correspond to what another person wanted or needed and when he needed it. A third problem was that the value of what one craftsman had did not always correspond to what another had to offer, and a fourth problem was that the value of a commodity was not stable but fluctuated according to its "availability on the market" (*Oik.* 20). The various problems that afflicted the market exchange of goods was solved by monetization. "For this reason, then, people coined gold, silver, and copper, and by this means they set prices for all items. They established this convention so that a man could obtain what he needed at the time of his need" (*Oik.* 21). In short, money was created so that humans could more easily acquire the objects needed "to make life good" (*Oik.* 22).

One of the features of Bryson's work that makes it distinctive is this discussion of the origins of money and the theory of economic production and market exchange that he sets forth. Other works on household management do not do this, so Bryson is pioneering in this regard. This first section also makes it clear that the city, with numerous craftsmen and a market for the exchange of goods, is part of the context for Bryson's discussion of the economy. But the city is hardly the focus of his concern. The city's importance is tied to the setting it provides for commerce in the marketplace. When he speaks of slaves and servants in part 2, he explicitly mentions the need for many slaves to manage the country estate (*Oik.* 55, 58). The important point is that Bryson's views on estate management have a pronounced ethical character, which make the principles equally applicable to urban and rural settings alike.

As we have noted, Bryson begins with the need of each human to manage his or her own body by providing it with food to eat and clothes to wear. He proceeds next to the management of one's life and its various affairs. Successful life management depends on the crafts, which through the markets provide humans with the objects that make life good. But efficient markets require monetary exchanges, and through market exchanges, people have the ability to acquire property and build wealth. Bryson's treatise shows us a member of the elite who had interest in markets and in making money. In keeping with that interest, in section 2, Bryson takes up the topic of acquisition of property.

Instead of focusing on *how* to acquire property, however, Bryson in this section deals with three moral failings that hinder acquisition: wrongdoing, outrage, and baseness. As far as wrongdoing is concerned, defrauding one's customers is not only unethical but also a bad business practice. He illustrates wrongdoing by giving several examples. "Wrongdoing," he says, "consists . . . in giving short weight, not filling the measure, practicing deception in the account, evading the truth, [and] alleging untruth." Wrongdoing in business creates a bad reputation – cheated customers don't return to trade with the dishonest businessman but rather tell others about him, and these potential customers also avoid the cheat like the plague.

The second moral failing, outrage, "consists of insulting and slapping and things like that"; and the third, baseness, occurs when one abandons a noble ancestral profession that he is capable of practicing, in order to purse a "more dishonorable craft," such as singing, piping, and other sordid professions. It is one thing, in Bryson's view, to be born into one of the lesser esteemed professions and to practice it; it is quite another to be born into a family that traditionally has practiced an esteemed trade and to abandon it for a baser one.

The third section deals with the preservation of wealth. Here, he sets forth five theses, all sensible in nature. First, "what a man expends should not be greater than what he acquires" (*Oik*. 32). That is, expenses should not exceed revenue. Second, "what he expends should not be equal to what he acquires" (*Oik*. 33). That is, do not spend all one's income – retain a portion so that one has savings as a "surplus" in case of "an accident, disaster, or commercial losses" (*Oik*. 33). Third, "a man should not undertake something he is incapable of sustaining" (*Oik*. 36). For example, a man may have sufficient funds to acquire livestock, but if he does not also have sufficient funds to feed the livestock, he should not acquire them (*Oik*. 36). "When someone ventures on the acquisition of something beyond his capacity, there is an immediate risk that not only the profit will be lost, but his capital will also disappear" (*Oik*. 37). Fourth, a "man should not invest his money in anything that is slow to leave his hands" (*Oik*. 38). This means giving thought to what we would call the issue of "supply and demand." Do not, he says, invest in items that few people want. His two illustrations are of interest: gemstones, which only kings want, and scholarly books, which only scholars demand (*Oik*. 38)! Fifth, a "man should be quick to sell his merchandise but slow to sell his real estate, even if his profit from the former is small while his profit from the latter is large" (*Oik*. 39). The reason for this counsel is doubtless because real estate, that is, land, is foundational for agricultural production, and if that is sold, even at considerable profit, the basis for future revenue is forfeited.

The fourth and final section of part 1 is concerned with the expenditure of wealth. Like the second section, it is written from a moral perspective and deals with five ethical failings: sordidness, meanness, profligacy, extravagance, and bad management (*Oik*. 40). Each of these failings is defined and illustrated. "Sordidness," for instance, "consists in holding back from spending on the categories of the Good, such as supporting relations, benefiting friends and clients, and charity to the needy, as far as he can and is capable" (*Oik*. 41). "Meanness" involves restricting his family's access to essential items such as food (*Oik*. 42). "Profligacy consists in being engrossed in lusts and pleasures" (*Oik*. 43). "Extravagance consists in a man overstepping the expectations of his class in regard to his food or the clothing he might wear due to a desire to show off" (*Oik*. 44). "Bad management" entails poor budgeting and expenditures. For example, "if he is profligate in one" area of household management and thus overspends, he will have to cut back in another, and "his affairs will be out of step with each other" (*Oik*. 45). Of these five failings, the fifth is the most serious. "Worst of all is the condition of the man who is a bad manager, for he is in fact undone because he understands neither the amounts of expenditure nor the occasions for it" (*Oik*. 50).

Good household management, by contrast, involves the avoidance of these failings and the practice of the virtues that stand in contrast to them. The good household manager recognizes and desires the categories of the Good and makes them incumbent upon himself. He is economical on his spending, not profligate, and his expenditures are in keeping with what people in his socioeconomic class can afford. He has a good household budget. "He knows the amounts justified by each category of his [household] needs, and he spends on [each] according to the value of its claim. He is not excessive in one category and then obliged to be restrictive in another" (*Oik.* 51). As a result of being a good manager, he not only has enough revenue or profit to provide for himself and his family, but also "has a surplus which he spends in part on supporting his relations, his friends, clients, [and] in part on supporting his poor and his beggars" (*Oik.* 53). His surplus, moreover, gives him a reserve that he may call upon when the vicissitudes of life demand it (*Oik.* 54). But a reasonable surplus is all the head of the household needs. "He must not demand more than this, since the demand for more is avarice" (*Oik.* 54).

Conclusion

As this brief and selective survey indicates, the earliest Greek discussions of the economy focused on the household. Such a focus was natural since the household was the basic social and economic unit of society. This focus begins with Xenophon and is continued by both Theophrastus and Bryson. Even Philodemus, who has nontraditional ideas about the household, reflects an awareness of its importance. The self-sufficiency of the household was a widespread ancient ideal, but in actual practice there was almost always some degree of interdependence, especially in times of need. Bryson's discussion in part 1 of his treatise reflects his awareness of this interconnectedness and economic interdependence, and he places a premium on moral considerations playing a decisive role in human interactions, including economic ones. Similarly, Xenophon invokes the ethical ideal of justice in discussing interstate relations in the *Poroi*, which is the first Greek treatise to offer economic solutions for the problems of urban poverty. As the preceding survey has indicated, ethics plays an important role in early Greek economic thought.

Notes

1 Finley's *magnum opus* was *The Ancient Economy* (rev. ed. 1999), but his first major study of the ancient economy was devoted to the *horoi*; that is, the marble or limestone steles that functioned as "boundary markers" (Finley, 1952). They are mentioned in the *Iliad* (12.421–423; 21.404–405), where they mark the extent of private property. But Finley in this study focused not on Homeric *horoi* but on those coming from ancient Athens, where they were used to indicate property that had been pledged to secure a loan or some other kind of obligation. Solon's reforms in ca. 594 BCE had included the cancelation of debts, which entailed tearing up these *horoi* or visible symbols of fiscal indebtedness.
2 For the influence of Polanyi on Finley, who participated in Polanyi's famous economic history seminar at Columbia from 1948 to 1953, see Morris (1994: 352–4). Neoclassical economics also influenced Finley, imprinting on him "a sharp contrast between pre-capitalist and capitalist institutions" (Saller, 2013: 60).
3 Ideals are rarely achieved, if at all. Cartledge (2002: 14) thus refers to "the ideally (yet rarely) self-sufficient *oikos*."

4 On the economy of the Aegean in the Bronze Age, see Bennet (2007); on the economy of Early Iron Age Greece, see Morris (2007); on the archaic Greek economy, see Kloft (1992: 98–110) and Osborne (2007); on Homeric (and Hesiodic) society and economy, see Raaflaub (1997) and Donlan (1997).

5 All translations of the *Iliad* and the *Odyssey* are those of Fagles (1991, 1997).

6 Others who use the term "political economy" as appropriate for the *Poroi* include Frolov (1973: 189), Cartledge (1997: 166), and Jansen (2007: 17–18).

7 The forthcoming translation of and commentary on the *Poroi* by David Whitehead in Oxford's Clarendon Ancient History series will render the title as *Revenue-Sources*.

8 The alternative date of 346 BCE, prompted in part by Xenophon's allusion (*Vect.* 5.9) to the Phocian sack of Delphi and the plundering of its treasury (see also Diodorus Siculus, *Bib. hist.* 16.14.3–5; Buckler, 1989), is problematic for various reasons; see esp. Bloch (2004) and Jansen (2007: 54–6). The sack, which prompted the Third Sacred War, occurred in 356/355 BCE and thus was a recent event when Xenophon wrote the *Poroi*.

9 Emphasis mine. All translations of Xenophon's *Poroi* are those of Waterfield (1997), sometimes, as here, slightly modified.

10 On the links between peace, friendship, and reconciliation, see Fitzgerald (2001).

11 Some of his claims are indeed implausible (Schorn, 2012: 706), but it should be noted that Gauthier (2010: 135) not only regards Xenophon "as more realistic than Isocrates" but also argues that his ideas are derived from contemporary fourth-century patterns of thought and images of democracy (2010: 126–35). On Xenophon and Athenian democratic ideology, see also Seager (2001). For a different view, see Schütrumpf (1982), who sees Xenophon as espousing an oligarchic conservatism.

12 Aristotle is mentioned once in the work (col. XXI.28), in relation to Metrodorus.

13 See frag. 661–2 FHSG (Stobaeus) and frag. 663–4 FHSG (Eustathius).

14 Book 3, which is notoriously difficult to date, may not even have been written when Philodemus was active.

15 Book 1 of Philodemus's *On Wealth* is preserved in P.Hercul. 163, which was edited by Tepedino-Guerra (1978). More recently, Armstrong and Ponczoch (2011) have shown that P.Hercul. 1570 probably contains fragments of another book of this same treatise.

16 All translations of Bryson are by Swain (2013).

Bibliography

Ambler, Wayne H. "Aristotle on Acquisition." *Canadian Journal of Political Science/ Revue canadienne de science politique* 17 (1984): 487–502.

Amemiya, Takeshi. *Economy and Economics of Ancient Greece.* Routledge Explorations in Economic History. London: Routledge, 2007.

Anderson, J.K. *Xenophon.* New York: Scribner's, 1974.

Armstrong, David, and Joseph A. Ponczoch. "[Philodemus] On Wealth (*PHerc.* 1570 Cols. VI–XX, PCC. 4–6a): New Fragments of Empedocles, Menander, and Epicurus." *Cronache ercolanesi* 41 (2011): 97–138.

Asmis, Elizabeth. "Epicurean Economics." Pages 133–76 in *Philodemus and the New Testament World.* Edited by John T. Fitzgerald, Dirk Obbink, and Glenn Holland. NovTSup 111. Leiden: Brill, 2004.

Badian, Ernst. "Xenophon the Athenian." Pages 33–53 in *Xenophon and His World.* Edited by Christopher Tuplin and Vincent Azoulay. Stuttgart: Steiner, 2004.

Bennet, John. "The Aegean Bronze Age." Pages 175–210 *The Cambridge Economic History of the Greco-Roman World.* Edited by Walter Scheidel, Ian Morris, and Richard P. Saller. Cambridge: Cambridge University Press, 2007.

Bloch, David. "The Date of Xenophon's *Poroi.*" *Classica et Mediaevalia* 55 (2004): 5–16.

Buckler, John. *Philip II and the Sacred War.* MnemosyneSup 109. Leiden: Brill, 1989.

Carlà, Filippo, and Maja Gori, eds. *Gift Giving and the 'Embedded' Economy in the Ancient World.* Akademiekonferenzen 17. Heidelberg: Universitätsverlag Winter, 2014.

Cartledge, Paul. "The Economy (Economies) of Ancient Greece." Pages 11–32 in *The Ancient Economy.* Edited by Walter Scheidel and Sitta von Reden. New York: Routledge, 2002.

———. Introductions and Notes to *Xenophon: Hiero the Tyrant and Other Treatises.* Translated by Robin H. Waterfield. London: Penguin Books, 1997.

Centrone, Bruno. "The Pseudo-Pythagorean Writings." Pages 315–40 in *A History of Pythagoreanism.* Edited by Carl A. Huffmann. Cambridge: Cambridge University Press, 2014.

Dillery, John. *Xenophon and the History of His Times.* London: Routledge, 1995.

———. "Xenophon's *Poroi* and Athenian Imperialism." *Historia* 42 (1993): 1–11.

Donlan, Walter. "The Homeric Economy." Pages 649–67 in *A New Companion to Homer.* Edited by Ian Morris and Barry Powell. MnemosyneSup 163. Leiden: Brill, 1997.

———. "The Unequal Exchange between Glaucus and Diomedes in Light of the Homeric Gift-Economy." *Phoenix* 43 (1989): 1–15.

Dreher, Martin. "Social War, Classical Greece." *Encyclopedia of Ancient History* (2013): 6303.

Fagles, Robert, trans. *Homer: The Iliad.* Introduction and Notes by Bernard Knox. New York: Penguin Books, 1991.

———, trans. *Homer: The Odyssey.* Introduction and Notes by Bernard Knox. New York: Penguin Books, 1997.

Figueira, Thomas J. "Economic Thought and Fact in the Works of Xenophon." Pages 665–87 in *Xenophon: Ethical Principles and Historical Enquiry.* Edited by Fiona Hobden and Christopher Tuplin. MnemosyneSup 348. Leiden: Brill, 2012.

Finley, Moses I. *The Ancient Economy.* Rev. ed. Sather Classical Lectures 48. Berkeley: University of California Press, 1999.

———. *Studies in Land and Credit, 500–200 B.C.: The Horos Inscriptions.* New Brunswick: Rutgers University Press, 1952.

———. *The World of Odysseus.* New York: Viking, 1954.

———. *The World of Odysseus.* Rev. ed. with an Introduction by Bernard Knox. New York: New York Review Books, 2002.

Fitzgerald, John T. "Paul and Paradigm Shifts: Reconciliation and Its Linkage Group." Pages 241–62 in *Paul Beyond the Judaism/Hellenism Divide.* Edited by Troels Engberg-Pedersen. Louisville: Westminster John Knox, 2001.

———. "The Stoics and the Early Christians on the Treatment of Slaves." Pages 141–75 in *Stoicism in Early Christianity.* Edited by Tuomas Rasimus, Troels Engberg-Pedersen, and Ismo Dunderberg. Grand Rapids: Baker Academic, 2010.

Frolov, Eduard. "Staat und Ökonomie im Lichte schriftlicher Quellen des 4. Jahrhunderts v. u. Z.: Zum Traktat des Xenophon 'Über die Einkünfte'." *Jahrbuch für Wirtschaftsgeschichte* 4 (1973): 175–89.

Gauthier, Philippe. *Un commentaire historique des Poroi de Xénophon.* Hautes études du monde gréco-romain 8. Geneva: Droz; Paris: Minard, 1976.

———. "Xenophon's Programme in the *Poroi.*" Pages 113–33 in *Xenophon.* Edited by Vivienne J. Gray. Oxford Readings in Classical Studies. Oxford: Oxford University Press, 2010.

Janko, Richard. Review of *Philodemus, On Property Management,* by Voula Tsouna. *Bulletin of the American Society of Papyrologists* 52 (2015): 329–31.

Jansen, Joseph N. "After Empire: Xenophon's *Poroi* and the Reorientation of Athens' Political Economy." PhD diss., Austin, TX: The University of Texas at Austin, 2007.

―――. "Strangers Incorporated: Outsiders in Xenophon's *Poroi*." Pages 726–60 in *Xenophon: Ethical Principles and Historical Enquiry*. Edited by Fiona Hobden and Christopher Tuplin. MnemosyneSup 348. Leiden: Brill, 2012.

Jensen, Christian, ed. *Philodemi Peri oikonomias qui dicitur libellus*. BSGRT. Leipzig: Teubner, 1906.

Kloft, Hans. *Die Wirtschaft der griechisch-römischen Welt: Eine Einführung*. Darmstadt: Wissenschaftliche Buchgesellschaft, 1992.

Laurenti, Renato. *Philodemo e il pensiero economico degli Epicurei*. Testi e Documenti per lo Studio dell'Antichità 39. Milan: Istituto Editorale Cispalpino-la Goliardica, 1973.

Morris, Ian. "The Athenian Economy Twenty Years after the Ancient Economy." Review of *Athenian Economy and Society: A Banking Perspective*, by Edward E. Cohen. *Classical Philology* 89 (1994): 351–66.

―――. "Early Iron Age Greece." Pages 211–41 in *The Cambridge Economic History of the Greco-Roman World*. Edited by Walter Scheidel, Ian Morris, and Richard P. Saller. Cambridge: Cambridge University Press, 2007.

O'Keefe, Tim. "The Epicureans on Happiness, Wealth, and the Deviant Craft of Property Management." Pages 37–52 in *Economics and the Virtues: Building a New Moral Foundation*. Edited by Jennifer A. Baker and Mark D. White. Oxford: Oxford University Press, 2016.

Osborne, Robin. "Archaic Greece." Pages 277–301 in *The Cambridge Economic History of the Greco-Roman World*. Edited by Walter Scheidel, Ian Morris, and Richard P. Saller. Cambridge: Cambridge University Press, 2007.

Polanyi, Karl. *The Great Transformation*. New York: Farrar & Rinehart, 1944.

Pomeroy, Sarah B. *Xenophon: Oeconomicus: A Social and Historical Commentary*. Oxford: Clarendon, 1994.

Raaflaub, Kurt A. "Homeric Society." Pages 624–48 in *A New Companion to Homer*. Edited by Ian Morris and Barry Powell. MnemosyneSup 163. Leiden: Brill, 1997.

Saller, Richard P. "Household and Gender." Pages 87–112 in *The Cambridge Economic History of the Greco-Roman World*. Edited by Walter Scheidel, Ian Morris, and Richard P. Saller. Cambridge: Cambridge University Press, 2007.

―――. "The Young Moses Finley and the Discipline of Economics." Pages 49–60 in *Moses Finley and Politics*. Edited by William V. Harris. Columbia Studies in the Classical Tradition 40. Leiden: Brill, 2013.

Salmon, J.D. *Wealthy Corinth: A History of the City to 338 B.C.* Oxford: Clarendon, 1984.

Schorn, Stefan. "The Philosophical Background of Xenophon's *Poroi*." Pages 689–723 in *Xenophon: Ethical Principles and Historical Enquiry*. Edited by Fiona Hobden and Christopher Tuplin. MnemosyneSup 348. Leiden: Brill, 2012.

Schütrumpf, Eckart, ed. and trans. *Xenophon: Vorschläge zur Beschaffung von Geldmitteln, oder, Über die Staatseinkünfte*. Texte zur Forschung 38. Darmstadt: Wissenschaftliche Buchgesellschaft, 1982.

Seager, Robin. "Xenophon and Athenian Democratic Ideology." *Classical Quarterly* n.s. 51 (2001): 385–97.

Sudhaus, Siegfried. "Eine erhaltene Abhandlung des Metrodor." *Hermes* 41 (1906): 45–58.

Swain, Simon. *Economy, Family, and Society from Rome to Islam: A Critical Edition, English Translation, and Study of Bryson's Management of the Estate*. Cambridge: Cambridge University Press, 2013.

Tepedino-Guerra, Adele. "Il primo libro sulla ricchezza di Filodemo." *Cronache ercolanesi* 8 (1978): 52–95.

Tsouna, Voula. *The Ethics of Philodemus*. Oxford: Oxford University Press, 2007.

———, trans. *Philodemus, on Property Management*. WGRW 33. Atlanta: Society of Biblical Literature, 2012.

Tsouna-McKirahan, Voula. "Epicurean Attitudes to Management and Finance." Pages 701–14 in Vol. 2 of *Epicurismo greco e romano: Atti del congresso internatzonale, Napoli, 19–26 maggio 1993*. Edited by Gabrielle Giannantoni and Marcello Gigante. 3 vols. Naples: Bibliopolis, 1996.

Waterfield, Robin H., trans. *Xenophon:* Hiero *and Other Treatises*. Introductions and Notes by Paul Cartledge. London: Penguin Books, 1997.

Zhmud, Leonid. "What Is Pythagorean in the Pseudo-Pythagorean Literature?" *Philologus* (2018): 1–23.

3 Benefactors, markets, and trust in the Roman East

Civic munificence as extramercantile exchange*

Arjan Zuiderhoek

Markets and beyond

The great French historian Fernand Braudel once noted, apropos a discussion of the economy of sixteenth-century Castile, that "60 percent or perhaps 70 percent of the overall production of the Mediterranean never entered the market economy to which our methods of accounting mistakenly seek to assimilate it" (Braudel, 1972: 1:425; cited by Whittaker, 1990: 112 n. 15). The exact percentages can of course be debated, but if Braudel's estimate is anywhere along the right lines, this would mean that even in the early modern Mediterranean, the market was hardly the dominant mechanism for allocating goods and services. Would things have been different in the Roman world? With C. R. Whittaker, I am inclined to think that they were not. As in early modern Europe, there was, of course, regional variation: especially in central Italy, to take the most obvious example, the voracious demand of the Roman megalopolis had strongly commercializing effects on the region's economy. Yet throughout much of the empire's vast agrarian spaces, most peasant production would at all times mainly have served household consumption needs. What was transferred to others would often have flowed through neighborhood or village social networks (but note that some produce would inevitably have to be sold if households were required to pay rents or taxes in coin rather than kind). Elite landowners brought the produce of their estates to urban markets, sometimes over considerable distances, but often provided for the needs of their household and (slave) personnel internally. Even in the empire's bustling cities, substantial amounts of wealth, goods, and services appear to have been produced, distributed, and consumed within extended *familia* networks, hardly touching the market, and within other urban social institutions, such as *collegia*, as well as in elite social circles.

At the risk of stating the obvious, I should point out that there is nothing "primitive" or "underdeveloped" about this. In terms of economic sophistication, the Roman Empire was probably a good match for much of later medieval and early modern Europe, and for other great agrarian empires such as Qin/Han China or the Mughal Empire (Scheidel, 2009, 2015; Bang, 2008). We should also remember that "the market" is not necessarily always and everywhere a synonym for sophistication or efficiency, as we, in the modern West, would understand these terms. Antedating capitalism by millennia, premodern markets (often created by the clustering of population – and especially social elites – in urban centers, and/ or by the need of imperial rulers to raise tribute to pay armies, and using coined money to do so – see Graeber, 2011 on this latter aspect) were generally character-ized by much friction, fragmentation, and uncertainty (Bang, 2008, 2016). Even in modern market economies, as the economist Ronald Coase has pointed out long ago, many transactions can be more cost-effectively concluded by avoiding the market altogether and "internalizing" them into social institutions: that, after all, is why companies exist (Coase, 1937). Nonmarket or extramercantile transac-tions and transfers probably exist in all societies: the more interesting questions to address are (1) why, in a specific society, these transfers took the form(s) that they did, and (2) why, in some societies, such transactions and transfers appear to have been more common than in others. In this chapter, I shall focus on one particular form of nonmarket transfer that was very common in the Greco-Roman world, namely elite benefactions, and explore if and how these related to the market and to the broader political culture of the cities under the empire. My remarks chiefly pertain to the Greek cities in the Roman imperial East during the first, second, and early third centuries CE.

Euergetism as extramercantile exchange

Extramercantile transfers can take multiple forms. One type found in many soci-eties is the gift. Greco-Roman society knew various kinds of gift giving, but one of the most prominent and most visible in the sources was elite public giving, or euergetism. Civic euergetism became ever more widespread in Hellenistic Greek poleis but reached its greatest proliferation in the early Roman Empire of the first and particularly the second centuries CE (Veyne, 1976; Gauthier, 1985; Zuider-hoek, 2009). Elite benefactors used their private resources to contribute to temples and other public buildings (including baths, gymnasia, and theaters), to festivals, games, public banquets, distributions, and occasionally also to civic infrastruc-ture such as roads, aqueducts, and the like. In recent decades, several historians, including myself, have argued, against an older consensus (Veyne, 1976; Wörrle, 1988), that civic euergetism actually was a form of gift *exchange* between elites and ordinary citizens, in which the former gave gifts in return for privileges and honors awarded to them by the citizen community (Rogers, 1991a, 1991b; Zui-derhoek, 2009; Domingo Gygax, 2016, and see also this volume). This model of euergetism, I would argue, has two important interpretative consequences. The first is that it implies a politically active citizenry, which via the public assembly played a crucial role in the allocation of honors to elite donors, and thus exercised a level of control over the munificent behavior of the wealthy. The second is that the exchange between elite and people is viewed as a dynamic *political* process, a form of politics indeed, which turns *euergesia* into a rather fluid and flexible concept: those deeds, and only those, that were in the course of this political pro-cess actually recognized as benefactions deserving the appropriate honors would be considered acts of euergetism. This afforded the people considerable leeway in the allocation of honors and, consequently, in the manipulation of the public behavior of often fiercely competitive elite families (Zuiderhoek, 2008a, 2009).

Let us pause for a bit here, though, and take a step back. For to argue that euergetism constituted a form of gift exchange is one thing. Actually to understand *how*, precisely, as a form of exchange, it affected other facets and institutions of Greco-Roman civic society, is quite something else. For instance, to what extent was euergetic exchange, in fact, truly *extramercantile*; that is, disassociated from the market? The exchange of gifts for honors did not occur via the market mechanism, to be sure. Yet what can we say about possible links between munificence and urban economy and society in a wider sense, including the urban market?

On the basis of the work of anthropological pioneers such as Bronislaw Malinowski, Marcel Mauss, Karl Polanyi, and other scholars inspired by them, it has long been argued that gift exchange constituted an alternative socioeconomic sphere that functioned parallel to, or even instead of, the market. "Gift economies," considered typical of so-called primitive, usually pre-state societies, were thought chronologically to have preceded economic systems based on other forms of exchange, such as barter, redistribution, or the market (which, in turn, were associated with more "developed" sociopolitical frameworks such as chiefdoms and states). For Marcel Mauss, the gift was a total social phenomenon, encompassing all spheres of social life: economic, legal, political, and religious (Mauss, 1923–1924), so that, following this line of thought, one could even speak of gift societies, in which the various social spheres were embedded within one another and had not separated, as they arguably had in modern Western society. Others, most notably Karl Polanyi, argued that various types of exchange, including the market, did function alongside one another in historical societies, but that market exchange became the dominant form of exchange only with the rise of capitalism in the (early) modern West (Polanyi, 1944). More recently, scholars involved in comparative ethnographic, archaeological, and historical research on different forms of exchange have begun to argue that there is, in fact, little or no evidence for societies that were wholly dominated by gift exchange or barter, and that the ideal-typical gift economy of anthropological discourse never existed (Graeber, 2011; Carlà and Gori, 2014). Gift exchange, barter, credit, and commerce appear to be almost as old as human society, and were often strongly interlinked. Not only did (and do) such forms of exchange exist side by side in many societies, but they also interact and influence one another. More specifically for the gift, it has been proposed that, rather than the market and gift exchange standing in structural opposition to one another, gift exchange might, in fact, facilitate commercial transactions through its creation of trust between the individuals and communities involved (e.g., Carlà and Gori, 2014; Verboven, 2014; Molm, Whitham, and Melamed, 2012).

Benefactions, the urban economy, and trust

This revisionist view of gift exchange offers a good point of departure to think further about euergetic gift exchange and its relation to broader economic and social life in the post-Classical polis. In what way(s), if any, did euergetism inter-act with the economy, in terms of the satisfaction of material wants, and more specifically, with that part of it that was effected through market exchange? As said, the exchange of gifts for honors did not involve a market transaction, even though it did often require a lot of institutionalized (and partly ritualized) bargain-ing between the benefactor-to-be, his or her elite peers, and the people. There are, however, a number of ways in which euergetic exchange *indirectly* interacted with broader (market-) economic processes.

Euergetic foundations are a case in point. These were set up by their donors to finance a recurrent benefaction, say, a periodic festival, or for the maintenance of some public building. The capital (consisting of either a cash fund or land/ real estate), which was often entrusted to the civic government, of course needed to generate returns to finance the benefaction (see Laum, 1914, for a large col-lection of relevant, mostly epigraphic, documents). We know from several texts (e.g., *SEG* 13, 1956, no. 258 = Hands, 1968, D 71; Buckler, 1937: 1–10; *REG* 19 1906: 231–48 = Laum, 1914, 2: no. 102) that foundation cash funds were lent out at interest, often in smallish portions, and even though the inscriptions provide hardly any information about the identity of the borrowers or what they used the money for, it seems reasonable to assume that it was used productively. That is, there is a strong likelihood that it was invested in some economic enterprise, whether in agriculture, urban manufacture, or service provision, if only because the sum had to be paid back with the interest accrued. The same line of reasoning can be applied to foundation-related real estate, which in most cases consisted of land, but sometimes also of urban properties (workshops, houses): rent had to be paid by the tenants, so we may reasonably assume that they put their rented land or properties to productive use. In this way, euergetic foundations potentially served as an important source of investment capital and capital goods in Greco-Roman cities, perhaps especially for middling groups who had only limited reserves of capital themselves (Broekaert and Zuiderhoek, 2015: 157–62).

Munificence also had an impact on the workings of the urban food market, partly through such euergetic measures as *parapraseis* (subsidized, i.e., low-cost food provisions to the urban community by elite benefactors, often made in times of scarcity; see Zuiderhoek, 2013), public distributions and banquets, but more importantly via elite contributions toward civic grain funds. These were run by especially designated officials, the *sitōnai*, and in many cities of the Roman East functioned as a financial reserve used to import grain from abroad during local periods of dearth (Strubbe, 1987, 1989; Erdkamp, 2008; Zuiderhoek, 2008b; Solonakis, 2017). Food-related benefactions do not appear to have been espe-cially numerous, though, and outside crisis periods, we may assume that the food supply was mostly left to the market, with some oversight, however, by urban officials (Erdkamp, 2005).

From food-related gifts it is but an easy step to contributions by benefactors to broader public goods that had a direct positive feedback on living standards, such as gifts toward the upkeep of water supply and drainage systems (aqueducts, sewers), the construction and upkeep of roads, the building of schools, and the like. These, however, constitute only a small subset of euergetic contributions; that is, they are by no means the norm (Zuiderhoek, 2009). The more mainstream euergetic gifts, those toward buildings, festivals, and games, will nonetheless also have had (market-) economic consequences to the extent that manpower and materials were acquired commercially, and festivals in particular, drawing throngs of people to the city in question, might give a boost to the local economy (see, e.g., Dio Chrysostom, *Or.* 27.5–6). Thus, in several different ways, euergetic gift exchange interacted with and impacted upon processes of investment, production, exchange, and consumption in the urban economy.

I would argue, however, that, interesting though these various interactions with day-to-day economic processes are, a far more challenging perspective on euergetism is offered by the issue of trust and its relation to gift exchange that is raised by recent work on the gift (e.g., Molm, Whitham, and Melamed, 2012). Gift exchange, though indeed frequently involving the exchange of material goods, often served primarily to create and maintain a social bond, and thus a level of trust, between the parties involved. This building up of trust, in turn, facilitates economic transactions between the groups or individuals concerned, or other forms of social or political interaction or cooperation (see Verboven, 2014, for an important analysis along these lines; also Molm, Whitham, and Melamed, 2012). It is in this wider sense that gift exchange might have had a major impact on economic life and, it should be said, political and social life. Indeed, it might explain why we find it in many societies (including our own) operating side by side and often in interaction with market exchange and, especially in modern societies, even despite the existence of more formalized economic and bureaucratic practices and (state) institutions (Mathews, 2017). Did euergetic gift exchange generate trust in this sense? The answer, I think, is complex, and potentially reveals much about the sociopolitical dynamics in the cities of the Roman East, and perhaps in cities in other parts of the empire as well.

Trust has been called "a multifaceted and relational concept" that is highly context-specific. It can operate at the microsocial level (between individuals) and at the macrosocial level, involving larger social groups or even society as a whole; it can be unconditional and unquestioned (trust in god, a child's trust in his or her parents) or indeed conditional, reflective, rational, and calculating (Marková, Linell, and Gillespie, 2007: 9–11, quote from p. 9). I would argue that euergetism contributed to the building and maintaining of trust in several ways. Being publicly generous was part and parcel of the behavior of every self-respecting elite citizen in a Greco-Roman city. To use a term from evolutionary biology, it was a costly signal to one's fellow citizens (see Wandsnider, 2013) that one cared about the community, was prepared to make sacrifices on its behalf, and could thus be trusted with social power and political office. At both the individual and the group level, therefore, such behavior earned the civic elite legitimacy for its elevated social and political position, a position that was encouraged by the Roman authorities, given that they depended on the provincial urban elites for local administration, tax gathering, and keeping the peace. This kind of social power was difficult to justify in the ideological context of the polis, with its emphasis on the basic political equality of all adult male citizens, unless legitimated through clear and visible efforts, by the wealthy, to benefit their poorer fellow citizens. Legitimization was effectively realized by means of public rituals of praise in which the benefactor concerned was honored by the grateful *dēmos*, in the theater or some other public venue. Such rituals were, of course, situations that served to reinforce the web of loyalty tying elite and non-elite citizens, and citizens *tout court*, together, through a shared public performance of the drama of elite/non-elite reciprocity (Zuiderhoek, 2009). Additionally, benefactors also often gave things that reinforced social cohesion, and hence trust: public buildings that served as markers of civic identity, but also as venues for social activities that reinforced civic bonds – think of the bathhouse, the gymnasium, the theater, and so forth. In particular, benefactors contributed a lot to what Pauline Schmitt Pantel has called "collective activities" (*pratiques collectives*; Schmitt Pantel, 1990), festive public events involving the entire civic community or substantial sections of it, such as games, festivals, distributions, processions, and public meals (Wörrle, 1988; Rogers, 1991b). Such events symbolically united the citizenry, cemented their sense of a collective civic identity and thus their notion of belonging to a wider but clearly circumscribed and identifiable group, which constitutes the basis for macrosocial trust. To be sure, euergetism was not the only source from which such events were financed, but to the extent that benefactors were involved, their gifts can be argued to have contributed indirectly to the manufacture of trust via civic collective practices. How precisely such trust might have facilitated other social transfers, particularly market transactions, is difficult to say at first glance, and would be a very interesting topic to investigate further. For now, at least, we might suggest that the repeated ritual affirmation of shared citizenship will have created and maintained the notion of an "in-crowd" of, at the furthest remove, trusted strangers, with whom it would, therefore, be easier to cooperate and do business than with complete foreigners.

Intra-elite competition

Again, however, I think we need to take a step back, for with this tale of euergetic exchange promoting civic trust and social harmony, we have heard only half the story. That is, we have focused solely on the part best reflected in the language of the honorific inscriptions with their constant references to the elite's *eunoia pros ton dēmon* ("goodwill toward the people") and in the emphasis placed on *homonoia* ("concord") among the citizens in inscriptions, civic coins and political rhetoric (see, e.g., Sheppard, 1984–1986 on *homonoia* within the city and between cities in the Roman East). Other sources, however, hint at a different scenario, providing snapshots of fierce conflicts between elite families generated by the struggle for prestige and dominance in the public sphere, often driven by competitive gift giving. The orator and politician Dio Chrysostom's seemingly endless feuds with some of his elite peers in his native Prusa in Bithynia over a euergetic building project are a case in point (e.g., *Or.* 40.8–14). So too is the Younger Pliny's remark, in a letter to an acquaintance, about an Ephesian benefactor who had been dragged into court by his invidious peers (*Ep.* 6.31.3). Sometimes such conflicts got so out of hand that word of them reached even the emperor's ear (as indeed happened in the case Pliny referred to in his letter). Latter-day *stasis* might ensue in the city in question, and political thinkers warned of the mess that would result once the imperial authorities felt the need to intervene (Plutarch, *Mor.* 814f – 815a *[Precepts of Statecraft]*). Moreover, such conflicts might considerably delay public works that were (partly) euergetically financed, leaving projects unfinished for years. There were costs for individual elite families as well. Some texts even refer to benefactors ruining themselves, in a euergetic race to the bottom with their peers (*IG* IV^2 ,1 65 = Hands, 1968, D 15; Dio Chrysostom, *Or.* 46.3–4; Plutarch, *Mor.* 604b *[On Exile]*). A *topos*, surely, yet one with a clear basis in reality, as is *inter alia* suggested by a reference to the phenomenon in the legal sources (*Dig.* 50.2.8: "It is permitted to supply with provisions decurions who have lost their property, especially if they have exhausted their patrimony through munificence towards their native city" *[Decurionibus facultatibus lapsis alimenta decerni permissum est, maxime si ob munificentiam in patriam patrimonium exhauserint]*, taken from the first book of Hermogenianus's *Iuris epitomae*, a compilation of classical Roman law).

Did such conflicts and their associated effects, such as families overspending, increase in number over time? This is difficult to say. Ancient civic elites had always been relatively open, characterized by upward as well as downward social mobility. Some families simply dropped out of the elite after a generation or two through impoverishment, which might be a consequence of having to divide the family patrimony among too many surviving heirs (the result of a combination of partible inheritance practices and demographic volatility), but might, of course, equally well be caused by euergetic overstretch. Nonetheless, there were some factors that arguably caused intra-elite competition to stiffen during the early and high empire, such as the heavy responsibilities that the Roman authorities placed on the shoulders of the local elites, which gave the latter a lot of power and opportunities for enrichment (tax gathering!) and, as a consequence thereof, the increase in value of the prizes (not just in terms of material wealth but also, crucially, in terms of political power, status, and prestige) that were to be gained at the top of the civic social hierarchy.

At the same time, slow but sustained population growth throughout the empire during the first and much of the second century CE (Frier, 2000: 813–16, 2001; Scheidel, 2001, 2007) also meant that elites, who were mostly large landowners, became considerably richer. In addition, it meant that families owning medium-sized estates over time, through rising rent incomes, became wealthy enough to join the lower ranks of the bouleutic *ordo*, causing civic elites to broaden (Zuiderhoek, 2009). The broadening of local elites might in due course have led to what Peter Turchin and Sergey Nefedov have called "elite overproduction." This refers to a situation, generally occurring during a period of population growth and increasing elite prosperity, in which the number of wealthy, well-educated, and ambitious elite individuals eventually starts to outrun the available number of positions of power, authority, and prestige, resulting in increasing frustration among those losing out. Usually, in Turchin and Nefedov's analysis, such a situation leads to loss of social and political unity among the elite, to discord and intra-elite feuding, and eventually, in a worst-case scenario, to revolution or civil war (Turchin and Nefedov, 2009). The conflicts that we hear of among local elites and in provincial cities, especially from the late first century CE onward, could well have resulted from such a situation of elite overproduction. Anyhow, can we match this side of the reality of euergetism's role in civic sociopolitical life, of euergetism as a tool in, even a source of, intra-elite conflict, to the tale of trust and social harmony generated by euergetism that was sketched earlier? Are these scenarios at all compatible?

I think they are. Overall, I would argue, cities managed to keep just the right balance between the disruptions caused by euergetism-generated intra-elite conflicts and social harmony-enhancing euergetic rituals. Despite occasional disruptive elite conflicts, even if these increased in number over time, it cannot be denied that the *forms* this intra-elite competition mostly assumed, that is, competitive public gift giving, striving for public honors and for political influence in council and assembly, were by and large beneficial to the civic community and the city as a whole. New public buildings, infrastructure, festivals, and games were surely much to be preferred to violent conflict and civil war. During the first and second centuries CE, at least, the socially positive impact of euergetic acts arguably mostly canceled out their potentially negative side effects, even if serious (albeit mostly nonviolent) civic crises may not have been particularly rare.

This leaves us with one further question to consider; namely, why, in this particular case, elite overproduction (if that was indeed the situation) did not lead to more violent and socially disruptive forms of conflict, or even an overthrow of the existing order? Or, to reframe the issue, why did civic provincial elites during the early and high empire choose to compete in these particular, socially fairly nondestructive ways? To some extent, their behavior can be explained by path dependence: the institutional, political, ideological, and even physical context of the polis (think of the shape of public buildings, the physical structure of public space, and the ideas and attitudes associated with it: see Zuiderhoek, 2014) simply invited these forms of elite public competitiveness. The long institutional and political tradition of elite generosity, stretching back to classical, even archaic, times (Domingo Gygax, 2016), ensured that the entire polis setting was geared toward, and stimulated, this type of behavior, and thus guaranteed that as a route to social and political prestige, it was less costly than possible, more violent alternatives. It would require a serious, probably exogenous shock (or series of shocks) to the system to make elite behavior, and polis politics more generally, fundamentally change gear. Empire, whether in its Hellenistic or Roman form, had not provided such a shock. To be sure, it had acted upon and molded elite behavior and civic political life, but it had not fundamentally changed its character. As already suggested earlier, the heavy demands that the Hellenistic royal administrations, but particularly the Roman imperial authorities, placed upon the local elites, and the effects of oligarchization that these had, gave a major boost to civic euergetism, which reached its apogee in the second century CE. Empire thus strongly stimulated the age-old polis tradition of competitive elite public generosity (Zuiderhoek, 2009).

In addition, possible elite tendencies toward predation were held in check: first, by the fact that the polis did not possess much in the way of an institutional (state) apparatus of repression, such as a police force, that the elite could use to subdue the citizens (Zuiderhoek, 2017a: 150–9 for references) and, second, by a strong desire on the part of the elite to avoid central government interference, the inevitable result of civic disturbances caused by predation. Such interference would immediately cancel out the highly profitable and powerful position local elites enjoyed in the under-bureaucratized imperial structure of the principate (Plutarch, *Mor.* 814f–815a *[Precepts of Statecraft]*; Dio Chrysostom, *Or.* 46.14). A far more profitable route to prestige, then, was to interact with the *dēmos* and acquire status, prestige, and power through assembly politics and competitive euergetic display. The fierce intra-elite competition resulting from this was partly mitigated, however, by yet another phenomenon that was a specific product of the socioeconomic conditions of the early and high Roman Empire, namely expanding and increasingly well-off middling groups in civic society, whose members dominated the professional associations *(collegia)* and the public assemblies (Zuiderhoek, 2008a, 2017a: 122–30, with many references). While population growth made elites, as landowners earning higher rent incomes, richer, and broadened their numbers, the growing demand generated by the expansion in number and size of cities, and not least the demand exercised by those very same wealthier and larger urban elites and their extensive households, led to the rise of fairly prosperous middling groups of urban craftsmen, traders, shop owners, service providers, and so forth. These urban middling citizens were among the prime recipients of elite generosity, but did not bear the burden of exploitation, which mostly fell on the rural population working the elite estates. The middling groups, or *plebs media*, then, probably acted as a sociopolitical buffer, constraining elite ambition to some extent (not least through their dominant position in the assemblies, which played a crucial role in the allocation of honors among the elite) and, at the same time, providing a stable political mass with whom the elite could interact peacefully via the public reciprocity of euergetism and patronage.

Conclusion

In Greco-Roman cities, the public exchange of gifts for honors between elites and the people, or euergetism, constituted an important and highly visible sphere of extramercantile transfers. We have seen that, in accordance with recent findings on gift exchange, euergetism interacted in crucial ways with broader (market-) economic processes in the cities. On a more fundamental level, the civic rituals and collective practices associated with munificence arguably also served to reinforce the degree of social trust in the cities, at least among those participating in these events, which frequently was the entire citizenry, and sometimes even groups beyond it (Zuiderhoek, 2017b). This may well have been beneficial to social and economic development in a broader sense. At the same time, however,

I would suggest that the case of civic euergetism also shows that we should not be *too* complacent about the possible trust-generating and social harmony-enhancing effects of gift exchange. Surely, these were present, but there was a competitive, disruptive, and potentially destructive side to gift exchange as well, which, in the case of civic euergetism in the East during the early and high empire, was mitigated by various propitious circumstances both internal and external to Greco-Roman civic life. We may add, finally, that many of the phenomena and conditions referred to earlier (the low level of imperial bureaucracy, the consequently important administrative role of provincial civic elites, the growth of the population, the expansion of civic elites and middling groups, the continuing influence of the people in urban politics, etc.) came to an end, or were modified, in the third century. Intriguingly, this was also precisely the period when the types of local elite behavior that we have been exploring in this chapter seem to disappear from view.

Note

* To the memory of my father, Dries Zuiderhoek (1950–2019).

Bibliography

Bang, Peter Fibiger. "Beyond Capitalism: Conceptualising Ancient Trade through Friction, World Historical Context and Bazaars." Pages 75–89 in *Dynamics of Production in the Ancient Near East 1300–500 BC*. Edited by Juan Carlos Moreno García. Oxford: Oxbow, 2016.

———. *The Roman Bazaar: A Comparative Study of Trade and Markets in a Tributary Empire*. Cambridge: Cambridge University Press, 2008.

Braudel, Fernand. *The Mediterranean and the Mediterranean World in the Age of Phillip II*. Translated by S. Reynolds. London: Collins, 1972.

Broekaert, Wim, and Arjan Zuiderhoek. "Society, the Market, or Actually Both? Networks and the Allocation of Credit and Capital Goods in the Roman Economy." *Cahiers du Centre Gustave-Glotz* 26 (2015): 141–90.

Buckler, William H. "A Charitable Foundation of A.D. 237." *Journal of Hellenic Studies* 57 (1937): 1–10.

Carlà, Filippo, and Maja Gori, eds. *Gift Giving and the 'Embedded' Economy in the Ancient World*. Heidelberg: Universitätsverlag Winter, 2014.

Coase, Ronald H. "The Nature of the Firm." *Economica* n.s. 4.16 (1937): 386–405.

Domingo Gygax, Marc. *Benefaction and Rewards in the Ancient Greek City: The Origins of Euergetism*. Cambridge: Cambridge University Press, 2016.

Erdkamp, Paul. "Grain Funds and Market Intervention in the Roman World." Pages 109–26 in *Feeding the Ancient Greek City*. Edited by Onno M. van Nijf and Richard Alston. Groningen-Royal Holloway Studies on the Greek City after the Classical Age 1. Leuven: Peeters, 2008.

———. *The Grain Market in the Roman Empire: A Social, Political and Economic Study*. Cambridge: Cambridge University Press, 2005.

Frier, Bruce W. "Demography." Pages 787–816 in *The High Empire, AD 70–192*. Vol. 11 of *The Cambridge Ancient History*. 2nd ed. Edited by A.K. Bowman, P. Garnsey, and D. Rathbone. Cambridge: Cambridge University Press, 2000.

————. "More Is Worse: Some Observations on the Population of the Roman Empire." Pages 139–59 in *Debating Roman Demography*. Edited by Walter Scheidel. Leiden: Brill, 2001.

Gauthier, Philippe. *Les cités grecques et leurs bienfaiteurs*. Athens: École française d'Athènes, 1985.

Graeber, David. *Debt: The First 5,000 Years*. Brooklyn: Melville House, 2011.

Hands, Arthur R. *Charities and Social Aid in Greece and Rome*. Ithaca: Cornell University Press, 1968.

Laum, Bernhard. *Stiftungen in der griechischen und römischen Antike: Ein Beitrag zur antiken Kulturgeschichte*. 2 vols. Leipzig: Teubner, 1914.

Marková, Ivana, Per Linell, and Alex Gillespie. "Trust and Distrust in Society." Pages 3–27 in *Trust and Distrust: Sociocultural Perspectives*. Edited by Ivana Marková and Alex Gillespie. Charlotte, NC: Information Age Publishing, 2007.

Mathews, Martin. "Gift-Giving, Reciprocity and the Creation of Trust." *Journal of Trust Research* 7 (2017): 90–106.

Mauss, Marcel. "Essai sur le don: Forme et raison de l'échange dans les sociétés archaïques." *L'Année sociologique* n.s. 1 (1923–1924): 30–196.

Molm, Linda D., Monica M. Whitham, and David Melamed. "Forms of Exchange and Integrative Bonds: Effects of History and Embeddedness." *American Sociological Review* 77.1 (2012): 141–65.

Polanyi, Karl. *The Great Transformation: The Political and Economic Origins of Our Time*. New York: Farrar & Rinehart, 1944.

Rogers, Guy M. "Demosthenes of Oenoanda and Models of Euergetism." *Journal of Roman Studies* 81 (1991): 91–100. (1991a).

————. *The Sacred Identity of Ephesos: Foundation Myths of a Roman City*. London: Routledge, 1991. (1991b).

Scheidel, Walter. "Demography." Pages 38–86 in *The Cambridge Economic History of the Greco-Roman World*. Edited by Walter Scheidel, Ian Morris, and Richard Saller. Cambridge: Cambridge University Press, 2007.

————. "Progress and Problems in Roman Demography." Pages 1–81 in *Debating Roman Demography*. Edited by Walter Scheidel. Leiden: Brill, 2001.

————, ed. *Rome and China: Comparative Perspectives on Ancient World Empires*. Oxford: Oxford University Press, 2009.

————, ed. *State Power in Ancient China and Rome*. Oxford: Oxford University Press, 2015.

Schmitt Pantel, Pauline. "Collective Activities and the Political in the Greek City." Pages 199–213 in *The Greek City from Homer to Alexander*. Edited by Oswyn Murray and Simon Price. Oxford: Clarendon, 1990.

Sheppard, A.R.R. "*Homonoia* in the Greek Cities of the Roman Empire." *Ancient Society* 15–17 (1984–1986): 229–52.

Solonakis, Nicolas. *Surplus, Subsistence and Shortage: The Grain Supply of the Graeco-Roman Mediterranean, between Agrarian Economy, Markets and Civic Institutions (1st–3rd c. AD)*. PhD diss. Ghent: Ghent University, 2017.

Strubbe, Johan H.M. "The *sitonia* in the Cities of Asia Minor under the Principate (I)." *Epigraphica Anatolica* 10 (1987): 45–82.

————. "The *sitonia* in the Cities of Asia Minor under the Principate (II)." *Epigraphica Anatolica* 13 (1989): 97–122.

Turchin, Peter, and Sergey Nefedov. *Secular Cycles*. Princeton: Princeton University Press, 2009.

Verboven, Koenraad. "'Like Bait on a Hook': Ethics, Etics and Emics of Gift-Exchange in the Roman World." Pages 135–53 in *Gift Giving and the 'Embedded' Economy in the Ancient World*. Edited by Filippo Carlà and Maja Gori. Heidelberg: Universitätsverlag Winter, 2014.

Veyne, Paul. *Le pain et le cirque: Sociologie historique d'un pluralisme politique*. Paris: Seuil, 1976.

Wandsnider, LuAnn. "Public Buildings and Civic Benefactions in Western Rough Cilicia: Insights from Signaling Theory." Pages 176–88 in *Rough Cilicia: New Historical and Archaeological Approaches; Proceedings of an International Conference held at Lincoln, Nebraska, October 2007*. Edited by Michael C. Hoff and Rhys F. Townsend. Oxford: Oxbow, 2013.

Whittaker, Charles M. "The Consumer City Revisited: The *vicus* and the City." *Journal of Roman Archaeology* 3 (1990): 110–18.

Wörrle, Michael. *Stadt und Fest im kaiserzeitlichen Kleinasien: Studien zu einer agonistischen Stiftung aus Oinoanda*. Munich: Beck, 1988.

Zuiderhoek, Arjan. *The Ancient City*. Key Themes in Ancient History. Cambridge: Cambridge University Press, 2017. (2017a).

———. "Controlling Urban Public Space in Roman Asia Minor." Pages 99–108 in *Space, Place and Identity in Northern Anatolia*. Edited by Tønnes Bekker-Nielsen. Stuttgart: Steiner, 2014.

———. "Feeding the Citizens: Municipal Grain Funds and Civic Benefactors in the Roman East." Pages 159–80 in *Feeding the Ancient Greek City*. Edited by Onno M. van Nijf and Richard Alston. Groningen-Royal Holloway Studies on the Greek City after the Classical Age 1. Leuven: Peeters, 2008. (2008b).

———. "No Free Lunches: Paraprasis in the Greek Cities of the Roman East." *Harvard Studies in Classical Philology* 107 (2013): 297–321.

———. "On the Political Sociology of the Imperial Greek City." *Greek, Roman, and Byzantine Studies* 48 (2008): 417–45. (2008a).

———. *The Politics of Munificence in the Roman Empire: Citizens, Elites and Benefactors in Asia Minor*. Cambridge: Cambridge University Press, 2009.

———. "Un-Civic Benefactions? Gifts to Non-Citizens and Civic Honours in the Greek Cities of the Roman East." Pages 182–98 in *The Politics of Honour in the Greek Cities of the Roman Empire*. Edited by Anna Heller and Onno M. van Nijf. Leiden: Brill, 2017. (2017b).

4 Euergetism and the embedded economy of the Greek polis

Marc Domingo Gygax

The decrees issued by the Greek cities in honor of their benefactors are a major source of information for the study of ancient Greek society. In comparison to literary sources, these decrees have the advantage of usually referring to contemporary events and to persons who do not appear in literature. Although they tell us about every sort of honoree (artists, athletes, war heroes, and so on), a substantial portion of the individuals rewarded had dedicated time and resources to their community. The impression these documents create is that Greek cities were full of benefactors and that a significant portion of the polis's economy rested on their contributions. But we must be very careful when drawing conclusions from this material. Benefactors are overrepresented in comparison with other actors in Greek society. We have many honorary decrees because one of the rewards benefactors often received was precisely the inscription of the honorific decree on stone. Cities took many other decisions that were not recorded on stone, including resolutions regarding the organization of public finances. Evaluation of the economic role of benefactors is thus a complicated matter, and as we will see, there are many disagreements among scholars regarding this aspect of Greek society.

Some terminological questions

Before I begin my analysis of the role of benefactors, some terminological issues must be addressed. The term *euergetism* used in the title of this chapter is a modern word coined after the ancient Greek words *euergesia* ("benefaction"), *euergetēs* ("benefactor"), and *euergeteō* ("to be a benefactor") by André Boulanger (1923: 25). After it was used by Henri-Irénée Marrou in his *Histoire de l'éducation dans l'Antiquité* (1948: 161, 405), it became widespread among ancient historians with the publication of Paul Veyne's *Le pain et le cirque* (Veyne, 1976) and its English translation in 1990. In the field of Greek history, the publication of Philippe Gauthier's *Les cités grecques et leurs bienfaiteurs* (Gauthier, 1985), with a long introduction that was very critical of Veyne's work, also contributed considerably to the spread of the term. As a result, in the last three decades many articles and books about euergetism in different ancient places and historical contexts have been published. But not all scholars understand "euergetism" the same way. Most use the term to refer merely to the phenomenon of voluntary gift giving to the community by individual citizens or external agents such as foreigners, Hellenistic kings, or Roman emperors (e.g., Spawforth). This conception of euergetism emphasizes the actions of benefactors rather than the reactions of beneficiaries, and treats euergetism essentially as munificence. It has also been argued, however, that benefactions were only one part of the complex, ongoing process of euergetism. Benefactions attracted honors and informal (unofficial) counter-gifts from the entire community; euergetism was characterized by reciprocity rather than one-way benefit. On this way of looking at the matter, euergetism was an *institution* and was essentially related to gift exchange (Domingo Gygax, 2003; Zuiderhoek, 2009).

This chapter deals with both "euergetisms." On the one hand, it takes into account donations by citizens to the archaic and classical polis that I personally do not consider manifestations of euergetism – because they could not be publicly recognized as benefactions through honors – but that fit a broader definition of the term. Although Engen (2010: 66–7) speaks of an "archaic, aristocratic euergetism," few scholars regard these as instances of euergetism due to the influence of Veyne, for whom euergetism does not begin until the Hellenistic period; the precondition for its emergence being the existence of Hellenistic notables. But these donations, despite not being expressions of an exchange of benefactions and honors, are much more closely related to this type of euergetism than they seem. They partly coincide with a time when foreigners were already rewarded as *euergetai*, and there were even citizens – victors in Panhellenic games – who received such treatment from their poleis. In other words, such donations occurred in an environment that was already "euergetic." Moreover, they were often part of a relationship of reciprocity with the community, in which context they were exchanged for informal gifts such as political support instead of honors.

On the other hand, this chapter considers the euergetism of benefactions and honors, a euergetism that should not simply be understood as an exchange of donations and honors. This euergetism includes benefactions that were not donations, such as heroic acts of war, athletic victories, artistic accomplishments, and political and diplomatic favors from foreigners; that is, services that scholars who understand euergetism to be "the phenomenon of gift giving to the community" normally do not take into account. These noneconomic benefactions were the earliest in the history of euergetism, and donations were incorporated into the institution only later on. The consideration of this type of euergetism, which can be characterized as an institution, is crucial to understand how and why many donations occurred. Despite having started with noneconomic benefactions, this euergetism ended up becoming an economic instrument of the polis (Domingo Gygax, 2016).

Models, theories, and paradigms

When in 1981 G. E. M. de Ste. Croix published his chapter "The Destruction of Greek Democracy" in *The Class Struggle in the Ancient Greek World* (de Ste. Croix, 1981: 300–26), the thesis that the Hellenistic age represented a period of crisis or of decline of the polis was prevalent among ancient historians. In accord with this view, de Ste. Croix offered an interpretation of the Hellenistic world in which the poleis were dominated by the Hellenistic monarchs and polis elites. Although in some poleis the kings did not interfere in internal affairs, in others, they appointed magistrates and overseers (e.g., *epimelētai*) and established garrisons. Elites cooperated with the kings, often against the interests of the rest of the community; citizen assemblies became increasingly controlled by royal officers, magistrates, and councils, and popular law courts *(dikastēria)* gradually disappeared. Last, but not least, de Ste. Croix made an observation that is particularly relevant for our study: magistracies were assimilated to liturgies by the attachment of special burdens to the performance of offices, as a way of both concentrating political power in the hands of a wealthy minority and avoiding having to introduce taxes. In de Ste. Croix's words, the purpose of the liturgization of magistracies was

> to keep the poorer citizens out of office without having to pass invidious legislation to that end, and even more to serve as a substitute for the one thing the wealthy Greeks would never tolerate: a legally enforceable taxation system under which the burden of maintaining the state would fall mainly upon those who derived most benefit from it and were best able to bear that burden.
>
> (de Ste. Croix, 1981: 306)

Apart from contributions that were indispensable for the smooth functioning of the polis, elites provided "charity" to the demos as compensation for its loss of political power:

> They offered to the lower classes a certain amount of *charity*, to be granted or withheld at their own pleasure. When things were not going well for them the charity could be cut down, without anyone having the right to complain. They were prepared on occasion to enforce upon recalcitrants among their own number the performance of expensive tasks which were really necessary; but inessential offices involving some outlay could at a pinch, in very hard times, or when no one could be persuaded to shoulder the burden, be conferred upon some obliging god or hero, who could scarcely be expected to make the customary expenditure.
>
> (de Ste. Croix, 1981: 306)

Although de Ste. Croix is considered a "singular" ancient historian – because he was a Marxist, but also because his Marxist approach focused on class struggle rather than on the mode of production – at the time he wrote these lines, his ideas about the Hellenistic polis and euergetism, based on the work of A. H. M. Jones (1971, 1940), were largely shared by students of the ancient Greek world. Claire Préaux believed that decrees in honor of *euergetai* reflected great economic inequalities and the concentration of wealth and political power in the hands of a few individuals who tried to obtain economic advantages and maintain the established order through political positions and donations (Préaux, 1978: 435–48). Similarly, Pierre Lévêque maintained that the rich, in order to mitigate the intensity of the contradictions between rich and poor, had no choice but to redistribute part of their wealth through the "system of euergetism," the only way in which the façade of *homonoia* could be safeguarded. Yet Lévêque, unlike de Ste. Croix, did not attribute an important role in the financing of the polis to euergetism; its function, as he saw it, was to mask the reality of social relations through the redistribution of a minimal part of the surplus accumulated by the ruling class (Lévêque, 1977: 96–103, 148). Likewise, Hans-Joachim Gehrke argued that elites tried to reinforce their superiority in the social structure by using their position and wealth to make public contributions (Gehrke, 1990: 67–9, 181–2). Both Gehrke and Lévêque describe a process that explains how the situation portrayed by them as well as by de Ste. Croix was reached: in the Hellenistic period, the economic and social gap between elites and the rest of society progressively increased due to a concentration of land in the hands of the rich, who also accumulated money through trade.

Veyne (1976) and Gauthier (1985) offer interpretations of euergetism considerably different from those of de Ste. Croix, Lévêque, and Gehrke, but also relate the phenomenon to "the crisis" of the polis. For Veyne, the emergence of euergetism had mainly to do with two developments: (1) the polis's loss of political significance in an international context dominated by the Hellenistic monarchies, which led to a devaluation of public offices; and (2) the establishment of regimes of city notables; that is, of governments of rich individuals who spent time and money performing public functions in formally democratic institutions in the conviction that polis politics were "their business," while the rest of the citizens gave up any political responsibility. In addition, Veyne reminds us of a sort of universal law expressed by Max Weber: "Toute démocratie directe tend à se convertir en un gouvernement des notables" (Veyne, 1976: 201).[1] According to Veyne, euergetism had nothing to do with a need on the part of elites to distribute wealth in order to maintain their privileged position. The demos did not ask for a social balance it did not know; it conformed to circumstances and did not question the regime of the notables or their wealth. The only social pressure came from the fact that a sort of historical pact obliged notables to be generous. But the main reason they performed onerous magistracies and made ostentatious gifts was the need of every elite group to express its superiority, its "social distance" with respect to the rest of society (Veyne, 1976: 299, 304, 311, 317–19, 326–7).

Gauthier, in principle, does not relate euergetism to a decline of the polis but quite the contrary: euergetism arose before the Hellenistic period, in the fourth century, and did so not in contradiction with the spirit of the classical polis but as a manifestation of the solidarity and patriotism of good citizens. But at the same time, Gauthier attaches great significance to the benefactions of the Hellenistic monarchs in the evolution of euergetism: thanks to their wealth and power, they could make large donations to cities, and when the Hellenistic monarchies experienced a crisis in the late Hellenistic period, great citizen benefactors emerged to fill part of the vacuum left by the kings. They financed festivals, buildings, and food distribution and were rewarded with high honors, giving rise to a superior class of citizens (Gauthier, 1985: 39ff., 53ff.).

In the last thirty years, the view of the Hellenistic polis on which these explanations of euergetism are based has been increasingly challenged. Scholars working on the archaic and classical polis, particularly Mogens Herman Hansen and his collaborators in the Copenhagen Polis Centre, have stressed that in the pre-Hellenistic Greek world, many small and middle-sized city-states did not enjoy much autonomy, since they were dominated by larger poleis or by the Persian king. For these secondary communities, the transition to the political conditions of the Hellenistic world did not represent much of a change (Hansen and Nielsen, 2004). Hellenistic historians, for their part, have contested the thesis of the decline of the Hellenistic polis. Since Erich Gruen published his influential paper "The Polis in the Hellenistic World" (Gruen, 1993), many articles and books have been written attempting to demonstrate that in Hellenistic cities the assemblies were well attended; citizens discussed and decided on political issues relevant to them; the demos had the capacity to exercise pressure on the elite; the term *dēmokratia* was a reflection of democratic institutions rather than of a republican regime; references to "freedom" and "autonomy" in negotiations between poleis and kings did not indicate how threatened but how valued these statuses were, and reflected the role of the kings in protecting them; many poleis were international actors who took advantage of rivalries among kings and had the capacity to sign treaties among themselves and to act as arbiters in inter-city conflicts; and, finally, thanks to all these circumstances, the exchange of donations and honors between elite and demos was not a sign of "decadence," but testimony to the communal spirit of benefactors and beneficiaries and of their attachment to the polis.

In line with these views, in recent years, two extensive monographs devoted entirely to showing the vitality of Hellenistic democracy – or, as many prefer, "democracies" – have been published (Grieb, 2008; Carlsson, 2010). It has also been stressed that even under Roman imperial rule, many aspects of traditional Greek democracy – especially the role of popular assemblies in decision-making – survived at least until well into the third century CE (Brélaz, 2013; Oppeneer, 2018). Finally, scholars have argued that the finances of the Hellenistic and imperial poleis were not as bad as has traditionally been assumed. Poleis had their own income from various fees and the leasing of public land, and obtained loans they were able to repay. Recourse to benefactors was necessary only in exceptional situations (e.g., crises caused by war, bad harvests, or earthquakes). The material aid to cities by Hellenistic kings was an extraordinary measure; it was instead the kings who depended on the poleis for their finances (Migeotte, 2006; Zuiderhoek, 2009; Strootman, 2014).

It is important to take this change in the interpretation of the Hellenistic polis in recent scholarship into consideration when evaluating the role of euergetism (see Domingo Gygax and Zuiderhoek, forthcoming). But we must also bear in mind that this new perception is the result not of the discovery of new evidence but of a paradigm shift connected to major cultural, political, and economic developments in the last thirty years (Hasegawa, 2017). The influence of postcolonial studies in the humanities (e.g., Said, 1978) has led to the traditional narrative of the evolution of the polis and democracy in the classical and Hellenistic periods being seen as Eurocentric (Athenocentric) and to reevaluation of the role of the multiple poleis that made up the Hellenistic world. But the change of paradigm is also related to ideas of a different nature derived from the end of the Cold War, the apparent success of Western democracy and capitalism over communism (Fukuyama's "end of history") and the crises of Marxism and of interpretations centered on class conflict, specifically ideas about the organizational superiority of democracy, its capacity for resistance to totalitarian empires, its relationship to economic success, its tendency to become universal, and its condition as the *natural* political system of humankind. Moreover, the Hellenistic world, due to its enormous political plurality – many poleis and democracies – multiculturalism, ethnic and religious diversity, fluidity of borders between kingdoms, political instability, multipolarity, cosmopolitanism, and freedom of movement, has become a paradise for the postmodern historian. This has led to the detection of aspects of political life that were overlooked in previous paradigms, but also to a certain idealization of the Hellenistic polis. Much as the positive view of the Hellenistic world of many late nineteenth-century and early twentieth-century historians is related to their conception of European imperialism rather than to the corpus of information available to them (Ellis-Evans, 2017), the new positive vision has less to do with the discovery of new inscriptions, papyri, coins, or other material evidence than with ideological changes. The same examples that have been cited to demonstrate the vitality of the Hellenistic assemblies had already been mentioned by de Ste. Croix in his analysis of the destruction of democracy (de Ste. Croix, 1981: 305). Despite recent trends in scholarship, Hans-Ulrich Wiemer, using the same information, has written an essay on the Hellenistic polis that incorporates the revisionist view of the early Hellenistic polis but offers a clear "decline" narrative in his analysis of the evolution of the polis after the mid-second century BCE (Wiemer, 2013). Likewise, Phillip Harding (2015) has recently published a book with the illustrative title *Athens Transformed, 404–262 BC: From Popular Sovereignty to the Dominion of Wealth*, while in his monograph on the history of democracy Paul Cartledge entitled the chapter on the Hellenistic period "Hellenistic Democracy? Democracy in Deficit c. 323–86 BCE" (Cartledge, 2016: 219–28).[2]

In conclusion, in our current state of knowledge, a good way of arriving at new conclusions about the economic role of euergetism would seem to be not to consider the Hellenistic material yet again, but to turn to the earlier stage of euergetism. This phase has been neglected due to the influence of Veyne's idea that euergetism begins in the Hellenistic period. But an examination of Greek attitudes toward gifts in the classical and even archaic periods, and of the circumstances in which the practice of honoring citizens was established in Athens, can shed new light on the question.

The meaning of gifts

Giving to the community was an act of generosity and solidarity, and is recognized as such in multiple honorary decrees, in which we read, for example, that a citizen "is good and has performed services for the community and in particular to each citizen" (e.g., *TAM* II 160), while many similar phrases refer to the *eunoia* ("goodwill"), *aretē* ("virtue"), *philotimia* ("love of honor") and *philanthrōpia* ("humanity") of certain citizens (Veligianni-Terzi, 1997; Gray, 2013). But this does not mean that we should understand euergetism simply as an expression of the goodness, altruism, and patriotism of certain citizens and of the promotion of these virtues by the polis. The Greeks had a complicated relationship with both donations and honors. Literary texts and inscriptions are full of references to the obligation to reciprocate gifts (e.g., Aristotle, *Eth. nic.* 1167a 14–16; Pseudo-Aristotle, *[Rhet. Alex.]* 1446b 36–8).[3] The ancient authors reflect on the feeling of indebtedness of those who receive a gift, their sense that a counter-gift will not be perceived as a gift but only as the cancelation of a debt, how this affects their attitude toward givers, the superiority/inferiority relationship between giver and receiver while the receiver is in debt after the exchange, and possible strategies to transform this inferiority into superiority. In his Funeral Oration, Thucydides's Pericles maintains that "he who owes [a favor] is more listless in friendship [than the benefactor], knowing that when he repays the kindness it will count not as a favor bestowed but as a debt repaid" (Thucydides 2.40.4, trans. Smith), while Demosthenes maintains that "the recipient of a benefit ought to remember it all his life, but the benefactor ought to put it out of his mind at once, if the one is to behave decently and the other with magnanimity," and considers that "to remind a man of the good turns you have done to him is very much like a reproach" (Demosthenes 18.69, trans. Vince). Aristotle believes that "[the great-souled man] is fond of conferring benefits but ashamed to receive them, because the former is a mark of superiority and the latter of inferiority"; for this reason, "he returns a service done to him with interest, since this will put the original benefactor into his debt in turn and make him the party benefited" (*Eth. nic.* 1124b 9–18, trans. Rackham).[4]

As these quotations indicate, receiving was not just an act of enrichment, but also had its downsides. Although the ancient Greeks had the notion of the "free gift" – "a 'gift' is a 'giving that needs no giving in return'" (Aristotle, *Top.* 125a 15) – the fact that it was usually necessary to reciprocate created a feeling of debt that lasted until the receiver found an opportunity to pay off. This feeling of indebtedness could be increased by pressure from the donor. The passage from Thucydides quoted earlier, in fact, is preceded by the observation that "he who confers the favor is a firmer friend, in that he is disposed, by continued goodwill toward the recipient, to keep the feeling of obligation alive in him" (Thucydides 2.40.4, trans. Smith). The benefactor exerted pressure, because the lack of a counter-gift not only represented a loss for him but also could convey the false impression that his gift was not a gift but a counter-gift.

Accepting a gift often implied entering into a power relationship in which the receiver was the weaker party. By means of his act of giving, the giver obliged the receiver to reciprocate, and his gift determined the dimension of the counter-gift (since only an equivalent counter-gift would cancel the debt). Moreover, the giver was normally in a position of moral superiority not only while he was owed a counter-gift but also after he had received it, since by taking the initiative he had ventured it not being reciprocated or being insufficiently compensated. As Aristotle indicates in the sentence quoted earlier, the receiver could reverse this superiority of the giver by reciprocating with an obviously greater gift that put the giver in his debt in turn (*Eth. nic.* 1124b 9–18). But this was not easy, due to the incommensurability that usually characterized the gifts exchanged and the custom of taking into account the means and circumstances of the two parties in the calculation of the degree of equivalence between gifts (Aristotle, *Eth. eud.* 1243a 15–31). As Thucydides's Pericles observes in one of the passages cited earlier, a counter-gift was normally perceived as mere compensation (Thucydides 2.40.4).

But gifts were problematic not only because of the dynamics of gift exchange but also for how they reflected on the social status, wealth, and personal circumstances of the actors involved. Whereas the gifts of guest-friendship that some individuals brought home after travel abroad made manifest their connections to the elites of other communities (e.g., Homer, *Od.* 7. 10), the grain others were forced to accept from their neighbors showed how hard life in the countryside could be (e.g., Hesiod, *Op.* 345–55). Whereas some people could afford to reciprocate small gestures with spectacular gifts (e.g., Herodotus 3. 139–40), many could respond to gifts only with subordination. In short, gifts revealed social, economic, and political relationships among individuals, and sometimes what they showed was demeaning. A gift exchange between individuals with different capacities to give – asymmetric gift exchange – reduced inequality through the material gift or favor of the one who enjoyed a position of superiority, but simultaneously increased it, since the contrast between gift and counter-gift made the inferiority of the weaker party even more visible.[5]

In classical Athens, asymmetric exchanges were far more widespread than most scholars suspect. By asymmetric exchange in this context, I mean exchanges between individuals who could afford to do favors and make gifts on a regular basis, on the one hand; and people of lower status, on the other, who could not match these gifts in a sufficient fashion, indebting them and leaving them at the disposal of their benefactors, obliged to provide services when necessary. The fact that the Greeks lacked the explicit rules and terminology of the Romans to explain asymmetric relationships has obscured the existence of patrons and clients in classical Athens, although the existence of such relationships has been recognized by some scholars (Millett, 1989; Mossé, 1994; Jones, 2004: 78–85; Morris, 2000: 139–44; Zelnick-Abramovitz, 2000; Domingo Gygax, 2016; Maehle, 2018).

In Attica, poor peasants did not have the same capacity as the rich did to face bad harvests, epidemics, and the impact of war on agricultural manpower. Few Athenians could live only from the *misthoi* and doles of the Theoric Fund (Maehle, 2018: 59, 75), and many needed the protection offered by rich citizens such as Cimon, who allowed anyone who wanted to gather produce from his fields and always had dinner available in his house for the needy (*FGrHist* 115 F 89 and F 135, *apud* Athenaeus 12. 532f – 3c; Pseudo-Aristotle, *[Ath.]* 27. 2–3). The wealthy, for their part, used these needy people to influence the council, the assembly, and the jury courts; to spread rumors that increased their prestige and discredited their rivals; and as additional labor for the harvest.[6] As Socrates tells Diodorus when he recommends that he transform a poor man named Hermogenes into his client, "It is worth many servants to have a willing, loyal, staunch subordinate capable of doing what he is told" (Xenophon, *Mem.* 2.10.3, trans. Marchant).

The Athenians were thus familiar with asymmetric exchanges of patronage, and the passages of Greek authors cited earlier show that they must have been very much aware of the drawbacks of this type of relationship for the weaker party, no matter how convenient it was for some people to engage in such a relationship to improve their living conditions. In fact, one of the first things Socrates tells Diodorus is that Hermogenes would be ashamed to take a favor from Diodorus without making a return, which shows Hermogenes's concern about the recipient's indebtedness – an indebtedness he will not be able to avoid with a return gift, since Diodorus's goal is to have a "staunch subordinate capable of doing what he is told." It is symptomatic that the Greeks tried to disguise the nature of this type of relationship by presenting it as a type of *philia* ("friendship") in which patron and client were both *philoi*.[7] This was a fiction, however, which could not always be maintained: the term *philos* coexisted with terms such as *kolax* ("flatterer"), *parasitos* ("parasite"), and *prostatēs* ("one who stands in front, protector") (Zelnick-Abramovitz, 2000: 78–80; Maehle, 2018: 67). Aristotle, who defines this type of relationship as "*philia* based on utility," notes that he calls it *philia* only because people use the term *philoi* to refer to people who interact in this way (*Eth. nic.* 1157a 25–35; Zelnick-Abramovitz, 2000: 67).

The Athenians were also aware that the patron-client relationship could exist between not only individuals but also an individual and his community; that is, that it could take the form of what one could, borrowing Finley's terminology, call "community patronage" (Finley, 1983: 35–9).[8] In reality, the difference between private and public gifts was not as clear as Veyne imagines (Veyne, 1976: 188–9). In the Hellenistic inscription quoted at the beginning of this section, the benefactor is rewarded for his "services for the community and in particular to each citizen." The perception of favors and gifts to individuals as a contribution to the common good and a benefit to the entire polis was also very much present in classical Athens. In trials, defendants try to win jurors over by describing their services to individual citizens (e.g., Lysias 16.14), and present themselves as benefactors by describing their *euergesiai*, in which they move from public to private gifts as if these were essentially the same thing (e.g., Andocides 1.147; Lysias 19.57–9; Demosthenes 18.267–8). Just as everyone was aware that many of the alleged community services offered to individuals were simultaneously services of a relationship of personal patronage, they must also have been aware that public gifts could function as benefits in a patron-client relationship between the benefactor and the community. Patrons usually had a network of clients, and the community could be imagined as an extension of this network. In fact, one task of clients was to get the entire community to behave like clients of their patron.

In classical Athens, gifts to the polis by wealthy citizens must have been reminiscent of the way the elite in the predemocratic polis related to the rest of society. The members of the archaic elite dedicated time to unpaid public functions and assumed public expenses that could not be covered by the polis with income drawn from fines, war booty, or rents on communal land. Consequently, in Draco's time, "appointment to the supreme offices of state went by birth and wealth," whereas under Solon, income was the only criterion for access to public positions (Pseudo-Aristotle, *[Ath.]* 3. 1; 7. 3–4). Some contributions to the polis took place through *leitourgiai* (literally, "work for the people"), that is, voluntary or obligatory services to the polis assigned to individuals who were required to supply the means needed to perform them (Pseudo-Aristotle, *[Oec.]* 1347a11–14; Pseudo-Xenophon, *[Ath.]* 1. 13; Wilson, 2000: 15; van Wees, 2013: 64–8, 98–100; Domingo Gygax, 2016). The strange form of "exchange" *(antidosis)* that regulated some aspects of the assignment of liturgies was considered by the Athenians of the classical period to be very old (Demosthenes 42.1) and fits better in archaic society, where wealth was easier to estimate than it was in classical Athens (Gernet, 1957: 75). The *naukrariai*, mentioned in several laws of Solon, predate the Solonian age (Pseudo-Aristotle, *[Ath.]* 8. 3; schol. Aristophanes, *Nub.* 37) and seem to have been subdivisions within the citizenry to equip and maintain ships that were led by *naukraroi* – originally "ship commanders" – who added resources from their own assets (van Wees, 2013: 44–61). The census classes of Solon, which defined political rights and military duties, were a good basis for determining which Athenians were capable of performing liturgies.

The members of the elite used these contributions – indispensable for the functioning of a polis of which they were, in fact, the greatest beneficiaries – to symbolically increase their social distance from the demos and fellow elite members, but also to justify their political privileges and economic superiority. Echoes of this way of thinking are found in one of the most conservative works by Isocrates, the *Areopagiticus*, in which mention is made of a golden age in which

> the less well-to-do among the citizens were so far from envying those of greater means, that they were as solicitous for the great estates as for their own, considering the prosperity of the rich a guarantee of their own well-being.
>
> (Isocrates 7.32, trans. Norlin, adapted)

The Pisistratidae also acted as patrons of the demos, as was even more necessary for them, since their autocratic power required more support and more extensive efforts at legitimation (Lavelle, 2005: 159; Hall, 2014: 253–5). Some ancient sources draw connections between the Pisistratidae and Cimon's liberalities, which included many more gifts than the ones mentioned earlier and represent a continuation of the typical munificence of archaic elites. Theopompus attributes to Pisistratus the same policy of letting anyone enter his fields who wished to do so (*FGrHist* 115 F 89 and F 135, *apud* Athenaeus 12.532f – 3c), while the author of the pseudo-Aristotelian *Athēnaiōn Politeia* says that Cimon performed his liturgies in a magnificent way because he "had an estate large enough for a tyrant" (*[Ath.]* 27.2–3). Both authors probably drew on a common fifth-century source that compared Pisistratus's and Cimon's generosity, as well as their means of financing their actions (Domingo Gygax, 2002).

Avoiding (and accepting) gifts and honors in classical Athens

In the classical period, the Athenians tried to prevent citizens' gifts from leading the community into indebtedness, reminiscent of the patron-client relationship between the archaic elite – including tyrants – and the demos, as well as of contemporary patronage. In the early classical polis, Cimon still behaved a great deal like a member of the archaic elite. In addition to the services already noted and others, such as contributing to funeral expenses, distributing clothes, and assisting individuals who occasionally asked for help, Cimon made huge public gifts outside the context of liturgies. Plutarch mentions his participation in the erection of the Long Walls, his planting of plane trees in the Agora, and his enhancement of the Academy with gardens (*Cim.* 13.7–8), and he may have been involved in constructing the Stoa of the Herms and the Theseion. Peisianax – perhaps Cimon's brother-in-law – seems to have contributed significantly to the construction of the Stoa Poikile, originally named the Stoa of Peisianax, while the law courts of Callias and Metiochus were likely also named after the individuals who funded their construction.

But after Ephialtes's revolution (462 BCE) and the radicalization of the democratic regime that followed, public gifts outside the context of liturgies seem to disappear. Cimon was ostracized in 461 BCE, and the Athenians who in the fifth century BCE continued to use public generosity to gain political support, thus perpetuating to some degree "community patronage" – men such as Nicias and Alcibiades – made public gifts only in the context of liturgies (Thucydides 6.16.3; Plutarch, *Nic.* 3.2–5; *Alc.* 16.3). There is even some suggestion of gifts being rejected by the demos (*IG* I³ 49; Plutarch, *Per.* 14.1–2).

The most successful fifth-century Athenian politician, Pericles, was a liturgist early in his career (*IG* II² 2318. 9–11), but he never used public gifts as a major element of his political strategy. Instead, he sponsored the distribution of money among the Athenians through the establishment of jury payments from public funds. The *Athēnaiōn Politeia* compares this measure to Cimon's strategy based on private and public munificence, and notes that it meant "to give the multitude what was their own" (Pseudo-Aristotle, *[Ath.]* 27.3–4; see also Plutarch, *Per.* 9.2–3). Plutarch understands the building program endorsed by Pericles in a similar way, and claims that he argued against his critics that this would enable groups of citizens to get "a beneficial share of the public wealth" (*Per.* 12.5–6). Although Plutarch's account may be anachronistic, it has been argued that he may be following a fifth-century source and thus be reflecting a view of the classical period (Stadter, 1989: 153).

Given these attitudes toward public gifts and the immense resources Athens drew from the empire in this period, one may wonder why the Athenians organized liturgies, services that allowed the elite to display their superiority and to indebt the demos through great generosity, as Cimon, Nicias, and Alcibiades did. But many factors explain the existence of liturgies in fifth-century Athens. To begin with, the financial contributions of the wealthy were essential in the early decades of the democratic polis, when no resources from the empire were available. Moreover, as noted earlier, liturgies were not an invention of the democratic regime but a legacy of the archaic polis. In addition, we must take into account that liturgies were not only a way to finance activities but also a manner to arrange them, in that liturgists were in charge of complex organizational matters. At the same time, liturgies offered the demos the possibility of feeling superior to the elite, since the polis decided who would have to assume a liturgy and when and how he had to perform it; members of the liturgical class who might have preferred not to serve were nonetheless obliged to do so. In principle, liturgies were not gifts but "counter-gifts," services owed to a community that offered multiple advantages, with each citizen contributing according to his abilities and capacity. Wealthy individuals who failed to do what was expected of them were considered to be depriving their fellow citizens of something that belonged to them (Xenophon, *Oec.* 2.6).

Not all rich Athenians, of course, accepted the official discourse on liturgies, and even among those who considered liturgies legitimate, some felt that they were being asked for too many or too costly services, or were contributing more than their share. There were liturgists who openly complained about their duties, as well as individuals who tried to avoid them by hiding their wealth or using legal mechanisms such as *antidosis* and *skēpsis* (exemption due to age, fulfillment of certain offices, or other reasons).[9] Even members of the demos agreed that the contributions of certain liturgists went beyond what was owed the city, as demonstrated by the fact that defendants in trials often try to gain acquittal by enumerating and describing their liturgies; that is, by presenting them as benefactions to the polis (e.g., Lysias 26.4; Demosthenes 21.169; Lycurgus 1.139).

This controversy surrounding liturgies was closely related to another controversy over public gifts: the debate about granting honors – public praise, crowns, statues, tax exemptions, dinner in the Prytaneion – to citizens in return for benefactions. Some benefactors tried not only to have their actions recognized as benefactions but also to have them publicly rewarded with honors, an effort that encountered resistance from part of the polis. It may seem obvious that a polis reluctant to recognize public services as gifts would be against awarding honors that unequivocally sanctioned certain contributions as benefactions. But the reality was more complicated. In principle, bestowing honors offered advantages to the polis. Honors were not simple tokens of gratitude but counter-gifts with the ability to pay off the debt created by a gift. Indeed, both benefactions and honors were called *dōreai* ("gifts") [e.g., *IG* II³ 298 = *SIG* 206], and an exchange of benefactions and honors was one in which the polis had the possibility of reciprocating with honors at the level of the benefaction. Demosthenes, in his *Against Leptines*, reflects on the importance of granting honors proportional to benefactions: "Grants ought . . . to be so apportioned that each man may receive from the people the exact reward *(dōrea)* he deserves" (*Lept.* 122, trans. Vince). Some Athenian honorific decrees highlight the claim that the honors they confer are worthy of the benefactions (e.g., *IG* II³ 519).

But honors were also highly problematic. For the polis, granting honors implied renouncing the possibility of trying to depict the gift as a counter-gift. As noted earlier, even in a balanced gift exchange, the party who reciprocated often came out of the transaction symbolically debilitated. Although the option existed of replying to the benefactor with grossly excessive honors that would in turn indebt him, the polis could do this only with foreigners – where such behavior was, in fact, common (Domingo Gygax, 2009) – and not with citizens. In the passage from Demosthenes quoted earlier, the orator is referring to citizens when he says that every benefactor must receive the *exact* reward he deserves. Honors perceived as disproportionate were criticized (e.g., [Pseudo-]Demosthenes 13.22–3; Demosthenes 23.196–9).

A person honored as a benefactor was identified as someone who could act again as such; that is, as a permanent potential benefactor, meaning that he supposedly had special qualities and was superior to most citizens. The solemn ritual in which the honors were received was remembered. The memory of the ceremony might be revived every time someone else encountered or referred to him. Honors such as the right to preferential seating at public spectacles and invitations to free meals in the Prytaneion were gestures that paid regular homage to the benefactor. A stele reproducing the honorific decree or a statue went even further, since these were constant expressions of recognition and potentially eternal. They even suggested, insofar as they signified permanent homage and an act of endless reciprocation, the idea that the debt to the benefactor could never be satisfied.

Granting honors to citizens implied the institution of an "order" of *euergetai* that stood in contradiction to the egalitarian ethos of democratic Athens. Probably this is the reason why even in the Hellenistic period, when honoring citizens became a widespread practice, the granting of the title *euergetēs* continued to be avoided for citizens (Gauthier, 1985: 33–4). But Athens also had problems with honoring citizens that other poleis did not have, which derived from having posthumously awarded honors to the tyrant-slayers Harmodius and Aristogiton in the early years of the democracy (Azoulay, 2017). The importance of their benefaction set the bar for obtaining rewards much higher, and honoring other citizens also made these two symbolic figures of democracy look less extraordinary.

Despite the problems arising from public gifts and honors, throughout the fourth century BCE the Athenians gradually accepted voluntary donations made outside liturgies, and increasingly granted honors for this type of benefaction as well as for benefactions related to liturgies. Most of the data come from the second half of the fourth century, but there is also information dating back to the final years of the Peloponnesian War (Andocides 2.17–18; Isocrates 18.61), as well as evidence indicating that these practices were habitual in the first half of the fourth century ([Pseudo-]Demosthenes 50.13; Isocrates 15.94). The most notorious reward for a fourth-century benefactor is the gold crown offered to honor Demosthenes's donations during his supervision of the reconstruction of the city walls and his administration of the festival fund in 337 that sparked his speech *On the Crown* (*Cor.* 112–13, 117–19, 299, 311; Aeschines 3.17). But throughout his career, Demosthenes made many more gifts – some probably dating to 357 and 360/359 BCE (MacDowell, 2009: 133–4, 425–6) – and received honors on a number of occasions, and after his death he was recognized in a decree of 280/279

BCE for "having relinquished his property for the common good" (Plutarch, *Mor.* 850f–851c). Demosthenes's references to other benefactors – Nausicles, Diotimus, Charidemus, and Neoptolemus – demonstrate that when he wrote *On the Crown*, it had become common for officials to make donations in the context of the performance of their duties and to be honored for them (*Cor.* 114).[10] In the time of Lycurgus, we even find donations made outside office and honors in return for such contributions, including an honor as exclusive as a statue (*Mor.* 841d, 843f–844a).

What led the Athenians to accept more and more donations, and to grant more and more honors? The Peloponnesian War represented a great economic effort for the city that already in 428/427 BCE led to the imposition of a war tax on the wealthy, the *eisphora* (Thucydides 3.19.1). After the defeat at the end of the century, the city's financial situation was dramatically more difficult: it had lost the tribute paid by the allies as well as other resources drawn from the empire (Harding, 2015: 84–5), and the income from the state-owned silver mines was interrupted. Although the Athenian economy and finances soon began to recover, thanks in particular to the vitality of the Piraeus harbor, Athens would never again have a source of income comparable to the empire.

One of David Pritchard's main conclusions in his recent study of public spending in classical Athens is that fifth-century Athens did not rely on imperial income to finance its democracy (Pritchard, 2015). By contrast, military expenses – according to Pritchard, substantially higher than spending on festivals and politics combined – were essentially paid for from imperial tribute and from nontribute imperial income (tolls, sacred land, and booty). In the fourth century, Athens continued to spend much more on defense than on festivals and politics, but since it did not have the same external resources, it was forced to rely to a greater extent on its wealthy citizens to cover military costs. The fourth-century institutional history of the *eisphora* and the military liturgy, the *trierarchia*, reflects the difficulty Athens had in financing its own defense (Christ, 2006: 164–71). In 378 BCE, the *eisphora* was reorganized with the introduction of *symmoriai* (groups of contributors) to reduce problems in collecting the tax. This reform was followed somewhat later by the establishment of *proeispherontes* in charge of paying the *eisphora* of their tax group in advance. In 358/357 BCE, problems surrounding the recruitment of trierarchs and the collection of debts led to the institution of naval *symmoriai* made up of members who shared the costs and duties of the *trierarchia*. This system was modified in 340 BCE to improve the allocation of costs within the *symmoriai* via the introduction of contributions in proportion to the property of the contributors.

The Athenians' difficulties in financing their defense affected the financing of other areas of the state as well: the contributions of the rich covered only part of military expenses, and the rest had to be paid with public money diverted from other issues. Moreover, the payment of *eisphorai* and the performance of trierarchies meant that some rich men could not fulfill their festival liturgies in the same way that members of the liturgical class could when they were financially less stressed. Under these circumstances, Athens increasingly welcomed the gifts of wealthy citizens willing to contribute to the community. Gifts even became part of the financial strategy of the polis, as is shown by the establishment of a naval *epidosis* in 357 BCE. An *epidosis* ("donation") was a voluntary contribution requested by the assembly or the council. There is controversy as to whether the naval *epidosis* consisted of the voluntary assumption of a trierachy, paying the costs of running a ship without commanding it, or donating the ship itself (Migeotte, 1992: 16–17; Gabrielsen, 1994: 2001–6). But it is evident that the naval *epidosis* represented moving the trierarchy from the ambiguous realm of the liturgy – where whether the service was a gift or a return was unclear – to the sphere of euergetism, where it was unquestionably a benefaction deserving a reward.

Giving in to benefactors' pressure to honor them was part of the price Athens had to pay to obtain additional funding. This step was facilitated by the fact that during the Peloponnesian War it became normal to award honors to citizens for military accomplishments (e.g., Andocides 2.18; Xenophon, *Hell.* 1.33) and even for benefactions with an economic dimension, such as supplying grain (Andocides 2.10–12, 17–18; Isocrates 18.61, 65). In addition, from at least 408/407 BCE on, it was customary to bestow a crown on the best prytany of the year (*Agora* XV.1, 1–30), and before the mid-fourth century it had become habitual to grant a crown to the entire council for successful management in its year of office (Demosthenes 22.5, 8, 36–7). But honors to the rich citizens who offered gifts to the community were not only a concession but also an instrument to attract further contributions. As a result, from the 340s BCE on, we find decrees that award honors to citizens "so that others may also show love of honor *(philotimia)*" (e.g., *IG* II³ 338; 355; 360; 416). The link between honors and economic strategy is also clear in the proliferation of honors to non-elite foreigners for trade-related services (Engen, 2010: 145–6, 151, 159, 171).

To conclude, the main characteristics of Hellenistic euergetism are already visible in fourth-century Athens: honors to citizens and not only foreigners; gifts made in connection with the performance of an office, as well as gifts made outside of office; and huge donations by citizens unequivocally recognized as benefactions, such as naval *epidoseis* and some gifts offered in the time of Lycurgus. But at the same time, the development of euergetism meets a certain resistance. There is a tendency to limit gifts to donations made under some degree of state control (i.e., to donations in the context of a liturgy or in the course of fulfillment of an office). Known gifts not linked to a public function are very few in number. Honors are the object of controversies, in which whether they are proportional to the services performed or exaggerated is debated. In the case of gifts made by liturgists, attempts are made to present these as services owed the polis rather than benefactions. Finally, there is a considerable difference between the euergetism of classical Athens and that of the Hellenistic polis: the former coexists with a system of obligatory liturgies and *eisphorai* that constitutes a substantial source for financing the polis, whereas the latter is typical of a polis in which there are no liturgies, or liturgies are voluntary in nature.

Conclusion

This chapter began with a discussion of the main theses regarding Hellenistic euergetism advanced in the last few decades. According to some interpretations, Hellenistic euergetism was related not to the economic needs of the polis but to political ones. On this way of looking at the situation, the Hellenistic polis had sufficient resources to avoid having to finance some of its activities and projects through benefactors, and the main function of euergetism was to reduce tensions between rich and poor by means of a limited redistribution of wealth. We have also seen that Hellenistic euergetism has been understood as a manifestation of some of the main values promoted by the democratic polis; that is, solidarity and cooperation among citizens for the common good. The Hellenistic polis was thus, on this interpretation of the evidence, democratic; and euergetism was not an institution imposed by the elite but one supported by the majority of citizens, who saw in it their best means to get some benefit from the revenues enjoyed by the wealthy.

The analysis offered above of euergetism in classical Athens, where the exchange of benefactions and honors between citizens and the polis was first systematically developed, suggests different conclusions. In Athens, both public gifts and honors were perceived as highly problematic. Gifts were viewed with great concern because of their capacity to subordinate the recipient and to be used as instruments of domination by elites. Honors, despite being counter-gifts with which the demos could try to manipulate the rich, were also regarded as dangerous, because they introduced a formal inequality within the citizenry and provided the honorand with symbolic capital the polis could not control. In Athens, the euergetism of citizens – unlike the euergetism of foreigners – had to overcome considerable resistance in order to develop, and the fundamental factor in its growth seems to have been the need to look for new forms of financing in the face of the economic difficulties of the polis. (Other factors would have been the proliferation of honors for military benefactions during the Peloponnesian War and the attempt to improve the administration of the polis by rewarding men who exercised public functions.) Euergetism progressed largely as a concession to elites – who demanded recognition of their efforts to finance the polis – and as a complement, not an alternative, to the system of liturgies and *eisphorai*, which in democratic Athens never ceased being more important to the economy of the polis than euergetism was. Despite the similarities between the two systems – from the moment Athens began to grant honors for benefactions linked to liturgies, they overlapped to some extent – euergetism and liturgies were very different. What euergetism represented for the demos in Athens is best understood if we consider what liturgies and *eisphorai* meant for the elite, or for part of it. Criticism of liturgies started long before the increase of the fiscal pressure on the rich in the fourth century (Pseudo-Xenophon, *[Ath.]* 1. 13); indeed, one cause of the oligarchic coup of 411 BCE was liturgies and *eisphorai* (Thucydides 8.48.1; Christ, 2006: 164, 190). During the regime of Demetrius of Phaleron (317–307 BCE), the system of liturgies was suppressed, and afterwards it was never fully reestablished but was replaced by a system of voluntary donations by the wealthy, who in turn were recognized as benefactors (Harding, 2015: 89–97; Cartledge, 2016: 242). In early Hellenistic Athens, euergetism, the arrangement that suited the elite better, acquired a key function in the financial structure of the polis, as is shown by several honorific decrees (e.g., *IG* II³ 1160; for further examples, see Oliver, 2007: 193–227).

Classical Athenian euergetism should be given more consideration by scholars of Hellenistic euergetism and the Hellenistic polis than it has been to date. The implication of the present study is that there were more differences between classical Athens and the Hellenistic polis than some recent interpretations assume, or alternatively that Hellenistic euergetism is different from what the previous theses maintain and far more similar to de Ste. Croix's characterization than is generally posited. That there was still great concern in the Hellenistic period about the debt gifts created, at any rate, is shown by the many Hellenistic decrees stressing that these honors are gifts equivalent to benefactions (e.g., *SIG* 374 and 493).

Notes

1 In this reference and the following ones to the work of Veyne, I quote the pages of the French edition, since the English edition is not a translation but an abbreviated version of the French text.
2 In the closing paragraph, he writes: "The life of democracy in the Hellenistic period presents much scope for interpretative confusion. Although the *polis*-form as such retained its legitimacy and vitality, the constitutional trend in political actuality was firmly toward various shades of oligarchy. . . . Overall, the conditions of this Hellenistic mode of democracy was one of some durability, no doubt, but far more one of decline from an earlier, full-blooded political mode. Hellenistic *demokratia*, lacking to a greater or lesser degree the key qualitative defining elements of freedom, both internal and external, and political, civic equality, simply could not have been anything much like *demokratia*" (Cartledge, 2016: 244–5).
3 On gifts and reciprocity in ancient Greece, see Gill, Postlethwaite, and Seaford (1998), Domingo Gygax (2013), Carlà and Gori (2014), and Domingo Gygax (2016).
4 In another context, Aristotle, like Thucydides, also reflects on the fact that "benefactors seem to love those whom they benefit more than those who have received benefits love those who have conferred them" (Aristotle, *Eth. nic.* 1167b 17–19, trans. Rackham). He says that this is usually explained as a result of one party being interested in being reciprocated, whereas the other is not in a hurry to reciprocate, but Thucydides's explanation seems to be different.
5 There are cases in which one could consider that the gift of the weaker party was superior, but these are situations in which the exchange is between gift exchange and exploitation, since the compensation the weaker party offers to the stronger one for its theoretical service – leadership – is made under coercion. The Homeric world offers many examples: Donlan (1981/1982: 158–61), Scheid-Tissinier (1994: 224–9, 234–44, 251–3), van Wees (2013: 18, 19, 21, 23), and Domingo Gygax (2016: 62–3).
6 E.g., Lysias 15.1–6, 10; 28.9; 29.6–7, 12; Xenphon, *Mem.* 2.6.26–7; 2.9.1–8; 2.10.1–6; Aeschines 2.184; Demosthenes 18.143; 21.112–13, 139–40; [Pseudo-]Demosthenes 53.1–14; 59.72. For further examples, see Zelnick-Abramovitz (2000) and Maehle (2018).
7 On the parallel situation in Rome, where relationships of patronage could be described as a form of *amicitia*, see Saller (1982).

8 Finley's concept of patronage, however, is broader, and includes obligatory liturgies that were regarded by the demos not as gifts that indebted the community but as services owed to the polis (Finley, 1983: 35).
9 E.g., Xenophon, *Oec*. 7.3; Pseudo-Aristotle *[Ath.]* 56.3; Lysias 2.24; 21.12; 28.3; 29.4; 32.23; Isocrates 7.35; 8.128; 15 *passim*; 17.1–11; Is. 2.47–9; 4.29; 5.35–7; 7.40; 11.47; Aeschines 1.101; Demosthenes 2.24; 8.21–3; 14.25; 20.1; 21.154–6; 28.7, 22–24; 42 *passim*; 45.66.
10 Additional literary and epigraphic information corroborates this conclusion: Demosthenes 23.145, 188; Hyperides 1.17; Plutarch, *Mor.* 844a; *IG* II³ 338, 348.

Bibliography

Azoulay, Vincent. *The Tyrant-Slayers of Ancient Athens: A Tale of Two Statues*. New York: Oxford University Press, 2017.

Boulanger, André. *Aelius Aristide et la sophistique dans la province d'Asie au IIe siècle de notre ère*. Paris: Éditions de Boccard, 1923.

Brélaz, Cédric. "La vie démocratique dans les cités grecques à l'époque impériale." *Topoi* 18 (2013): 367–99.

Carlà, Filippo, and Maja Gori, eds. *Gift Giving and the 'Embedded' Economy in the Ancient World*. Heidelberg: Universitätsverlag Winter, 2014.

Carlsson, Susanne. *Hellenistic Democracies: Freedom, Independence and Political Procedure in Some East Greek City-States*. Stuttgart: Steiner, 2010.

Cartledge, Paul. *Democracy: A Life*. New York: Oxford University Press, 2016.

Christ, Matthew R. *The Bad Citizen in Classical Athens*. Cambridge: Cambridge University Press, 2006.

De Ste. Croix, Geoffrey E.M. *The Class Struggle in the Ancient Greek World: From the Archaic Age to the Arab Conquests*. London: Duckworth, 1981.

Domingo Gygax, Marc. *Benefaction and Rewards in the Ancient Greek City: The Origins of Euergetism*. Cambridge: Cambridge University Press, 2016.

———. "Euergetismus und Gabentausch." *Mètis* n.s. 1 (2003): 181–200.

———. "Gift-Giving and Power Relationships in Greek Social Praxis and Public Discourse." Pages 45–60 in *The Gift in Antiquity*. Edited by Michael L. Satlow. Oxford: Wiley-Blackwell, 2013.

———. "Peisistratos und Kimon: Anmerkung zu einem Vergleich bei Athenaios." *Hermes* 130 (2002): 245–9.

———. "Proleptic Honours in Greek Euergetism." *Chiron* 39 (2009): 163–91.

Domingo Gygax, Marc, and Arjan Zuiderhoek. *Benefactors and the Polis: Origins and Development of the Public Gift in the Greek Cities from the Homeric World to Late Antiquity*. Cambridge: Cambridge University Press, forthcoming.

Donlan, Walter. "Reciprocities in Homer." *Classical World* 75 (1981/1982): 137–75.

Ellis-Evans, Aneurin. "Four Attitudes to Decline in the Hellenistic Period." Pages 19–28 in *Decline and Decline-Narratives in the Greek and Roman World: Proceedings of a Conference held at the University of Oxford in March 2017*. Edited by Takashi Minamikawa. Kyoto: Kyoto University, 2017.

Engen, Darel T. *Honor and Profit: Athenian Trade Policy and the Economy and Society of Greece, 415–307 B.C.E.* Ann Arbor: University of Michigan Press, 2010.

Finley, Moses I. *Politics in the Ancient World*. New York: Cambridge University Press, 1983.

Gabrielsen, Vincent. *Financing the Athenian Fleet: Public Taxation and Social Relations*. Baltimore: Johns Hopkins University Press, 1994.

Gauthier, Philippe. *Les cités grecques et leurs bienfaiteurs*. Athens: École française d'Athènes; Paris: Diffusion de Boccard, 1985.

Gehrke, Hans-Joachim. *Geschichte des Hellenismus*. Munich: Oldenburg, 1990.

Gernet, Louis. *Démosthène: Plaidoyers civils*. Paris: Les Belles Lettres, 1957.

Gill, Christopher, Norman Postlethwaite, and Richard Seaford, eds. *Reciprocity in Ancient Greece*. Oxford: Oxford University Press, 1998.

Gray, Benjamin D. "The Polis Becomes Humane? *Philanthropia* as a Cardinal Civic Virtue in Later Hellenistic Honorific Epigraphy and Historiography." Pages 137–62 in *Parole in movimento: Linguaggio politico e lessico storiografico nel mondo ellenistico; Atti del convegno internazionale Roma 21–23 febbraio 2011*. Studi ellenistici 27. Edited by Manuela Mari and John Thornton. Pisa: Fabrizio Serra Editore, 2013.

Grieb, Volker. *Hellenistische Demokratie: Politische Organisation und Struktur in freien griechischen Poleis nach Alexander dem Großen*. Stuttgart: Steiner, 2008.

Gruen, Erich S. "The Polis in the Hellenistic World." Pages 339–54 in *Nomodeiktes: Greek Studies in Honor of Martin Ostwald*. Edited by Ralph M. Rosen and Joseph Farrell. Ann Arbor: University of Michigan Press, 1993.

Hall, Jonathan M. *A History of the Archaic Greek World, ca. 1200–479 BCE*. 2nd ed. Malden, MA: Wiley-Blackwell, 2014.

Hansen, Mogens H., and Thomas H. Nielsen. *An Inventory of Archaic and Classical Poleis*. Oxford: Oxford University Press, 2004.

Harding, Phillip. *Athens Transformed, 404–262 BC: From Popular Sovereignty to the Dominion of Wealth*. London: Routledge, 2015.

Hasegawa, Takeo. "The Causes of Greek Decline Revisited: How Should We Consider Them in the 21st Century?" Pages 7–17 in *Decline and Decline-Narratives in the Greek and Roman World: Proceedings of a Conference held at the University of Oxford in March 2017*. Edited by Takashi Minamikawa. Kyoto: Kyoto University, 2017.

Jones, Arnold H.M. *The Cities of the Eastern Roman Provinces*. 2nd ed. Oxford: Clarendon, 1971.

———. *The Greek City from Alexander to Justinian*. Oxford: Clarendon, 1940.

Jones, Nicholas F. *Rural Athens under the Democracy*. Philadelphia: University of Pennsylvania Press, 2004.

Lavelle, Brian M. *Fame, Money, and Power: The Rise of Peisistratos and 'Democratic' Tyranny at Athens*. Ann Arbor: University of Michigan Press, 2005.

Lévêque, Pierre. "Forme politiche e rapporti sociali." Pages 39–155 in *Storia e civiltà dei Greci 7. La società ellenistica: Quadro politico*. Edited by Ranuccio Bianchi Bandinelli. Milano: Bompiani, 1977.

MacDowell, Douglas M. *Demosthenes the Orator*. Oxford: Oxford University Press, 2009.

Maehle, Ingvar B. "The Economy of Gratitude in Democratic Athens." *Hesperia* 87 (2018): 55–90.

Marrou, Henri-Irénée. *Histoire de l'éducation dans l'Antiquité*. Paris: Éditions du Seuil, 1948.

Migeotte, Léopold. "La planification des dépenses publiques dans les cités hellénistiques." Pages 77–97 in *Studi ellenistici 19*. Edited by Biagio Virgilio. Pisa: Giardini, 2006 (Pages 59–74 in Léopold Migeotte. *Économie et finances publiques des cités grecques. Vol. 2. Choix d'articles publiés de 2002 à 2014*. Lyon: Maison de l'Orient et de la Méditerranée Jean Pouilloux, 2015).

———. *Les souscriptions publiques dans les cités grecques*. Geneva: Librairie Droz; Quebec: Éditions du Sphinx, 1992.

Millett, Paul. "Patronage and Its Avoidance in Classical Athens." Pages 15–47 in *Patronage in Ancient Society*. Edited by Andrew Wallace-Hadrill. London: Routledge, 1989.

Morris, Ian. *Archaeology as Cultural History: Words and Things in Iron Age Greece.* Oxford: Wiley-Blackwell, 2000.

Mossé, Claude. "Les relations de 'clientèle' dans le fonctionnement de la démocratie athénienne." *Mètis* 9–10 (1994): 143–50.

Oliver, Graham J. *War, Food, and Politics in Early Hellenistic Athens.* Oxford: Oxford University Press, 2007.

Oppeneer, Thierry. "Assembly Politics and the Rhetoric of Honour in Chariton, Dio of Prusa and John Chrysostom." *Historia* 67.2 (2018): 223–43.

Préaux, Claire. *Le monde hellénistique: La Grèce et l'Orient de la mort d'Alexandre à la conquête romaine de la Grèce (323–146 av. J.-C.).* Paris: Presses Universitaires de France, 1978.

Pritchard, David M. *Public Spending and Democracy in Classical Athens.* Austin: University of Texas Press, 2015.

Said, Edward W. *Orientalism.* New York: Pantheon Books, 1978.

Saller, Richard P. *Personal Patronage under the Early Empire.* Cambridge and New York: Cambridge University Press, 1982.

Scheid-Tissinier, Evelyne. *Les usages du don chez Homère: Vocabulaire et pratiques.* Nancy: Presses Universitaires de Nancy, 1994.

Spawforth, Antony. "Euergetism." Page 546–7 in *The Oxford Classical Dictionary.* Edited by Simon Hornblower, Anthony Spawforth, and Esther Eidinow. 4th ed. Oxford: Oxford University Press, 2012.

Stadter, Philip A. *A Commentary on Plutarch's Pericles.* Chapel Hill: University of North Carolina Press, 1989.

Strootman, Rolf. *Courts and Elites in the Hellenistic Empires: The Near East after the Achaemenids, c.330–30 BCE.* Edinburgh: Edinburgh University Press, 2014.

Van Wees, Hans. *Ships and Silver, Taxes and Tribute: A Fiscal History of Archaic Athens.* London: Tauris, 2013.

Veligianni-Terzi, Chryssoula. *Wertbegriffe in den attischen Ehrendekreten der klassischen Zeit.* Stuttgart: Steiner, 1997.

Veyne, Paul. *Le pain et le cirque: Sociologie historique d'un pluralisme politique.* Paris: Éditions du Seuil, 1976.

Wiemer, Hans-Ulrich. "Hellenistic Cities: The End of Greek Democracy?" Pages 54–69 in *A Companion to Ancient Greek Government.* Edited by Hans Beck. Malden, MA: Wiley-Blackwell, 2013.

Wilson, Peter. *The Athenian Institution of the* Khoregia*: The Chorus, the City and the Stage.* Cambridge: Cambridge University Press, 2000.

Zelnick-Abramovitz, Rachel. "Did Patronage Exist in Classical Athens?" *L'Antiquité Classique* 69 (2000): 65–80.

Zuiderhoek, Arjan. *The Politics of Munificence in the Roman Empire: Citizens, Elites and Benefactors in Asia Minor.* Cambridge: Cambridge University Press, 2009.

5   The economic and cognitive impacts of personal benefaction in Hispania Tarraconensis

Rachel Meyers

[Testa]mento Cornelia[e P]roc[ulae ex rel]ictis HS(sestertium) N(ummis) XL et ad[iectis] HS(sestertium) [N(ummis) V(milia)[C]CCCXCV [de suo aedem] consum[mavit – – l]ib(ertus).

(*IRC* III, 36)[1]

This text informs us that in Emporiae in the first century, Cornelia Procula allocated forty thousand sesterces in her will for the construction of a temple, to which her freedman added 5,495 sesterces to complete the project. This inscription is an apt example to begin this chapter on civic munificence for it has several features shared with numerous other inscriptions. The text has been reconstructed from six disjointed fragments found through excavations carried out in the twentieth century, just as most inscriptions are fragmentary. It records the construction of a temple; architectural projects were one of the most common undertakings by benefactors. The benefaction was completed with funds bequeathed by the donor; posthumous donations are a small but significant number of the whole corpus of benefactions, which necessitate another individual – sometimes a family member or, as in this case, a freedperson – to bring the project to fruition. Finally, the plaque would have been mounted on the temple proclaiming in large letters the donor's name and her donation. The advertisement of one's generosity is paramount to the discussion of civic munificence in the Roman Empire.

This chapter addresses the economic and cognitive impacts of personal benefaction in Hispania Tarraconensis, a province of the Roman Empire encompassing the northeast region of modern Spain. Hispania Tarraconensis (also known as Hispania Citerior) was an important military, economic, and political center during Rome's wars against the Carthaginians in the late Republican period. Rich in natural resources and with quick accessibility by sea to Rome, it was one of the earliest Roman provinces and home to some of the earliest colonies, including Barcino, founded during the time of Augustus. Large-scale scientific excavations conducted since the 1980s have brought forth substantial remains of civic architecture, artworks, and inscriptions that permit scholars the opportunity to consider the nature of Roman society in these towns. Benefaction was practiced throughout the Roman Empire in a variety of ways.

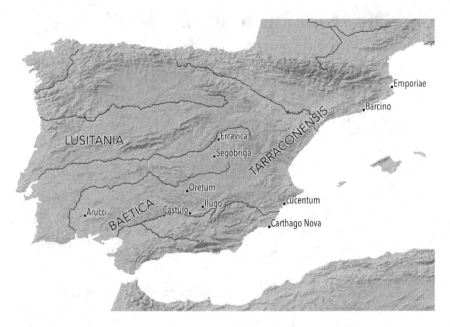

Map 5.1 Roman Iberia[2]

During the Imperial period, in particular, individuals and families financed public works, buildings, statues, foundations, and various forms of entertainment such as games, banquets, and performances. No other scholar has analyzed the broad impact of these donations on the towns in which they were bestowed. Evaluating the nuances of benefaction yields information about the cultural identity of a place. We can understand the demographic makeup of a town, what sorts of individuals or groups held authority and prestige, what kinds of buildings were desired, and what kinds of entertainment were enjoyed. The custom of benefaction tells us much more about society than a simple transaction. As a way of assessing both the financial and cognitive impacts of these benefactions over time, this chapter analyzes a selective corpus of inscriptions from Hispania Tarraconensis dating from the Augustan period through the late second century. After providing an overview of the evidence from the province, three towns will be examined in more detail with the aim of discerning the trends in actions of civic munificence over time.[3]

Methodology

The present study should be understood within the broader context of scholarly inquiries into the phenomenon of euergetism. The topic of euergetism – or, benefaction, as it is also called – has been the subject of numerous studies in the last forty years, but much of the scholarship has focused on the economic side of the practice.[4] In fact, a starting point for understanding benefaction is R. P. Duncan-Jones's numerous works on the Roman economy. Duncan-Jones (1982) has compiled price lists for Italy and the African provinces, namely the epigraphic evidence stating the costs of buildings and infrastructure, various forms of spectacles, cash distributions, taxes, land valuations, the price of wine and wheat, and several other expenditures. These are essential comparanda for other areas of the Roman Empire where no such comprehensive quantitative studies have yet been undertaken. My own corpus of benefactions from Hispania Tarraconensis, explained further ahead, is an initial effort for quantitative analysis in this province.

Leonard Curchin (1983) narrowed in on the epigraphic evidence from Spain, but his approach was to determine whether Spain's reputation for having some of the wealthiest cities in the empire held up to scrutiny. Therefore, he looked at the wealth of individuals by reviewing the monetary values recorded in inscriptions. He engages with Duncan-Jones's findings in Italy and North Africa, but he does not provide any in-depth analysis of any single benefaction or discern trends in place, time, or personal status of donations and donors. A few rich individuals in a variety of towns do not inform us about the overall livelihood of those towns.

Enrique Melchor Gil has done more than any scholar in focusing on euergetism in the Spanish provinces, especially in Baetica, where the most evidence has been recovered. He investigated the sources of wealth for some notable benefactors and found individuals and families involved in the silver mines, olive oil production, and the garum trade, among other pursuits (Melchor Gil, 1993–1994). In his assessment of six hundred and forty one benefactions in all of Spain, only forty-four have the costs included in the inscribed text, amounting to only 6.9% (1993–1994: 346). Of those with a declared cost, 36.4% of them show that the donor(s) spent less than ten thousand sesterces. Since most projects undertaken by the benefactors were not that costly, Melchor Gil concludes that they would have not have been a hardship.[5] However, a significant 20.4% of the texts describe projects involving more than one hundred thousand sesterces, indicating a substantial range in the amount gifted by donors.

In another study, Melchor Gil differentiated between donations given as part of what was required by local magistrates and what was given voluntarily (1994). He also attempted to understand the motivations for euergetism in Spain and the reasons for the decrease in the practice in the third century (Melchor Gil, 1994). Finally, Emily Hemelrijk (2015) on female benefactors – as well as her previous studies – must be mentioned, for, though she encompasses the entire Roman West, her methodology provides a useful framework for my own investigation.[6]

Most studies, therefore, have aimed for broad overviews of the evidence, cataloging and categorizing inscriptions, with a particular eye toward expressions of costs in the texts. All this work has helped from an economic perspective, as far as our understanding of costs, trade, municipal management, and individual wealth. In building on these previous studies, I have different goals in mind. First, my approach combines the established categories of benefaction with considerations of geography, frequency, and chronology. Another way in which my approach differs is in moving beyond the strict economic impact to consider the cognitive impacts: how these benefactions were received by the towns and their residents in their daily lives. Both residents and potential future donors would have been affected. To investigate this sort of effect, I analyze the function(s) and placement of the physical structures that were donated and the value – broadly speaking – of goods, games, or other intangibles.

Thus, the original context of these acts of civic munificence – as far as they can be determined – cannot be excluded from study. The baths, roads, temples, and porticoes were not simple financial transactions from donor to recipients. Considering only the financial resources required by any particular benefaction isolates the activity from its original setting. Buildings and monuments occupied physical space in and around towns for decades and even centuries. People used them and saw them on a regular basis and, undoubtedly, had opinions about them. Spectacles, banquets, and goods filled other needs for those who received them. One might even say that those sorts of activities made life enjoyable. I do not deny that tracking the finances is worthwhile, but it is also essential to grasp the functions of those costed expenditures and to ask the basic questions: what did donors get out of making the gifts, and what did the people get?

In order to answer these and other questions, I have assessed more than thirty-one thousand inscriptions from the Spanish provinces, available via the Hispania Epigraphica Online Database, which is a growing electronic collection of published inscriptions found in Spain and Portugal. I determined whether inscriptions record benefactions if they included at least one of a number of expressions in the text, such as *de sua pecunia, donum dedit, faciendum curavit* (or similar variations), or other indications that an individual provided funds for a structure, goods, or other activity for the public benefit. If inscriptions were too fragmentary, they were discarded from study. My goal is not to be exhaustively comprehensive but to have a reasonably complete sample to examine in meaningful ways.

Therefore, I have sorted out and analyzed sixty-one inscriptions from the province of Hispania Tarraconensis for the purpose of this study. Many of the inscriptions record more than one benefaction, but the item mentioned first in the inscription is used as the primary gift for ease in analysis. The different types of benefactions are the following: architectural, whether new or repairs; public works, such as roads, walls, bridges, aqueducts, baths, and other water features; spectacles, including all types of entertainment; one-time and foundational cash gifts; statues made with precious materials such as gold, silver, or gems; goods, namely public banquets; alimentary programs; and unspecified, in which cases the text is either in poor condition or omits any particular act of benefaction. In order to see the full range of benefactions in this province, a cross-section of the whole corpus is presented first, and then three towns are analyzed in further detail for the sake of space.

Overview of benefactions in Hispania Tarraconensis

Of the sixty-one inscriptions, twenty-five record some kind of architectural structure, and that number also includes two instances of land being donated for the explicit purpose of building a temple (see Figure 5.1).

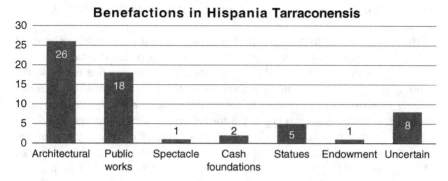

Figure 5.1 The benefactions in Hispania Tarraconensis included in the corpus under study

Financing of public works can be found in eighteen of the inscriptions that mention roads, city walls, bridges, towers, baths, aqueducts, or other water features. In addition to financing baths with her own money on her own land in Tagili and giving a public feast and circus games to celebrate, Voconia Avita also left two hundred thousand sesterces for the future care of the bathing structure (*AE* 1979, 352; *IRAl* 48). This benefaction falls into a small group of enterprises that were not simply ephemeral transactions but were established with the intent of providing goods, entertainment, or repair costs for the future enjoyment of townspeople.

Two of the benefactions were established as foundations with an initial large quantity of cash invested so that the interest could be used for various gifts in the future. In these two cases, one foundation paid out a small cash gift to various individuals in the town (known as *sportulae*) (*CIL* II, 4511), and the other established annual games and oil to be used at the public baths (*CIL* II, 4514). The final example of this type of endowment benefaction, which dates to the time of Augustus, is less clear whether the donor, Gaius Iulius Celsus, designated his financial gift to be used in a certain way. It appears that he bequeathed a sum of money to the town of Ercavica (in the region near Cuenca today), and the *decuriones* (members of the town council) decided to spend it, or a portion of it amounting to one hundred thousand sesterces, to build eight miles of roadway (*CIL* II, 3167).

Only one text records the financing of spectacles as the primary benefaction, though numerous other inscriptions include some kind of games along with the costlier gifts.[7] For example, as seen earlier, Voconia Avita sponsored games to celebrate the opening of a bath complex she financed. Though most often statues are designated as honorary, since they were set up to recognize an individual, rather than to benefit the broader community, I do include five statues here under benefactions.[8] These are not typical statuary dedications, as they were made from precious materials, which were much costlier than the common marble or bronze. Games or a cash distribution were given to mark the dedication of some statues. The final eight inscriptions in my corpus cannot be categorized because the text

is too fragmentary or the wording too vague to ascertain the precise type of benefaction, but other language in the inscription makes clear that a donor is being
recognized.

The amount given by this group of benefactors varies immensely. The most
expensive donations are those that involve some kind of construction, whether
a building or infrastructure, and these are the very donations that compose the
majority of my corpus to date. Ten inscriptions record the construction, renovation, or repair of temples, and eight record the same of nonreligious structures,
such as a council house, paving in the forum, and restoration of markets. Even
within the category of construction, there is a range of cash outlay, depending
upon the size, decoration, and types of materials used (among other factors).
Though it is outside this study, the highest recorded price in sesterces for the construction of a single building in the Roman West comes from the province of Hispania Baetica, where an inscription records that Baebia Crinita bequeathed two
hundred thousand sesterces for a temple in Arucci (*CIL* II, 964; *ILS* 5402; *ILER*
1760). However, the only inscription in my corpus from Hispania Tarraconensis
that includes the cost outlay for any building is that recording the bequest of forty
thousand sesterces by Cornelia Procula for a temple in Emporiae, as mentioned
earlier (*IRC* III, 36). The silence on the exact expenses is in keeping with general
trends, as the majority of inscriptions commemorating benefactions do not mention the amount of money spent (Curchin, 1983: 229).

The second highest recorded cost for a privately funded construction project
in the Spanish provinces is a bridge in the town of Oretum in Tarraconensis,
financed by Publius Baebius Venustus in the time of Hadrian and dedicated to the
divine imperial household, the *domus divina* (*CIL* II, 3221; Curchin, 1983: 229).
He spent eighty thousand sesterces on this project and gave circus games upon
its dedication. In the text, Venustus gives the full names of his father and grandfather, rather than the more standard format with only his father's name. Perhaps
Venustus wished to stress that his family had history in Oretum.[9] If his family had
established roots in the town – even though no offices or priesthoods are listed in
the text – that might explain why he actually undertook this enterprise or why the
ordo and people approached him with the request for a new bridge.[10] The careful
wording might also suggest that the construction of the bridge was something that
was needed by the town and not a frivolous expenditure by a wealthy benefactor.
A further implication is that the town itself did not have the resources available to
see to this infrastructure venture.

Aqueducts, another public works project, were among the costliest construction undertakings, costing millions of sesterces. In Gaul, there is record of a two
million sesterces bequest for an aqueduct (Curchin, 1983: 229 n. 16; *CIL* XIII,
596). Four inscriptions record the construction or repair of aqueducts in Tarraconensis, though unfortunately none include the amount expended. At the end of the
first century or beginning of the second century in the town of Ilugo, Annia Victorina sponsored an aqueduct and bridges, dedicated with a banquet on account
of the memory of her husband and son (*CIL* II, 3240). While this text does not
specify the amount she donated for the endeavor, it does state that Annia Victorina

took care of the costs on her own. If the aqueduct in Gaul is any indication, Annia Victorina allocated a very large amount of her resources for these undertakings, at least two million sesterces.

In forty of the sixty-one texts in my corpus, the gender and social rank of the donor can be determined with some degree of certainty (see Figure 5.2). At times, the personal status of the donor cannot be determined just from the name in the inscription, but often there are other clues if a certain office or priesthood is mentioned too. Established family names might help distinguish a senator from an equestrian, and the format of the name can sometimes identify a former slave. It is perhaps not surprising that most of the people responsible for financing the more expensive projects were members of the local decurial *ordo*. The architectural projects and public works, as has been established, are usually the costliest benefactions on record. Of the forty-three gifts in these categories, decurions were responsible for twelve, senators for two, and equestrians for two. However, female donors undertook seven of these costly projects too, and freedpeople carried out five of them.[11]

Of the few examples of freedmen financing costlier donations, a freedman – a *sevir Augustalis* named Marcus Popilius Onyxs – in Lucentum paid for the restorations of a temple. His former master's name is in the dative here, perhaps indicating that Onyxs made the restoration on behalf of his patron. The female donors, constituting 14.7% (nine of sixty-one examples overall), are involved in the same kind of benefactions as the male donors in Tarraconensis. Claudia Persina granted land for a temple in Tarraco (*CIL* II, 4265; *RIT* 363). Sempronia Arganta's name appears inscribed on monumental blocks from Segobriga, indicating that she was responsible for a large architectural structure (*AE* 1999, 938; *HEp* 10, 2000, 291). Finally, Domitia Pressilla financed a bridge, which her freedmen oversaw (*CIL* II, 5690).

This overview of the practice of benefaction in the province of Tarraconensis has demonstrated the range of benefactions, the variety of people who engaged

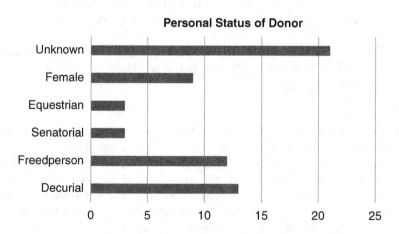

Figure 5.2 The personal or legal status of the donors

in the practice, and the incompleteness of the evidence.[12] By narrowing down the focus to a single town at a time, we can ask different questions of the evidence, leading us to a more nuanced view of munificent activities in a given locale. I have chosen to focus on Carthago Nova, Barcino, and Castulo, for they shared some traits – such as a change in their Roman civic status around the same time – yet also had different pre-Roman and early Roman existences. They have all been excavated to some degree and have multiple examples of benefaction for examination. These three were also prominent towns in their own regard in antiquity, whether serving as a port city or possessing natural resources.

Carthago Nova

Carthago Nova had a long history before the Romans established it as a Roman town. It was founded by the Carthaginian Hasdrubal, father of Hannibal ca. 229/228 BCE (Abascal Palazón and Ramallo Asensio, 1997: 11). It became a Roman *colonia* around the middle of the first century and was a significant port city in the Mediterranean, as well as being proximate to silver mines.[13] Excavation of the ancient town has been problematic due to the continued habitation at modern Cartagena. Excavations since the 1990s have been carried out at different places around the city, and they have begun to provide an overview of the urban framework (Ruiz Valderas and Martínez Andreu, 2017). One thing that is clear from the written sources is that Carthago Nova was known for its fortifications.

Sixteen of the benefactions in my corpus come from Carthago Nova, and they are some of the earliest datable texts as well. Of these sixteen, six were some kind of architectural structures, either new construction, renovation, or part of an existing structure. The other ten were public works, specifically sections of the city wall, gates, or towers. In fact, no other city has provided as many pieces of evidence for the construction of the city wall as Carthago Nova (Díaz Ariño, 2008: 225; Abascal Palazón and Ramallo Asensio, 1997: 11). Marcus Calpurnius Bibulus and Gnaeus Cornelius Cinna were two of the men who each financed sections of the city wall. The inscription recording Cinna's donation reads:

> Cn(aeus) Cornelius/ L(uci) f(ilius) Gal(eria) Cinna/ IIvir/ murum long(um) p(edes) CII/ ex d(ecreto) d(ecurionum) f(aciendum) c(uravit) i(dem)q(ue) p(robavit).

(CIL II, 3425; *ILS* 5332)[14]

The text specifies the length of wall (102 feet) and that Cinna took care of it according to a decree of the decurions. The inscription commemorating Bibulus's donation follows a similar format, though it is very fragmentary (*CIL* II, 3422).[15] The other eight inscriptions that record construction of sections of the city wall, gates, and towers use the same formulaic language without providing too much detail about the donors themselves. They record sections of wall from sixty to almost one hundred and fifty feet financed by each donor or group of donors. It is likely that all these infrastructure projects date to the very late first century

BCE or early first century CE (Abascal Palazón, 2002: 35). Very few inscriptions from the Roman Empire that record gifts of a city wall and associated structures make any mention of the amount of money donated or required for such projects. The physician Crinas was said by Pliny to have spent ten million sesterces on the walls and other structures at Massilia (*Nat.* 29.9). Depending upon the amount of reconstruction or new construction, which is impossible to know without further excavations, the walls at Carthago Nova must have cost millions of sesterces as well, with each donor providing a portion.

Most of the architectural benefactions cannot be precisely dated. One inscription, dated to the Augustan period, records that a donor, whose name is missing but who is described as *duovir designatus*, paid for pavement and something else with his own money *(de sua pecunia)*, though the location of this paving is unclear (*CIL* II, 5931). Another fragmentary inscription – known in duplicate – records the testamentary gift for *hoc opus* ("this work"), which should indicate a civic structure of some sort, especially as it was found in the forum area (*CIL* II, 3423 + 3424); it is dated from the late first to the early second century CE. A third datable architectural project is a *sacellum* to Jupiter Stator, financed and dedicated by the freedperson Marcus Aquinius Andro in the second quarter of the first century BCE, according to the text set in small white tesserae in the floor of the structure (*HEp* 6, 1996, 655; *AE* 1996, 926). Though Republican in date, this shrine is included here as one of the earliest recorded benefactions in this region and is the only documented shrine to Jupiter Stator in the whole empire.[16] Though unique from this perspective, it also fits into the pattern of architectural benefactions in the imperial period.

Two other architectural undertakings involve porticoes. In the last years of the first century BCE, two men financed a *porticus* (*CIL* II, 3430), and another man named Gaius Plotius Princeps paid for a crypt and porticus in the early first century CE (*CIL* II, 3428). The latter probably refers to the forum area, perhaps the Capitolium, as the inscribed stone was discovered next to the Plaza de San Francisco in Cartagena where the ancient forum is believed to have been situated (Abascal Palazón and Ramallo Asensio, 1997: 135).[17] Three or possibly four men (the stone is very fragmentary) dedicated a column in commemoration of the *genius* of Carthago Nova and also funded a parade and games in the late Republic or early Augustan period (*CIL* II, 3408). The exact nature of this *columna* recorded in the text is unknown; most mentions of columns in inscriptions allude to the construction or repairs of public buildings where they form part of the structure or stand out because of an unusual characteristic (Abascal Palazón and Ramallo Asensio, 1997: 154).

Like most inscriptions that record benefactions, all but one of this group are silent about the costs of the project. The unspecified *hoc opus*, mentioned earlier, was financed by Lucius Aemilius Rectus, according to his will, with the amount of two hundred and fifty pounds of silver, which his heir Lucius Aemilius Senex provided (*CIL* II, 3423 + 3424; Ramallo Asensio, 1997: no. 59). Since there were silver mines not far from Carthago Nova, it is not uncommon to find cash amounts provided as bullion, though figuring out the value of the silver can be challenging.

Curchin notes that the value of two hundred and fifty pounds of silver would be two hundred thousand sesterces, using the model developed for figures in North Africa (1983: 229 n. 11). However, the proximity of the silver mines might have made the cost of silver less expensive in Spain. The inscription for the *sacellum* to Jupiter Stator does not list the amount given by Andro, and temple costs that are stated in inscriptions range from three thousand in third-century Sarra (in Africa Proconsularis) to six hundred thousand sesterces in late second-century Lambaesis for a temple to the *genius* of the town (Duncan-Jones, 1982: 90–1). The latter is certainly atypical, as most of the costs cluster around twenty thousand to sixty thousand sesterces.

According to the inscriptions, all sixteen of these donations were one-time projects with no funds allocated for future repairs or commemoration. Thus, while most of these acts of civic munificence would have required a fair amount of cash to carry out, the donors were not required to contribute financing after they were finished. We will see examples of long-term investments in Barcino, but let us now consider the broader significance of these donations in Carthago Nova over the course of about two centuries.

The inscriptions make clear that in the second half of the first century BCE, there was a concerted effort at constructing new sections of wall and restoring parts of the older Carthaginian Barquid fortifications as well. Strabo (*Geogr.* 3.4.6) comments on the impressive nature of the city walls of Carthago Nova, but in the late first century there was little reason for such a sturdy enclosure. In fact, the areas known for intense mining efforts became less densely populated, while in other areas new settlements developed (Orejas and Sánchez-Palencia, 2002: 587). Rather than signaling a time of insecurity, the efforts directed at improvements for the city wall correspond to its change in civic status. Carthago Nova became a Roman *colonia* in the mid-first century BCE. Three of the named benefactors were among the earliest magistrates of the colony, while others lack any official offices and were presumably part of the wealthy elite. Residents and officials of the new colony pursued the sort of urban infrastructure they thought the new status required (Abascal, 2002: 35). A new cityscape was being formed in the first century BCE, as evidenced by a number of structures serving the religious, political, and entertainment needs of the city's populace (Ruiz Valderas and Martínez Andreu, 2017: 34–8).

Though a new city wall might have helped create the sort of urban look residents desired to go along with the new civic status of Carthago Nova, so many private benefactions for this sort of infrastructure are puzzling when weighed against other evidence. In the municipal charters from Urso, Malaga, and other cities in Spain, we learn that public funds may be used by the *duoviri* and other magistrates for the construction and maintenance of roads, city walls, sewers, and so on.[18] Why are private individuals taking on this financial burden when the towns themselves were supposed to fund the sorts of construction that benefited the town as a whole? Was Carthago Nova a special case? Though ten recorded examples may seem insignificant when compared with the thousands of individuals who lived in Carthago Nova in the Augustan period, in no other city represented in my study are private benefactors responsible for so many projects of civic infrastructure. Perhaps the importance of Carthago Nova during the Republican period inspired special pride in their fortifications.

Another consideration behind the number of sections of wall financed by private individuals is competition. All of the extant texts recording the donations for sections of the city wall, towers, and gates date to about the same time period. There might have been a coordinated effort by multiple donors to take on responsibility for parts of the whole construction project, especially if the city did not possess the funds for such a massive undertaking. However, the donors might have been driven by a sense of competition after one or two individuals allocated funds for the structures. A donor inserts himself into the town fabric through his or her donation and the subsequent commemoration of that gift. Donors broadcast their own wealth and social status by engaging in such a public activity as benefaction. Everyone coming and going through the city gates would have seen the plaques commemorating the donors' generosity. A certain degree of jealousy might prompt others to make similar or even larger donations to receive the same kind of recognition given to earlier benefactors. The desire to contribute to the wall, in particular, might have been increased due to the recent designation of Carthago Nova as a Roman *colonia* and the significance of city walls as an emblem of that status. This sense of competition is naturally difficult to find among the fragmented stones bearing the records of donations, yet it is entirely plausible based upon the short time period in which the city wall was reconstructed.

The benefactions for buildings in Carthago Nova would have allowed donors the same privilege of marking their identity into the fabric of the city. Although we do not know for certain where the structures were located, with the exception of the *sacellum* to Jupiter Stator (Sánchez et al., 1995), they were probably within the city center and therefore visible to passersby on a daily basis. Through the monuments and the monumental writing inscribed on commemorative plaques, individuals incorporate themselves into the larger whole. A "primary function of monuments in the early Empire was as devices with which to assert the place of individuals within society" (Woolf, 1996: 29). Buildings endured for generations; thus, generations of people saw the donor's name affixed to a temple, porticus, or other civic building. Furthermore, the arrangement of buildings dictates how people approach them and how people experience their city. As Valone puts it, "Buildings mold the physical and cultural environment of a place" (2001: 317). The donors received prestige for their donations while also impacting the daily lives of thousands of people as they negotiated their way through their city. From the type of benefactions undertaken – mostly architecture and infrastructure – it is clear that at least a small group of families in Carthago Nova had substantial wealth and used it as a way of asserting their own roles within the city.

Barcino

Barcino was established as a Roman *colonia* in the last part of the first century BCE and known officially as *colonia Iulia Augusta Paterna Faventia Barcino*. It occupied a strategic position on the coast, while also having communication with the interior of the province via the Rubricatus river (Mar, Garrido, and Beltrán-Caballero, 2012). It experienced steady development as a Roman town over the course of the first and second centuries, and many of its residents pursued careers in imperial administration.

While in Carthago Nova, the private benefactions were divided between architectural and public works; in Barcino, there is more variety in the types of gifts provided by benefactors. Indeed, there is a notable lack of any type of architectural donation, and just one donor financed a portion of city wall. Two donors gave statues, one pair jointly financed the construction of baths, and two set up recurring gifts. Thus, the six benefactions in Barcino represent a range of types. Of the four that can be dated, three were made during the second century.

A concise inscription, dated to the Augustan era, commemorates the financing of walls, towers, and gates by a Gaius Coelius (*IRC* IV, 57; *AE* 1978, 441).[19] The text simply states: *C(aius) Coelius Atisi f(ilius)/ IIvir quin(quennalis) mur(os)/ turres portas/ fac(iendas) coer(avit)*. This reconstruction – or construction *ab initio* – coincides with the period in which Barcino became a Roman colony. A recent analysis of the remains of the Roman city walls visible in Barcelona concludes that the first wall, constructed at the end of the first century BCE, was made with local sandstone, had a perimeter of 1,315 meters, a height of eight meters, and was two meters thick (Corso, Casals, and Garcia Almirall, 2017). Four gates allowed traffic in and out of the town. Since there is no indication of the length of the wall or how many towers or gates were financed by Gaius Coelius, a cost estimate is impossible. Certainly the cost of the walls, towers, and gates at Barcino must have extended into the millions, based upon the sparse evidence we have. Just like at Carthago Nova, here at Barcino the elevation to the status of *colonia* seems to be the impetus for improving the city walls.

When he died in the Antonine period, Lucius Minicius Natalis Quadronius Verus left one hundred thousand sesterces so that the income from interest on the gift could finance *sportulae* annually on his birthday for the *seviri Augustales* and the *decuriones* (*CIL* II, 4511). The rates are missing due to the fragmentary nature of the inscribed stone, but Duncan-Jones (1964: 205) suggests that, in comparison with other known rates, the conjecture of three denarii per *sevir Augustalis* and five denarii per decurion is highly plausible. Therefore, one hundred decurions would benefit and two hundred and fifty Augustales. During his lifetime, Quadronius and his father financed baths with porticoes and water channels on their own land (*CIL* II, 4509). The gift of the baths is overshadowed by the long list of offices, priesthoods, and titles for both men, occupying the majority of the inscribed stone slab.[20]

Lucius Caecilius Optatus had a military career as a legionary centurion and was honorably discharged under the emperors Marcus Aurelius and Lucius Verus before serving as *duovir* and *flamen Romae divorum et Augustorum* in Barcino. He bequeathed seven thousand five hundred sesterces to the town of Barcino such that a portion based on 6% of the annual interest was to be used annually on June 10 (probably his birthday) for boxing matches and to provide oil for bathers at the public baths (*CIL* II, 4514). Specifically, two hundred and fifty denarii could be spent on boxing matches, and twenty denarii should be used for the distribution of oil. Optatus further specified that this bequest was accompanied with a condition: that unless his freedmen and freedwomen were spared taking up the office of the sevirate, the whole sum of money would be transferred to the city of Tarraco, which would be obliged to carry out the same distributions. This is the only such stipulation in a donation in this province and carries with it an element of distrust. Perhaps the donor worried about the handling of his gift to Barcino. From the inscription, Optatus has no apparent connection with the colony of Tarraco, so his reason for establishing it as the alternate beneficiary remains unclear.

While statues of individuals do not necessarily fall into the purview of civic munificence, statues of gods or emperors, and any statue made from precious metals or decorated with jewels could, indeed, be considered a gift for the public good. There are two statue dedications from Barcino, neither of which can be dated specifically, that are included in the present corpus. One inscription, recording a statue dedicated to Aequitas Augusta by Lucius Minicius Myron (*IRC* IV, 1; *AE* 1962, 395), explicitly states the reason for the gift: *ob honorem VIvirat(us) (on account of the honor of the sevirate)*. The other inscription is very fragmentary, though it can be discerned that a Marcus Porcius Martialis dedicated a statue of Venus Augusta (*CIL* II, 4500). This statue might have also been dedicated *ob honorem VIviratus*, but the stone is too fragmentary to be certain. While some scholars have previously considered that dedications made *ob honorem* were closely connected to the contribution required of local offices and priesthoods, Duncan-Jones (1974: 86–7) asserts that this type of donation is, indeed, a form of euergetism. Melchor Gil (1994: 203–5) has compiled a study with fifty-seven donations made *ob honorem* in the Spanish provinces, not all of which were statues. Neither of these inscriptions mention the type of material used or any special decorations. It is, therefore, likely that they were marble statues, which could cost anywhere from a few thousand sesterces to over twenty thousand (Duncan-Jones, 1962: 83–8).

With this range of civic munificence in Barcino, the economic impact of all the gifts varies considerably from just a couple thousand sesterces to hundreds of thousands and millions. The costliest project presumably was the undertaking of walls, towers, and gates. Even without knowing whether this gift included the whole circuit of the wall or repairs to existing structures, this undertaking would have easily totaled millions of sesterces. Bathing complexes were also costly, especially when one considers water conduits, holding tanks, and even the land on which the structures were built. The data from Africa yield the range of one hundred thousand to four hundred thousand sesterces for the construction of a thermal complex (Duncan-Jones, 1982: 91). Apart from the architectural benefactions, we also see the establishment of recurring gifts of games, goods, and a cash distribution. While Optatus left behind the moderate amount of seven thousand five hundred sesterces for annual distributions, Quadronius Verus bequeathed one hundred thousand, which would have provided gifts for many more years. *Sportulae* had both an economic and a cognitive impact.

The Minicii family, of which Quadronius Verus was a member, was one of the most well known in the province, for a father and son both had extensive careers in imperial administration and are known from multiple inscriptions, not only in their hometown of Barcino, but also in other towns in Spain and even in North Africa, where they were stationed (Andreu Pintado and Ferré, 2006; Eck, 2009: 82–3). As Eck points out, these men were well known in Barcino; the inscriptions recording their civic munificence did not need to include all their offices and titles, as they would have been identifiable simply by their names alone (Eck, 2009: 82). However, by memorializing their careers, the men demonstrate their connections to the emperors Trajan and Hadrian, and tout their lifetime accomplishments. The large cash gift left by the younger Minicius exhibits clear signs of self-promotion. The recurring cash distribution would have lasted quite a few years, benefiting three hundred and fifty people (and their families) each year. The amount given to each individual was not substantial, and the recipients would have been some of the wealthiest residents of the town anyway. *Sportulae* did not function as charity; rather, they were a means by which a donor could be recognized for his goodwill and, in this case, that recognition continued for a number of years. While not tangible in the sense of a building in the middle of the forum, a recurring gift would have given the donor another sort of lasting fame after his death. The townspeople would continue to know the impact of the Minicii family for decades, which would benefit the rising generations of the family in the public sphere of Barcino.

Castulo

Castulo became a Roman *municipium* in the late Republic. It had been part of the province Baetica but was transferred into the province Tarraconensis through the territorial reforms by Augustus (Arboledas Martinez, 2008: 83). Tarraconensis was an imperial province, while Baetica was under senatorial authority. Several productive silver mines were located near Castulo, which might have been one motivation for the city's rezoning.

Just five benefactions are known from Castulo, and they are distributed from the mid-first to mid-second centuries. There is a mix of benefaction types as well. The earliest recorded act of civic munificence is unique in my corpus, as it names an emperor along with the other benefactors:

> [Ti(berius) Claudius Caesar Aug(ustus)] Germanicus p(ater) p(atriae) e[t/ P(ublius) Cornelius P(ubli) f(ilius) Gal(eria) Taurus et Valeria P(ubli) f(ilia) V]erecunda uxor d(e) s(ua) p(ecunia) f(ecerunt)/[P(ublius) Cornelius P(ubli) f(ilius) Gal(eria) Taurus f(ilius) ludis inpensa] sua factis dedicavit.
>
> (*CIL* II, 3269c)[21]

While emperors are known to have funded public works and architectural projects in Rome and around the empire, this is the only example in Tarraconensis that shows a (presumably) local couple in coordination with the emperor.[22] The inscription is known in triplicate from fragments of three stone slabs, which would have been mounted on the structure. Though unnamed in the text, the building has been identified as the amphitheater of Castulo (Gómez-Pantoja and Garrido, 2009). Due to the high construction costs of such a building, the emperor might have contributed funds from the imperial treasury. In fact, none of the amphitheaters in Spain were known to have been funded solely by private funds.[23] Since the text lacks any description of Taurus's career, the connection between him (or his wife) and emperor Claudius cannot be determined.

A benefaction dated to the Flavian period provided for a water conduit, tanks, and pipes (*CIL* II, 3280). The donor's name does not survive, but the gift came at the same time that a large thermal complex was constructed in Castulo (Pavía Page, 2016: 89). No donor can be matched with the costly undertaking of the bath structure itself. However, there might have been a number of private individuals who funded various aspects of this project, evidence for which has been recovered elsewhere in the empire.[24]

One benefaction from Castulo records the deeds of a Cornelia Marullina, who had financed silver statues (of whom, it is unknown), a public feast, and circus games in the first half of the second century (*CILA* III, 101; *AE* 1958, 4). When the city wished to erect statues of her and her son Lucius Cornelius Marullus to show its gratitude, she paid for the expense herself. It was a common practice for someone receiving an honorary statue to cover the costs associated with the statue – a sort of benefaction in its own right – signaled in the texts with expressions such as *honore accepto de pecunia sua* ("with the honor accepted, [she paid] from her own money") or *sua impensa* ("at her/his own expense"). Her heir Gaius Cornelius Bellicus dedicated those statues of Marullina and her son and provided additional circus games to celebrate. The full text of the base for the statue of Cornelius Marullus reads:

> L(ucio) Corn(elio) Marullo/ quod ordo Castulon(ensium)/ pro liberalitate Cor(neliae)/ Marullinae matris/ eius quod civitatem/ Castulonensium sta/tuis argenteis et epu/lo et circensib(us) decora/set statuam ei et filio su/o posit-eram se decre/verat Cor(nelia) Marulli/[n]a honore accepto/ d[e] pec(unia) sua poni iussit/ [h]oc donum illius/ C(aius) Co[r(nelius)] Bellicus heres eius/ d(edit) d(edicavit) edi[tis] circensib(us).
>
> (*CILA* III, 101; *AE* 1958, 4)[25]

There is nothing else known about Marullus; no titles, offices, or priesthoods are recorded in this inscription. He was the intended recipient of the town's praise, as he was listed first in the text, yet it was his mother's liberality that apparently provided the impetus for the council of Castulo to move that statues of them both be set up. Unfortunately, we know little else about Marullina either.[26] She was likely a widow by the time of the honor was conferred, since no husband or father was referenced in the inscription, as would have been customary. Certainly she had acquired substantial financial resources to make costly benefactions in her town, and perhaps she was trying to use her wealth to pave the way for her son's political career.[27] Her heir carried out the dedication of the statue so she must have died between the decreeing of the honorary statue and its actual installation.

In an eloquent, though unfortunately fragmentary, inscription, it is recorded that Lucius Licinius Abscantio gave theatrical shows and gladiatorial contests lasting multiple days for residents and citizens of Castulo, and dedicated a statue to the reigning emperor Antoninus Pius in 154 CE (*AE* 1976, 351; Ceballos Hornero, 2004: 227–9). He undertook these dedications after his time as *sevir* in Castulo, perhaps as a way of commemorating his own civic service. The base for the statue of the emperor was found in an area thought to have been part of the baths in Castulo (Mariner Bigorra, 1979: 407). While this text does not provide details for an entirely remarkable benefaction, it is significant for other reasons. This is the only base for a statue of any of the members of the Antonine family in Castulo, and Abscantio is the first *sevir* known from the town (Mariner Bigorra, 1979: 407).

Last, but certainly not least, the costliest of all benefactions in Castulo was financed by Quintus Thorius Culleo at some point in the mid-first to mid-second century. He was a procurator of Baetica but was probably from Castulo, as deduced from the scale of the projects he undertook there. According to the inscription on a statue base set up by the town in his honor, he repaired the city wall, paved a road after heavy rains damaged it, gave land for a bath complex, paid for statues of Venus Genetrix and Cupid for the theater, forgave a debt of ten million sesterces owed to him by the town, and provided circus games on top of everything else (*CIL* II, 3270). Taken together, this is the largest set of donations by a private individual to any town in the Western Roman Empire (Duncan-Jones, 1974: 80). In Italy, where comparative material is available, each mile of paved road could cost one hundred thousand sesterces (Duncan-Jones, 1982: 124–5, 152–3). The road connected Castulo to Sisapo, about ninety miles to the northwest. There has not been a complete excavation in this area, which passes through quite rocky terrain in parts, but the estimate of ten million to twelve million sesterces seems reasonable (Duncan-Jones, 1974: 81).

The donation of the land for the thermal structure indicates that Culleo owned substantial property in Castulo, as a bath complex necessitated a large expanse of flat land. This was apparently the second bath structure in Castulo, the first having been built in the Flavian period, to which the anonymous donor of *CIL* II, 3280 might have contributed with the financing of water conduits. The statues of Venus and Cupid were probably made from silver, which is a very common material for statues of deities in this area, given the proximity of the silver mines. Though details are not provided as to the length of the road paved or whether the whole circuit of the wall was reconstructed, Duncan-Jones (1974) has estimated the total financial outlay of certainly more than ten million and up to twenty million sesterces.[28]

While there are not many benefactions known from the small *municipium* of Castulo, those that were given were rather costly. To review, they comprise an amphitheater, water features probably connected to a bath structure, feasts and circus games, several days of gladiatorial and theatrical shows, costly statues, and all the projects financed by Culleo. Certainly the extravagant gifts by Culleo tip the scales. But what might have been the cognitive impact of this array of benefactions as well as the others? Given that the donations were spread over at least a century, there does not seem to be a pattern of competitive giving by the wealthy elite. Returning to the earliest benefaction, the amphitheater, funded by Publius Cornelius Taurus and his wife Valeria Verecunda, along with the patronage of the emperor Claudius, would have played a significant role in the society of Castulo. Having a venue for gladiatorial combats and other shows would set the town apart from others. Thousands of residents and visitors from the region would have enjoyed the entertainment for decades to come. Indeed, the gladiatorial shows sponsored by Abscantio in 154 CE must have taken place in this very amphitheater constructed a century earlier. An amphitheater was not a place where people visited daily or even weekly, yet when they did come, they would have seen the donors' names in large letters next to Claudius's name. Though we do not know the nature of the connection between Taurus and his wife Verecunda and the emperor, the fact of having their names on the same structure bearing the emperor's name is of an inestimable magnitude. The association must have lent respect to Taurus and his family. Such an immense physical structure also created a long-lasting memory of its donors, keeping the family name in the town's collective consciousness.

All of the gifts provided by Culleo were certainly important individually. Having a strong city wall was a characteristic of Roman towns, even when there was not any imminent danger of attack.[29] Repaving a road would have facilitated travel and commerce, and was especially crucial for mining operations in the area. According to the town charters of Irni and Urso, the construction and maintenance of roadways was under the direction of the *duoviri* or *aediles*. The fact that Culleo, who served in neither position in Castulo (according to the text of the dedication), spent such a large sum of his own money on such operations was remarkable. That said, the road in question served as an important route in mining operations, which could have benefited Culleo himself, his friends, or at least others in the town, since the silver mines nearby were an integral part of the local economy. Thus, while the undertaking of caring for the road was beyond what most private benefactors financed, it might not have been entirely selfless.

The two bathing facilities in Castulo would have been received enthusiastically, given the importance of such buildings in Roman society. Baths were places for so much more than simply bathing. People met up with friends, had a bit to eat and a drink, got a massage or other specialized services, and engaged in athletic activities. The grounds were landscaped with fountains, plants, and trees, and the interiors were decorated with statuary, mosaic, and marble revetment.[30] The baths were central to the lives of the Romans, and everyone entering or even walking by would have seen the names of the donors who made them possible.

Conclusions

Throughout this chapter, both the economic and cognitive impacts of benefactions in Hispania Tarraconensis have been highlighted. In terms of the economic impact on the donors, the benefactions run the gamut from inexpensive to very costly. Most would not have affected the finances of the donors to a great extent, nor would those such as *sportulae* have had much of an impact on the recipients. Another aspect of the economic impact relates to the broader market economy. A very large labor force was required for each of the construction projects under discussion. Materials and supplies had to be sourced and transported, whether from close in the vicinity or across the empire. The public banquets provided by some donors necessitated a great quantity of foodstuffs as well as workers to prepare the feast. All of these benefactions, therefore, created a large effect not just on those immediately involved but in the broader economy as well (Hoyer, 2013).[31] The structures funded by donors composed only a fraction of all buildings and monuments in a given town. Public funds, the resources derived from taxes, the obligatory fees assessed from local officials *(summae honorariae)*, and other income would have funded the majority of buildings and public works. The intangible impression of privately funded works is much harder to assess but undoubtedly more significant. Both recipients and donors benefited in ways that are hard to quantify.

Donors received acknowledgment for their munificent acts in a variety of ways. First and foremost is the inscribed plaque commemorating their gifts. Additionally, many donors were honored with statues erected in public, further thanking the donor for their generosity. The donation itself and the acknowledgment of the donation helped to seal the memory of the donor into the fabric of the city. A portico or the commemoration of a public banquet endured for decades or generations, making it possible for people to remember the benefactor. The desire for this type of lasting recognition certainly motivated some men and women to sponsor benefactions.

Diana Ng has recently argued that spectacles were valued more highly than buildings for their ability to keep a donor's memory alive since, in certain instances, even when an endowment for games had been exhausted, cities provided funds to continue them (2015: 1–23). According to her reasoning, buildings might fall into disrepair and unintentionally serve to tarnish the memory of the donor. However, Ng's conclusions, supported by the writings of jurists, philosophers, and a few epigraphical examples from the eastern provinces of the Roman Empire, do not correspond to my own findings in Tarraconensis where spectacles make up a small number of benefactions.

Furthermore, a sense of competition might have motivated donors to give ever more elaborate gifts, thus increasing the recognition they received as well.[32] In analyzing the effect of benefactions on other residents in a given town, I have focused on the physicality of architectural structures and also the enjoyment derived both from the amenities or activities offered in these buildings, as well as the entertainment provided by shows or public banquets. Having an organized town replete with richly decorated buildings and beautiful statuary can also bring a sense of joy to people's lives.

Not all donors were clearly motivated by the same circumstances. A number of people financed large building projects or other donations during their lifetimes, but some of the more expensive and more ostentatious gifts were made posthumously. That is, the gifts intended to bring more personal recognition to their donor were given through testamentary bequest. At first glance, the practice seems contradictory. Why wait until after death to give a large gift that could be received with thanks, an honorary statue, and inestimable personal capital? Perhaps, contrary to my arguments regarding a sense of competition among the elite and the desire for great recognition, there was a sense of modesty in some donors. Over the course of two hundred years, men like Cicero, Seneca, and the emperors Antoninus Pius and Marcus Aurelius cautioned people against lavish gifts, especially for ephemeral pleasures such as banquets and games and the construction of entirely new structures. Seneca advises:

> Let us give what is necessary first, then what is useful, then what is pleasurable, particularly things that will endure. But we should begin with necessities; for that which supports life impresses the mind in one way, that which adorns or equips life, in quite another.
>
> (*Ben.* 1.10.5–11.4)

Both Antonine emperors encouraged potential donors to see to more useful endeavors, such as the repairs of old structures rather than financing new buildings.[33] The contradictory nature of the evidence cautions us from making broad generalizations about all benefactors in the Roman Empire, or even in one province.

This analysis of inscriptions from Hispania Tarraconensis that record benefactions is one step in a larger study of assessing the nature of civic munificence in the Spanish provinces. Analyzing the expenditures made by donors is limited due to the fragmentary nature of many inscribed texts or the simple omission of these figures in the inscriptions. The fact that the majority of inscriptions are silent on the costs of benefactions should itself cause us to wonder if the amount of money mattered as much as other factors for the benefactors or those in the town. Clearly, other elements such as the functions of a building or activity sponsored by donors were also significant.

Notes

1 "According to the will of Cornelia Procula, with the amount of forty thousand sesterces, her freedman completed the temple with an additional 5,495 sesterces of his own money." All translations by the author.
2 Map made by David B. Hollander using QGIS, Natural Earth raster data, and the Ancient World Mapping Center shapefiles "Ba_rivers.shp," "Coastline.shp," and "Openwater. shp" (Accessed: May 31, 2018. http://awmc.unc.edu/wordpress/map-files/).
3 This chapter does not address the topic of civic patronage or the patron-client relationship, which, though they may encompass some of the same motivating factors, are quite different from the sort of civic munificence under discussion. For a detailed overview of civic patronage in Spain, see Melchor Gil (2018).
4 A full overview of the practice of benefaction is beyond the scope of this chapter. The beginnings of this line of inquiry, particularly as it relates to the Classical and Hellenistic periods, can be traced back to Veyne (1976), Gauthier (1985), and Quass (1993).

Rogers (1991) argues for a new approach to euergetism in the context of the Greek East during the Roman period. A growing body of scholarship, as cited throughout the chapter, has considered elements of benefaction in particular places and time periods in the Roman Empire.

5 Melchor Gil (1993–1994: 346) states that the entry into the decurionate in most large cities was 100,000 sesterces, whereas in smaller cities, the amount was around 20,000.

6 For benefactions by women in the East, as well as their public roles in general, see van Bremen (1996).

7 For a full study on the range of games in Roman Hispania, see Ceballos Hornero (2004).

8 Andreu Pintado (2004) also includes statues to individuals, emperors, and divinities as examples of euergetism since they add to the overall ornamentation of the city and provide public benefit.

9 Thank you to Arjan Zuiderhoek for this suggestion.

10 The phrase *petente ordine et populo* indicates that the town council and people sought out the donation.

11 If a man is designated as *sevir* or *sevir Augustalis*, I consider him a freedman since they tended to fill this priesthood most commonly, though some freeborn men known in this role. The sevirate was a priesthood whose members had duties in the imperial cult, among other things. However, I am hesitant to make assumptions solely based upon the name of an individual since a Greek cognomen does not always indicate freedperson status, especially later in the imperial period (cf. Liu, 2009: 172–3). On the sevirate in the Spanish provinces, see Rodà de Llanza (1993).

12 The range of benefactions, status of donors, and the chronological framework are all similar to the findings of Andreu Pintado (2004) in the province of Lusitania.

13 Abascal Palazón (2002) revises the date for the founding of the colony Carthago Nova from 45 BCE under Julius Caesar to 54 BCE during the governorship of Pompey based on numismatic evidence for the existence of *duoviri quinquennales*.

14 "Gnaeus Cornelius Cinna, son of Lucius, of the Galeria tribe, duovir, undertook the construction of (a section of) the wall 102 feet long, according to the approval of the town councilors." For more on the possible family connections of this Cinna, see Abascal Palazón and Ramallo Asensio (1997: 90–2).

15 This is not necessarily the same Bibulus who was consul in 59 BCE. See Abascal Palazón (2017: 120).

16 The *gens* to which this freedman belonged is known to have been involved in mining in the area near Carthago Nova starting in the mid-second century BCE. See Orejas and Sánchez-Palencia (2002) for discussion of mining activity and social structure in Roman Spain. For more on the discovery of the *sacellum*, see Sánchez et al. (1995).

17 Ceballos Hornero (2004: 622) suggests that this inscription refers to the theater, which was located at some distance from the forum. The theater was built during the time of Augustus, the same time when C. Plotius Princeps financed this construction project. There is no overwhelming proof for this suggestion, though inscriptions were commonly transported from the areas in which they were originally installed.

18 For example, see the *Lex coloniae genetivae Iuliae Ursonensis*, chapter 77, recorded on multiple bronze tablets (*CIL* II suppl. 5439; *ILS* 6007; *CIL* II², 594), which is a copy of the founding law of the colony of Urso, made during the Flavian era.

19 For more on the walls of Barcino, see Puig i Verdaguer and Rodà de Llanza (2007) and Ravotto (2017).

20 On the careers of the two men, see *PIR²* M 619, 620; E. Groag, s.v. *Minicius, RE* XV² n. 19, cols. 1836–42. Lucius Minicius Natalis Quadronius Verus is known from at least twenty inscriptions from around the empire, mostly coinciding with the military and political positions he held. Also see Eck and Navarro (1998) and Rodà (1978).

21 "The emperor Tiberius Claudius Caesar Augustus Germanicus, father of his country, and Publius Cornelius Taurus, son of Publius, Galeria tribe, and Valeria Verecunda,

daughter of Publius, his wife, made [this] with their own money. His son Publius Cornelius Taurus, son of Publius, Galeria tribe, dedicated [it] and gave games at his own expense."

22 Sánchez López (2015) suggests a reading of *eius iussu* in place of *et* at the end of the first line of the inscription. With that reading, the emperor would not have provided finances for the construction of the building. Instead, he would have given the order or suggestion that the local couple carried out. While the inscription is very fragmentary and does not rule out this reconstruction, it seems tenuous. Sánchez López provides no other inscriptions or references to the use of the phrase *eius iussu* in other situations. The expression is not commonly used at all in inscriptions, nor are there documented examples in which individuals pay for the construction of a building at the behest of the emperor. See Ceballos Hornero (2004: 203) for further bibliography on this set of inscriptions.

23 A fragmentary inscription with large letters found in the amphitheater of the ancient town of Segobriga provides the partial name Lucius Iulius and the word *testamento*, suggesting that this man bequeathed funds for the structure in his will (*HEp* 2, 1990: 384). The amphitheater at Tarraco was probably also financed, at least partly, by a private individual (*HEp* 4, 1994: 841; *AE* 1997: 882).

24 See Pliny, *Ep.* 10.39.3: *huic teatro ex privatorum pollicitationibus multa debenter, ut basilicae circa, ut porticus supra caveam* (referring to the theater at Nicaea). Duncan-Jones (1982: 224, no. 443) records other examples of shared benefactions, one of which was for the bath complex built at Corfinium in Italy through funds by at least three men as well as with public money.

25 "To Lucius Cornelius Marullus, because the ordo Castulonensis due to the generosity of his mother Cornelia Marullina, who had adorned the city of Castulo with silver statues and had given a banquet and circus games, had decreed a statue for herself and her son be erected, Cornelia Marullina, with the honor accepted, ordered this gift to be placed with her own money. Gaius Cornelius Bellicus, her heir, gave and dedicated [it] and gave circus games."

26 Another inscription (*CIL* II, 3265) records that she dedicated an altar to Pietas Augusta in memory of her son.

27 Eumachia might have been attempting the same, as her son was included in the dedication (*CIL* X, 808 + 809) she made of a building in the forum of Pompeii. Gómez Pantoja and Rodríguez Ceballos (2006: 356) suggests that Marullina's son might have already been deceased at the time the statue was dedicated since he does not possess any of the titles a man of his position normally would have acquired.

28 Duncan-Jones reasons that the mention of the ten million sesterces owed by the city might not be an additional expense but, rather, refer to the cost of repaving the road that led to Sisapo through the Castulonensis pass. There is a dearth of evidence in Spain for other private individuals undertaking road-building (1974: 82). This is the type of project that municipalities were generally responsible for. Since the town council erected the statue for Culleo and presumably decided on the language of the text, the inclusion of this act of munificence might signal the immense gratitude the council felt for Culleo and his contribution.

29 See Palmer (1980) for the use of city walls and gates as stations for the collection of customs and taxes on goods.

30 For more on baths in the Roman world, see Fagan (1999) and Yegül (2010).

31 Hoyer (2013) proposes some scenarios in which the local economy of Africa Proconsularis might have developed, especially in relation to benefactions such as banquets. This is one case study that pulls together archaeological and epigraphical evidence to reveal the possible impacts of benefaction on the wider economy. He does not consider non-market channels, such as the goods and services provided from the donors' own estates. The honorary texts themselves, however, are silent on such issues, complicating our own understanding of the nuanced effects of large benefactions of the local economy.

32 In a future publication, I will consider the impact of competition as a motivating force behind benefaction in Hispania.
33 *Digest* 50.10.7. Rescripts from Marcus Aurelius and Commodus in 177 CE put caps on how much could be spent for gladiatorial contests.

Bibliography

Abascal Palazón, Juan Manuel. "La fecha de la promocion colonial de Carthago Nova y sus repercusiones edlicias." *Mastia* 1 (2002): 21–44.

———. "Epigrafía y numismática de Carthago Nova." Pages 117–128 in *Cartagena: Colonia Urbs Julia Nova Carthago*. Edited by E. Conde Guerri, J.M. Abascal Palazón, et al. Roma: L'Erma di Bretschneider, 2017.

Abascal Palazón, Juan Manuel and Ramallo Asensio, Sebastián F. *La ciudad de Carthago Nova: La documentación epigráfica*. Cartagena: Universidad de Murcia, 1997.

Arboledas Martinez, Luis. "Aspectos sociales y fiscales en las minas romans del Alto Guadalquivir." *Pyrenae* 39 (2008): 71–99.

Andreu Pintado, Javier. *Munificencia pública en la Provincia Lusitania. (siglos I–IV d.C.)*. Zarazoga: Institución Fernando el Católico, 2004.

Andreu Pintado, Javier, and Oscar Curulla Ferré. "Un Nuevo documento sobre los Minicii de Tarraco." *Butlleti Arqueològic* 28 (2006): 199–210.

Ceballos Hornero, A. *Los espectáculos en la Hispania Romana: La documentación epigráfica. Cuadernos Emeritenses*. Vol. 26. Mérida: Museo Nacional de Arte Romano, 2004.

Corso Sarmiento, Juan Manuel, Jordi Casals Fernandez, and M. Pilar Garcia-Almirall. "Restitution of Barcelona at the End of the Third Century: Models and Diffusion of the Colonia Iulia Augusta Faventia Paterna Barcino." Pages 1–10 in *World Heritage and Disaster: Knowledge, Culture and Representation; Le Vie dei Mercanti; XV International Forum*. Edited by Ciro Ferrandes. Naples: La scuola di Pitagora, 2017.

Curchin, Leonard A. "Personal Wealth in Roman Spain." *Historia* 32 (1983): 227–44.

Díaz Ariño, B. "Las murallas romanas de Cartagena en la segunda mitad del siglo I a.e." *Zephyrus* 61 (2008): 225–34.

Duncan-Jones, R.P. "Costs, Outlays, and *Summa Honorariae* from Roman Africa." *Papers of the British School at Rome* 30 (1962): 47–115.

———. *The Economy of the Roman Empire*. 2nd ed. Cambridge: Cambridge University Press, 1982.

———. "Human Numbers in Towns and Town-Organizations of the Roman Empire: The Evidence of Gifts." *Historia* 13 (1964): 199–208.

———. "The Procurator as Civic Benefactor." *Journal of Roman Studies* 64 (1974): 79–85.

Eck, W. "There Are No *cursus honorum* Inscriptions: The Function of the *cursus honorum* in Epigraphic Communication." *Scripta Classica Israelica* 28 (2009): 79–92.

Eck, W., and F. Navarro. "Das Ehrenmonument der Colonia Carthago für L. Minicius Natalis Quadronius Verus in seiner Heimatstadt Barcino." *Zeitschrift für Papyrologie und Epigraphik* 123 (1998): 237–48.

Fagan, G.G. *Bathing in Public in the Roman World*. Ann Arbor: University of Michigan Press, 1999.

Gauthier, Ph. *Les cités grecques et leurs bienfaiteurs (IVe-Ier siècle avant J.-C.): contribution à l'histoire des institutions*. Paris: De Boccard, 1985.

Gómez-Pantoja, Joaquin, and Javier Garrido. *Epigrafia anfiteatrale dell'Occidente Romano, VII: Baetica, Tarraconensis, Lusitania*. Roma: Quasar, 2009.

Gómez-Pantoja, Joaquin, and Mariano Rodríguez Ceballos. "¡Fiesta! Una nota sobre los festivales y espectáculos ciudadanos de Hispania." Pages 359–84 in *Poder central y autonomía municipal: La proyección pública de la élites romanas de Occidente.* Edited by J.F. Rodríguez Neila and E. Melchor Gil. Córdoba: Universidad de Córdoba, 2006.

Hemelrijk, Emily. *Hidden Lives, Public Personae: Women and Civic Life in the Roman West.* Oxford: Oxford University Press, 2015.

Hispania Epigraphica Online Database: Roman Inscriptions from the Iberian Peninsula. http://eda-bea.es/.

Hoyer, Daniel. "Public Feasting, Elite Competition, and the Market Economy of Roman North Africa." *Journal of North African Studies* 18 (2013): 574–91.

Liu, Jinyu. *Collegia Centonariorum: The Guilds of Textile Dealers in the Roman West.* Leiden: Brill, 2009.

Mar, Ricardo, Ana Garrido, and José Alejandro Beltrán-Caballero. "Barcino y el urbanismo provincial romano." *Barcelona Quaderns d'Història* 18 (2012): 63–112.

Mariner Bigorra, S. "Basa de una estatua de Antonino Pío, dedicada en Cástulo el 154 d. C." Pages 407–15 in *Cástulo II.* Edited by J.M. Blázquez. Madrid: Ministerio de Educación y Cultura, 1979.

Melchor Gil, Enrique. *El patronato cívico en la Hispania Romana.* Sevilla: Universidad de Sevilla, 2018.

———. "Consideraciones acerca del origen, motivación, y evolución de las conductas evergéticas en Hispania Romana." *Studia Historica: Historia Antigua* 12 (1994): 61–81.

———. "Construcciones civicas y evergetismo en Hispania romana." *Espacio, Tiempo y Forma, Serie II, Historia Antigua* 6 (1993): 443–66.

———. "Las élites municipals de Hispania en el alto imperio: un intent de aproximación a sus fuentes de riqueza." *Florentia Iliberritana* 4–5 (1993–1994): 335–48.

———. "*Summae Honorariae* y donaciones *ob honorem* en la Hispania Romana." *Habis* 25 (1994): 193–212.

Ng, Diana. "Commemoration and Élite Benefaction of Buildings and Spectacles in the Roman World." *Journal of Roman Studies* 105 (2015): 1–23.

Orejas, Almudena, and F. Javier Sánchez-Palencia. "Mines, Territorial Organization, and Social Structure in Roman Iberia: Carthago Noua and the Peninsular Northwest." *American Journal of Archaeology* 106 (2002): 581–99.

Palmer, R.E.A. "Customs on Market Goods Imported into the City of Rome." *Memoirs of the American Academy in Rome* 36 (1980): 217–33.

Pavía Page, Marta. "Termas Públicas del Conventus Carthaginensis: Primera Aproximación a su catalogació y studio." *Cuadernos de Arquelogiá* 24 (2016): 81–101.

Puig i Verdaguer, F., and I. Rodà de Llanza. "Las murallas de Barcino: Nuevas aportaciones al conocimiento de la evolución de sus sistemas de fortificación." Pages 597–632 in *Murallas de ciudades romanas en el occidente del imperio: Lucus Augusti como paradigma; Actas del Congreso Internacional celebrado en Lugo (26–29, XI, 2005).* Edited by A. Rodríguez Colmenero and I. Rodà de Llanza. Lugo: Publicaciones de la Diputación Provincial de Lugo, 2007.

Quass, F. *Die Honoratiorenschicht in den Städten des griechischen Ostens: Untersuchungen zur politischen und sozialen Entwicklung in hellenistischer und römischer Zeit.* Stuttgart: Steiner, 1993.

Ramallo Asensio, S. *La Ciudad Romana de Carthago Nova: La documentación arqueológica.* Cartagena: Universidad de Murcia, 1989.

Ravotto, A. "La simbiosi entre muralla i ciutat de Bàrcino." *Auriga: Revista de divulgació i debat del món clàssic* 87 (2017): 10–15.

Rodà de Llanza, I. "Consideraciones sobre el sevirate en Hispania. Las dedicaciones 'ob honorem seviratus' en el 'conventus Tarraconensis'." Pages 399–404 in *Religio deorum:*

actas del coloquio internacional de epigrafía; Culto y Sociedad en Occidente. Edited by M. Mayer and J. Gómez Pallarés. Sabadell: AUSA, 1994.

———. "Le iscrizioni in onore di Lucius Minicius Natalis Quadronius Verus." *Dacia* 12 (1978): 219–23.

Rogers, G.M. "Demosthenes of Oenoanda and Models of Euergetism." *Journal of Roman Studies* 81 (1991): 91–100.

Ruiz Valderas, E., and M. Martínez Andreu. "Topografia y evolución urbana." Pages 25–38 in *Cartagena: Colonia Urbs Julia Nova Carthago.* Edited by E. Conde Guerri, J.M. Abascal Palazón, et al. Roma: L'Erma di Bretschneider, 2017.

Sánchez, Manuel Amante, Miguel Martín Camino, Maria Ángeles Pérez Bonet, Rafael González Fernández, and Maria Ángeles Martínez Villa. "El *Sacellum* dedicado a Iuppiter Stator en Cartagena." *Lengua e historia* 12 (1995): 533–62.

Sánchez López, Elena. "Nuevo fragment perteneciente a la inscripción *CIL* II, 3269." *Sylloge Epigraphica Barcinonensis* 13 (2015): 45–54.

Valone, Carolyn. "Matrons and Motives: Why Women Built in Early Modern Rome." Pages 317–30 in *Beyond Isabella: Secular Women Patrons of Art in Renaissance Italy.* Edited by Sheryl E. Reiss and David G. Wilkings. Kirksville, MO: Truman State University Press, 2001.

van Bremen, Riet. *The Limits of Participation: Women and Civic Life in the Greek East in the Hellenistic and Roman Periods.* (Dutch Monographs on Ancient History and Archaeology.) Amsterdam: J.C. Gieven, 1996.

Veyne, Paul. *Le pain et le cirque. Sociologie historique d'un pluralisme politique.* Paris: Le Seuil, 1976.

Woolf, G. "Monumental Writing and the Expansion of Roman Society." *Journal of Roman Studies* 86 (1996): 22–39.

Yegül, F. *Bathing in the Roman World.* Cambridge: Cambridge University Press, 2010.

6 New Institutional Economics, euergetism, and associations

John S. Kloppenborg

Introduction

Until quite recently, the prevailing orthodoxy regarding the function of the *collegia, thiasoi, koina, synodoi,* and other private associations that dotted the landscape of the Mediterranean is that they fulfilled mainly social and cultic roles; their raison d'être was not economic. In his classic work on professional associations, Jean-Pierre Waltzing, reasoning from his observations of workers' clubs in Belgium, concluded that the principal function of associations was social: "After a day devoted to work, a week spent in hard labour, workers came together in their clubhouse to relax and to meet with friends."[1] Three quarters of a century on, Sir Moses Finley spelled out the negative inference of Waltzing's view:

> Not only were there no Guildhalls in antiquity, there were no guilds, no matter how often the Roman *collegia* and their differently named Greek and Hellenistic counterparts are thus mistranslated. The *collegia* played an important part in the social and religious life of the lower classes, both free and slaves; they sometimes performed benevolent functions, as in financing burials; they never became regulatory or protective agencies in their respective trades, and that, of course, was the *raison d'être* of the genuine guilds, medieval and modern.[2]

Finley was not alone. Ramsay MacMullen, for example, had argued that although the swath of papyri from Egypt that record the tax payments and contracts of associations might lead to the conclusion that associations had a mainly economic function, that impression was misleading:

> The associative principle looks like an economic one simply because a barely literate society naturally put on paper only things like contracts and receipts. Exact obligations had to be set down in writing. But the dominance of business matters among papyri distorts the total record. Actually, unions were not formed for an economic end, they were merely handy to that purpose once formed. . . . Any analogy with a medieval guild or modern labor union is wholly mistaken.

> (MacMullen, 1974: 18–19)

Hence, for MacMullen and others, associations provided benefits to their members unrelated to their particular crafts (1974: 75). This "standard model" has been echoed by many: "They were not guilds or embryonic trade unions. Their purpose was social, recreational, and religious."[3] I adopted the same view in 1996 as did others both before and since.[4]

As will become clear ahead, this understanding now seems too simplistic. Nevertheless, I think it important to take note of the context in which the "standard model" developed: on the one hand, it was proffered to distinguish Greek, Greco-Egyptian, and Roman associations from modern labor unions, which in the context of contemporary industrial societies function in structural relationships with the means of industrial production and with governmental agencies – functions that they could not have had in antiquity, given its economic structures. And on the other, there was an effort to distinguish ancient collegia from medieval merchant guilds, which monopolized the long-distance trade in staples and medieval craft guilds, which tried to control the crafts, and are sometimes thought to have suppressed the number of laborers through the practice of apprenticeships.[5]

In order to distance ancient associations both from modern unions and from medieval guilds, it was routinely observed that there was little evidence of labor actions (strikes) or other occasions in which associations were responsible for disruptions in pursuit of some goal.[6] It was possible, of course, to cite a handful of examples of what might be instances of labor actions (IEph 215)[7] and what appears to be the monopolization of a commercial sector by a guild (P.Mich. V 245),[8] but these were treated as more exceptions than the rule. Moreover, if one were to adopt a Weberian view of the economy, actions of this order ought not be called "strikes" at all, since the goal of such disruptions did not occur within a framework defined by the pursuit of profit and economic growth, but instead in the context of the pursuit of honor, social advantage, or some other noneconomic end.

A second factor in the articulation of the "standard model" is that it relied heavily on a very small number of the documents, typically the well-known bylaws of the Collegium of Diana and Antinoüs from Lanuvium (*CIL* 14.2112; 136 CE) and the charter of the Iobakchoi (*IG* II² 1368; 164/165 CE). Neither of these suggests that the association *qua* association was engaged in any economic pursuit. Indeed, as Jonathan Perry notes, it is striking just how little the extant *nomoi* and *leges collegiorum* deal with matters pertaining to a craft. These charters are mainly interested in the collection of dues, the conduct of, and etiquette at, communal dinners, the honoring of patrons, and the provision of funerals for members.[9]

An examination of the thirty-eight inscriptions and papyri that record bylaws of associations, some complete and others quite fragmentary,[10] does not change this picture very much. Of these thirty-eight, only P.Mich. V 245 (Tebtynis, 47 CE) includes provisions that relate specifically to the regulation of the trade of the members (all salt merchants).

The relative silence of association charters should perhaps be put into perspective. While only one of the thirty-eight extant charters deals with matters pertaining to the trade, the majority of the extant bylaws come not from occupational guilds (as I will call them) but from cultic associations. Aside from P.Mich. V 245, the only other charters from occupational guilds are P.Mich. 243 (Tebtynis, time of Tiberius), a guild of Sheep and Cattle Owners, and P.Berl.Spieg. 3115 (Memnoneia, 109–108 BCE),[11] a guild of funerary workers (χοαχύται). And these two charters, rather than dealing with matters of commerce, prescribe schedules of banquets and elaborate etiquette at those banquets. That is, our dossier of association charters is badly skewed toward cultic associations. Although we know of hundreds of occupational guilds in Asia Minor,[12] not a single set of bylaws appears in the epigraphical record. Perhaps even more striking is the epigraphical profile of the guild of textile workers *(collegium centonariorum)*, attested throughout Italy and the Western Provinces. Jinyu Liu collected 234 Latin inscriptions from local clubs of *centonarii*; yet not one of them includes the bylaws of any of these associations.[13] This cannot be because the *centonarii* lacked bylaws: their clubs were large and relatively well off, they enjoyed a high profile within the cities in which they were found, and they were exempt from certain taxes. They must have had bylaws governing admission, dues, benefits, meetings, and banquets. Yet none is extant.

The absence of bylaws for the *centonarii* might be attributed to the chance survival of the epigraphic records. Stones bearing inscriptions often degraded owing to exposure to the elements, and they were reused in the construction of buildings and turned around so that the inscribed face is no longer visible. Yet this cannot have been the whole explanation, since it is not only the *centonarii* for whom we lack bylaws but also several other extremely well-attested Roman occupational guilds: the *fabri tignuarii* (builders and carpenters), *dendrophori* (tree-bearers), *fullones* (fullers), *pistores* (bakers), *navicularii* (sailors), *lenuncularii tabularii* (boatmen and registrars), *fabri navales* (ship builders), and *mensores frumentarii* (grain measurers). It would be incredible if none of these associations had bylaws, and equally incredible that *all* of the inscribed bylaws of these groups have been accidentally lost. It seems much more likely that their bylaws were kept on such perishable materials as wooden tablets or parchment that do not survive in most of the climates of Europe. In fact, the bylaws from the Latin West that *have* survived seem to have done so because they were parts of *other* epigraphic genres, appended for example to acknowledgements of the gifts and donations of influential persons. This is the case with the bylaws of the collegium of Aesculapius and Hygia *(CIL* 6.10234), the bylaws of the collegium of Diana and Antinoüs *(CIL* 14.2112), and the bylaws of the Familia Silvani *(AE* 1929, 161, Trebula Mutuesca, 60 CE). That is, in at least some instances where we have bylaws, the reason they were inscribed has less to do with the need to inscribe bylaws on stone and more to do with a need to acknowledge a donor's generosity in a durable manner and to indicate how the donor's funds will be allocated. Bylaws travel on the coattails of other epigraphical genres. Most of the Greek bylaws on papyrus that we have from Egypt come either from a single administrative archive, that of Kronion the κωμογραμματεύς of the village of Tebtynis at the time of Tiberius or, in the case of most of the Demotic bylaws, from the same village in the second century BCE, likely all from the same archive. Hence, our epigraphical data concerning association charters are weighted in favor of cultic associations, not occupational guilds, and the papyri containing association charters, meager as it is, comes from only a small number of administrative archives.

The "standard model" began to be problematized in the late 1990s by Onno van Nijf, not by focusing on association charters – although he did discuss P.Mich. V 245 – but by pointing to other documents, such as proconsular decrees and records of complaints about associations' attempt to monopolize certain markets.[14] For example, ISmyrna 712 (Smyrna, I/II CE) reflects a dispute apparently about the monopolization of ferry services; *IGRR* IV 352 (Pergamon) complains about the imposition of a surcharge by (a guild of) money changers; IEph 215 records disturbances in Ephesus provoked by bakers by apparently staging a strike; and Acts 19:23–28, probably written in the second century, tells a tale of a riot of the silversmiths allegedly occasioned by Paul's activities there.[15] On the other hand, he elided some of the differences between ancient occupational associations and medieval guilds, noting that medieval guilds were very interested in "piety, conviviality, charity, and sociality" no less that ancient associations.[16] And the degree to which medieval guilds were successful in forming cartels and controlling prices has been greatly exaggerated. Sylvie Thrupp's conclusion is that although medieval goldsmiths, butchers, and leather guilds had the reputation of forming cartels, as a generalization,

> in any medieval town, at any given time, the various gilds would have been strung out along the scale of economic power, with most of them bunched in positions in which they could have exercised little or no influence on selling-prices in local trade.[17]

Moreover, apprenticeship in medieval guilds was more a mechanism for securing cheap labor than it was an effort to control the labor supply.[18] This being the case, the distance between medieval guilds and ancient associations is somewhat reduced.[19]

Van Nijf's final point confronts the common assumption that occupational associations were marginal – socially, politically, and economically.[20] Perhaps this view is the residue of the jurists' invention of the category of *collegia tenuiorum*, a convenient legal term, but one that hardly corresponds to the complex array of occupational or cultic associations.[21] Van Nijf shows that there is good reason to suppose that many guilds of craftsmen were relatively well off. Cicero's complaint in *Pro Flacco* (17–19) to the effect that various craftsmen (cobblers, belt-makers, artisans, and shopkeepers) in Pergamon caused disturbances in the civic assembly – one could add Xenophon's lament that fullers, cobblers, builders, bronze smiths, farmers, and merchants made up the ἐκκλησία (*Mem.* 3.7.1–6) – suggests that artisans were not only members of the civic assembly in many Greek cities, but also may sometimes even have been in the majority.[22] A particularly striking example of a well-appointed craft guild is the linen workers of Saittai, who were assigned seats in the theater.[23] The morphology of the seat inscriptions is consistent in taking the form φυλῆς Ἀπολλωνιάδος, "(seat) of the tribe of Apollonias." Rows 36–41 are assigned to various subdivisions of the φυλ(ῆς) β' [λ]ινου[ργῶν(?)], "(seats) of the second tribe of linen workers."[24] Dittmann-Schöne concludes:

> Obviously one or two tribes of the city were named after crafts groups of linen workers. . . . The existence of such occupational groups indicates the social and economic standing of those handworkers in Lydian cities; at least in Sattai the prominent standing of linen production is well attested epigraphically.[25]

The same term, φυλή, to describe an occupational guild is found in two other Lydian inscriptions,[26] again striking because "tribe" (φυλή) was a term typically reserved for the groups composing the citizen body and hence, the civic assembly. This suggests that at least in Lydia, some of the craft guilds enjoyed "some formal political status."[27] Of course, this status of the Lydian linen workers cannot be generalized, as Pleket observes:

> The picture for Asia Minor is not unitary. There does not seem to have existed a bourgeoisie dominated by the manufacturers and merchants of luxury textiles. A few representatives of these occupational groups may have belonged to the civic elites; others – the majority – were under some conditions sufficiently wealthy to be able to be candidates for offices and civic councils, but they did not ultimately attain this goal. They operated in the "grey zone" between the elite and the higher strata of the people.[28]

Closer scrutiny of associative practices indicates indeed that the relationship of occupational guilds to civic and provincial administration was not casual or incidental, but routinized for purposes of taxation. Roger Bagnall, in fact, argued that occupational guilds in Egypt, at least, were "fiscal rather than social in character."[29] Whether Bagnall is right to juxtapose "fiscal" with "social" as he does remains to be seen, but we can no longer overlook the genuine economic roles of associations, at least occupational guilds. They engaged with the nome or provincial administration in at least three ways, each of which had to do with financial matters.

First, the imperial administration employed occupational guilds as the key link between the fiscus and individual craftsmen, and this meant that there was likely a strong incentive for individual craftsmen to join occupational guilds, since that was a key node for tax extraction. Guilds seem to have been required to provide official declarations of the names of their members for purposes of the imposition and payment of the χειρωνάξιον (tax on crafts and trades).[30] The material in *Stud. Pal.* IV: 58–83, lines 378–431, is a register of the craft taxes collected from two guilds, a guild of five rugbeaters and a guild of five potters. The rugbeaters paid sixty drachmas, that is, twelve drachmas per member, but the full tax for a potter was seventeen drachmas one-half obol, two chalkoi. One of the five had died in the course of year 4, and hence a portion of the craft tax was collected, but for year 5, the full amount of seventeen drachmas one-half obol, two chalkoi was deducted from the expected tax. The full tax was due, however, for one of the potters who had decamped during the previous year (year 3), and it was still expected to be paid for year 5. The liability of guilds collectively to pay craft taxes on behalf of their members helps to explain provisions such as that encountered in P.Mich. V 244.10–12 (Tebtynis, 43 CE):

10 τὸν δὲ ἀδωσιδικοῦντα καὶ μὴ

πληροῦντά τι τῶν δημοσίων λαογραφίας ἢ καὶ δαπανῶν ἐξεῖναι τῷ Κρονίωνι
ἐνεχυράζειν αὐτοὺς ἔν τε τῆι
πλατείᾳ καὶ ἐν ταῖς οἰκίαις καὶ παραδιδόναι αὐτοὺς ἢ σώματα αὐτῶν·

But if someone fails to pay his dues and does not pay some of the poll tax *[laographia]* or some of the expenses, Kronion shall have authority to exact a pledge from him, whether in the town square or in his house, and hand over either him or his slaves.[31]

Of course, this provision was effective only if the defaulter was still in the village.

While it is clear that the provincial administrations used guilds for the purpose of tax collection, and that Rome relied on various Ostian guilds to manage the supply of grain and other commodities,[32] it is hardly the case that the Roman administration set up these guilds or wanted to manage them directly.[33] That is, the raison d'être of occupational guilds, as Gibbs has recognized,[34] is not solely (or even principally) fiscal, even though provincial administrations recognized the utility of guilds both for fiscal purposes and for the supply of essential commodities.[35] Cracco Ruggini has suggested that the first-century guilds from Tebtynis, in fact, initiated this practice of their own accord, and not at the instigation of the provincial or nome administration.[36]

Second, the guild mediated the relationship between individual craftsmen and the marketplace, as is illustrated by *SB* 16.12695 (Oxyrhynchus, 143 CE), a report of the taxes collected from at least fifteen guilds for access to the market of the Sarapeion in Oxyrhynchus.[37] It is not that one did not necessarily have access to the marketplace without guild membership,[38] but guild membership likely facilitated the payment and recording of the market tax.

Third, the guild could (and did) act to protect the interests of its members, either against the actions of other guilds, or against what they regarded as unfair exactions of tax collectors, or other depredations. The text in P.Rain.Cent. 51 (Sestis, 99–50 BCE) records the complaint of the linen cleaners of a village in the Delta, who were upset that cleaners from a neighboring village had begun to do work in their area and so petition the *stratēgos* to summon the interlopers to judgment. A guild of fullers and dyers in the mid-second century protested to the procurator the new imposition of higher craft taxes on them.[39] And a guild of weavers complained to the *stratēgos* that four of its twelve members had been required to serve liturgies (guarding the grain boats), which, they alleged, severely affected their ability to complete an order of cloaks for the army.[40]

These and many other papyri that could be cited show that occupational guilds were centrally involved in the defense (if not promotion) of their craft and its members. Yet Bagnall's binary formulation, "fiscal rather than social" is too sharp. It is here that Andrew Monson's acute observations on the Ptolemaic religious associations become important theoretically, even though, as the title of his article indicates, his focus is on cultic associations rather than occupational guilds.[41] Monson notes that the fines levied by Demotic cultic associations – and one could argue the same of the many Greek and Roman associations that are extant – might be thought to serve as an economic incentive to fair-dealing with fellow association members, especially because, measured in relation to the cost of wheat, the fines are usually quite substantial. But for Monson fines are only a symptom of something more general. Drawing on the work of Charles Tilly, he argues that associations are "trust networks," which, in Tilly's words,

> stand out from other sorts of social relations precisely because they build controls over malfeasance and safeguards against consequences of mistakes and failures into their routine operation. For members of trade diasporas, well-knit lineages, and clandestine religious sects, the threats of shunning, shaming, and denial of reciprocity loom much larger than in everyday social networks.[42]

Tilly comes close to a key feature of New Institutional Economics when, citing work on Chinese trading networks, he argues that

> networks activate invisible ethical codes in a "low cost clublike institutional arrangement," which economize[s] on contract enforcement and information costs. . . . Social arrangements . . . reinforce or substitute for firms and markets by reducing transaction costs and stabilizing economic outcomes.[43]

Monson has indeed made a strong case that religious associations created trust networks with a combination of the constraints that they placed on misbehavior (the imposition of fines), the demand for the contribution of dues, which served as tangible indications of commitment, and undertakings to assist fellow members in times of distress. One could add communal dining and drinking, and the nearly ubiquitous requirement to participate in the funerals of members. The inscribing of bylaws had the effect of institutionalizing the boundary between the association and other groups, and lowered "the costs of cooperation because other members can be trusted."[44]

We might well ask what such "costs of cooperation" or "lower transaction costs" might look like in the context of a cultic association. Cultic associations collected dues, sometimes disbursed funds to members who had fallen on hard times, made loans, provided for funerals and, of course, had banquets. But since these activities are precisely the features that create a trust network, it is essentially tautologous to point out that the transaction costs involved in these activities are be reduced. One could suppose that membership in a cultic group could reduce transaction costs for transactions that lay *outside* the ostensible activities of the cultic association: for example, a member of a Sobek association who is a weaver dealing with a fellow member in relation to the purchase of oil or wine might achieve a benefit in lower transaction costs. But because these costs have nothing to do with the internal transactions of the cultic association, the model of New Institutional Economics is irrelevant here.

It seems reasonable to suppose that notwithstanding the general lack of association charters for occupational guilds, occupational guilds enumerated analogous sets of prescribed (and proscribed) behaviors for their members and that, accordingly, ancient occupational guilds could also be treated as trust networks. As such, and in accordance with NIE models, members would have benefited from lower transaction costs. This is what has been argued most recently by Cameron Hawkins and Philip Venticinque. Hawkins argues as follows:

> For artisans who joined such collegia [he is speaking of the *centonarii*], the chief benefit of the arrangement was greater opportunity to compete for a share of state contracts by subcontracting work from the association itself.[45]

Venticinque adduces a more complex set of theoretical considerations, including Brennan and Pettit's notions of esteem and reputational pooling as untradeable commodities that serve to generate social capital in "voluntary associations," to enhance collectively the reputation of all members, and to discourage free riding.[46] To this, he adds Robert Putnam's influential treatment of how networks "lubricate social life" and generate social capital for members of those networks, though not necessarily for others.[47] Then, adducing Tilly's model of trust networks, Venticinque tessalates this into an NIE approach to ancient associations:

> Operating within an association's institutional framework – indicated by charters and other documents related to group activities – enabled members to amass social capital by establishing interpersonal trust and developing a trustworthy reputation through repeated interaction, whether via feasts, funerals, meetings, loans or other transactions. Abiding by norms spelled out in charters also likely helped members secure credit and financial assistance and acquire and disseminate information about goods, services, prices, and potential partners. Ultimately, relying on trust, reputation, and social capital allowed members to further individual and group goals; to manage risk and uncertainty in economic, political, social and legal contexts; and in short, to reduce transaction costs.[48]

Very similar conceptualizations of the role of occupational guilds in reducing transaction costs have been mooted by Broekaert[49] and Hawkins.[50] As practices that cultivate trust, Broekaert, for example, points to the vetting or screening of members (to guarantee the trustworthiness of members), the likelihood of information exchange within the occupational guild network, disciplinary practices designed to ensure trustworthiness (and to eliminate free riders), the recruiting of patrons, and the use of fictive family language.[51]

Unfortunately, a good deal of this description is rather thinly attested among occupational guilds. First, vetting or, to be more precise, a *dokimasia*, is well attested among cultic associations;[52] it *may* have been used in occupational guilds, but the case is mainly circumstantial. Since P.Mich. V 245 says nothing of a process for the induction of new members, *a fortiori* there is no indication of whether there was a *dokimasia* or not. Second, while we might assume that a good deal of information was exchanged within occupational guilds concerning prices and costs, the best and almost the only instance is P.Mich. V 245, which is a rather singular case of a guild establishing minimum prices for members. It is routinely cited as a showcase example of an occupational guild attempting to control a market and thereby, presumably, to achieve some competitive advantage, but it is virtually the one bit of evidence to this effect.[53] Third, disciplinary practices are for the most part not oriented toward commercial matters except perhaps in three cases: P.Mich. V 245 establishes a minimum price for salt and requires that if a member wants to buy additional measures of salt, the others must sell to him jointly. *CIL* 6.33885 (Rome, period of Hadrian) required the expulsion of any *curator* responsible for the fraudulent induction of someone who was not a citrus wood or ivory dealer into the guild, one of the very few guilds that expressly restricted membership to the craftsmen or merchants of a single profession. And a sixth-century *lex* from a guild of fishermen (*SB* 3:6704) prohibits a member from interfering in another member's sale of a boat. And, finally, it is difficult to judge whether the use of fictive family language – Broekaert's example is *CIL* 13.8354, a guild member buried by his *fratres*[54] – is much more than a stereotypical way to refer to a fellow guild member, especially because the epithet is so widely attested in Latin guilds.[55]

Broekaert nevertheless assembles these practices into a general picture of the way in which the trust generated by associative practices might have redounded to the financial advantage of guild members:

> First, the association as a whole may provide some services to ease the individual member's business. For instance, in Rome, a collegium of *negotiantes* dedicated an inscription to the genius of the *horrea Agrippiana* (*AE* 1915, 97). It seems feasible that the association was using the common chest to hire storage space in the warehouse, which may have been put at the disposal of the *collegiati*. This way, the merchants did not have to search for a depot separately, but were better protected by the association against market fluctuations: in case the demand for certain products was temporarily satiated, the common store room could be used till sales would be profitable again. We have also an indication that a sixth-century Egyptian association of linen-weavers possessed private workshops, which were leased to the *collegiati* (*SB* XIV 12282).
>
> Secondly, *collegiati* may informally help each other in trying to reduce trading costs. The idea of informal mutual support may sound trivial, given the association's role in constructing sociability and promoting friendship.

No doubt, in the same way as with agency, membership and *amicitia* encouraged *collegiati* to advance money, grant low-interest or free loans, lend infrastructure, provide storage space, etc.[56]

It might be noted how many hypotheticals there are in this formulation – the auxiliary verb "may," and the phrase "it seems feasible," and how little one can appeal to evidence that transaction costs were, in fact, reduced to the competitive advantage of guild members.

Does the conceptual model of New Institutional Economics assist in thinking about ancient occupational guilds? The innovation of NIE is not that medieval guilds (or presumably ancient occupational associations) had some economic functions. That can be seen on other grounds. The specific goal of NIE, according to North and Thomas, is to account for the "causes of economic growth, defined as a *per capita* long-run rise in income," where the growth of the total wealth of a society exceeds the growth of its population.[57] Unlike classical and neoclassical economic theories, which focused on the relationship between production and consumption and imagine the economic actor as a *homo economicus* acting with rational self-interest, NIE pays attention to "institutions" – that is, sets of rules, formal and informal, which constrain behavior and regulate economic relationships.[58] For North, the specific foci of interest are "transaction costs," which represent a major challenge to growth. Transaction costs arise from the lack of knowledge, for example, of the reliability of those with whom they transact business;[59] free riders who cannot be compelled to share in transaction costs represent additional costs, and similarly, the lack of institutions that can guarantee and enforce property rights inhibit the smooth conduct of transactions.[60]

Accordingly, NIE proposes that the costs of transactions can be lowered by "institutions" that constrain behavior such as formal rules (laws) and informal codes (codes of conduct) that are institutionalized in organizations such as courts, schools, firms, unions, markets, clubs, and so on. Moreover, for NIE, it is not simply that institutions and the organizations that embody those institutions lower transaction costs, but that there is a *causal relationship* between the need to reduce uncertainty and hence, transaction costs, and the *generation* of the kinds of social arrangements and institutions that reduce those costs, "ranging from firms, markets, and property rights, to clubs, families, and associations."[61]

The mention of clubs and associations as organizations that potentially reduce transaction costs is significant here, since their mention appears to be the "hook" that potentially connects the study of ancient associations, both occupational guilds and cultic associations, with NIE. Ironically, perhaps, North and Thomas noted ambivalence in the functioning of medieval guilds in relation to the economy as a whole: in the thirteenth century, they made for an efficient division of labor in the textile industry that allowed Flemish textile manufacturing to undercut the price of textiles in England.[62] However, the monopolization of productive sectors in towns by medieval guilds also had the effect of driving some manufacturing into the countryside, precisely in order to circumvent the restrictive nature of guild-based economies. They point out, further, that guild control had the overall effect of stifling economic growth, although guilds undoubtedly were a boon to guild members and allowed them to profit and to rise in social standing.[63]

Observations of this nature coincide with those of Sheleigh Ogilvie, who noted that two perspectives on guilds are seldom brought into dialogue. On the one hand, economic historians often held that guilds, owing to their cartel-like functions, were a drag on the economy; and on the other, some political scientists and social historians argued that the effect of guilds was, as a whole, positive since they generated social capital that benefited the economy. Focusing attention on the region of Württemberg between the late sixteenth century and the early nineteenth, where there is a robust set of regulatory and economic data, Ogilvie made a strong case that early modern guilds were neither institutions that guaranteed high quality or even a basic quality, nor were they effective in controlling labor markets, nor did they uniformly encourage technological innovations, especially those technologies that were not labor intensive. The monopolistic practices of guilds might have encouraged innovation, but the closed membership policies of most guilds worked against this; the practices of "tramping" (journeymen) and apprenticeship might theoretically have been responsible for the geographical and intergenerational diffusion of skills, but regulations on apprenticeship and journeymen were not enforced, and while the spatial clustering of guilds might have insured the horizontal dissemination of skills, guilds were "neither necessary nor sufficient for spatial clustering which might have favoured technology transmission."[64]

While the notion that guilds, at least medieval guilds, were responsible in some way for economic growth remains uncertain, it does seem clear that guilds and similar organizations were effective in generating social capital for their members:

> Social networks generating a social capital of shared norms, common information, mutual sanctions, and collective political action may – in some forms – overcome problems posed by lack of trust, reputation, monitoring, and cooperation in developing economies. But the evidence presented in this article provides greater support for the possibility already acknowledged by Coleman – that social capital might reduce innovativeness and economic well-being by penalizing "deviant" actions that could have benefited the economy at large.[65]

Hence, as to the economic function of guilds, Oglivie cautions:

> The evidence presented here suggests grounds for skepticism about hypotheses that guilds arose and survived because they corrected market imperfections. Information asymmetries between producers and purchasers certainly existed, but many important and long-lived guilds – such as those in the Württemberg worsted industry – did not make any contribution to solving them. Imperfections in training markets may also have existed in pre-industrial economies, but the empirical evidence examined in this article provides reasons for doubting that guilds were an efficient institution for correcting them.

Imperfections in markets for innovative techniques exist in all economies, and no perfect institution for addressing them has yet been devised. But sober empirical investigation suggests little reason to believe that guilds were this institution.[66]

Returning to occupational guilds in antiquity, we might raise several questions in relation to the heuristic value of NIE. First, was the motor for the origin and/ or proliferation of guilds the perception that associative behavior could reduce transaction costs, as NIE suggests? Any answer to this question is, of course, hampered by the lacunary nature of our data and the very uneven distribution of occupational guilds in the Mediterranean.

In the first place, occupational guilds appear in the epigraphical record differently, and in most cases later, than do cultic associations. In Athens, cultic groups vastly outnumber occupational guilds prior to the Imperial period.[67] This striking disproportion might indicate that labor in Hellenistic Athens was not organized in such a way as to promote the formation of occupational guilds, or that for some reason the guilds that existed had not adopted an epigraphical habit. Or again, it might be that craftsmen were incorporated into cultic associations instead of associations organized along occupational lines, as is sometimes instanced in a few associations from Macedonia and Thrace in the Imperial period.[68] Arnaoutoglou points out further that on Rhodes, cultic associations are attested, but there are no craft guilds or professional associations at all.[69]

Professional associations involved in shipping are, of course, attested on Delos from the second century BCE alongside earlier cultic associations, and in Egypt groups (or guilds) of craftsmen are known from the third century BCE but, again, alongside earlier cultic associations.[70] On Delos, there are a few associations of merchant-shippers that were also cultic associations devoted to Poseidon or Herakles.[71]

Owing to the complexities of the epigraphic (and papyrological) record concerning the appearance of occupational guilds, it seems impossible to untangle whether they arose as part of cultic associations, or in imitation of cultic associations, or whether they developed quite independently. It is, at the very least, very difficult to make out a clear case that occupational guilds arose *in order* to lower transaction costs, as NIE claims.[72]

A second question then arises: irrespective of the raison d'être of occupational guilds, was the *result* of guild formation the reduction of transaction costs? And was such a reduction, if it occurred, generally beneficial to the economy as a whole? The answer is again hampered by an almost complete lack of financial data from which to draw any conclusion. Quite independently of the debate about NIE, Peter van Minnen in 1987 observed that despite their organization as collectives, there is almost no evidence of collective action:

> I have not been able to find joint measures concerning the care and exploitation of workshops, or collective hiring of wage-labourers in the papyri. Probably this is to be explained by the fact that there was no real competition (e.g.,

from villagers) or just to the simple fact that most craftsmen operated on an individual basis in their own workshop. I have not been able to find any trace of guild action in regard to quality. . . . Nor is there any trace of collective acquisition of raw materials, except in the case of government requisitions of course.[73]

In spite of new publications, the situation has not changed since van Minnen's comments: there is very little reason to suppose that occupational guilds were much concerned with supervising quality, as medieval guilds at least claimed to be, and there is little evidence of collective action. The very few instances of efforts at price control (or at least setting minimum prices) and efforts to lubricate commercial transactions – the regulations of the sixth-century guild of fishermen mentioned earlier[74] – are as rare as they are late.

Van Minnen also noted that while associations held funds collectively, these funds were used for a combination of underwriting the costs of banquets and drinking parties, providing funerals for members, and for giving loans to members, but there is no evidence of the use of collective funds for commercial purposes; that is, investment. They were "more of a social convenience for members in need."[75]

The rather pessimistic view of medieval craft guilds by Robert Lopez might apply equally to Greek and Roman associations, as he thinks it does:

> As a matter of fact, craft guilds reflected the modest possibilities of feebly capitalized and mechanized workshops, whose owners could hardly reach for unlimited gain without overworking their dependents or crowding out their colleagues. They functioned at their best in small towns, where security was more desirable than opportunity, or in those larger cities that were consumption centers rather than production hubs. . . . Insofar as they succeeded in regulating growth without stopping it, they spared their humbler members the extreme sufferings that were inflicted on the slave gangs of antiquity and the factory hands of the early Industrial Revolution. Their braking action, however, tended to maintain the entire craft at an economic level closer to Greco-Roman "golden mediocrity" than to the moving escalators of modern industrial capitalism.[76]

It is, of course, true that during the Imperial period, Roman administrators used guilds as the extraction point for taxation, and employed guilds to manage the shipping of grain, oil, and wine from Egypt, the Rhône Valley, and Spain. Yet this does not necessarily mean that they did so because this lowered administrative costs or that they understood that transaction costs within the guild were lower. There may have been a marginal benefit to individual guild members to have the guild president or treasurer funnel the craft tax to tax collectors but this system also cost the guild, since data show that the guild was even responsible for the craftsman tax of members who had decamped or were deceased, at least until appropriate proofs of the death or the absence of the member could be supplied and accepted.

Some occupational guilds indeed have impressive longevity, which likely means that they had developed efficient ways of collecting dues, replacing members who had died, and creating a stable network of trust. Jinyu Liu draws attention to several Italian guilds such as the *collegium fabrum tignuariorum* of Rome, which recorded at least forty-three *lustra* (five-year periods), which implies a life-span of at least 215 years.[77] There are, however, also conspicuous failures: a rather pathetic notice, posted by the *magister* and treasurer of an association devoted to Jupiter Cernenus in Albernus Major (Dacia, 167 CE), reported that of the fifty-four original members, only seventeen remained, and that the collegium had insufficient funds to pay for any more funerals. This implies that the collegium lacked the ability to collect fines or to compel members to contribute – that is, an inability to create social capital.

In sum, it seems to be very likely that occupational guilds, like cultic associations, created social capital through a complex of practices, including communal dining and drinking, contribution of fees, financial and other supports available to members, participation in members' funerals, reputational pooling, and the imposition of disciplinary practices that discouraged free riding and various forms of misconduct. That this array of practices produced a trust network is eminently likely, and participation in such a network was surely one of the attractions of membership. The thesis of NIE, however, is that organizations (guilds, etc.) instrumentalized the social capital (Putnam) and the trust (Tilly) that networks and associative behavior generated, and that they did this *for economic ends*, by reducing transaction costs, generating and exchanging knowledge of essential economic activities, and thus gaining a competitive advantage over those economic actors who could not guard against malfeasance and were unable to secure knowledge reliably about economic activities.

This conclusion is not as secure as the hypothesis concerning social capital. It remains unclear that occupational guilds mobilized the trust networks that they had built for economic ends, either for the economic advancement of the guild, still less for the competitive position of the guild vis-à-vis other economic agents. Occupational guilds, as Paul Erdkamp observes, undoubtedly enabled some agents to profit from relations of trust and reputation, but also likely imposed their interests on less powerful craftworkers.[78] Commenting on Peter Temin's *The Roman Market Economy* (2013), Erdkamp concludes:

> Many people in business undoubtedly profited from their dealings with the annona, but there is precious little evidence in support of their supposed role in reducing transaction costs beyond the provisioning of Rome.[79]

The study of ancient associations, both cultic associations and occupational guilds (as well as neighborhood groups and diasporic clubs) has indeed shifted significantly from the "standard view" that they met principally and essentially for social ends. The theoretical perspectives introduced by Putnam on social capital, Monson on trust networks, and Brennan and Pettit on reputational pooling, have, I think, been successful in making the case that associations generated social capital and esteem for their members and that this served as a key feature in the attraction of membership. And while the economic functions of occupational guilds are now clear, thanks to van Nijf and others, what is not so clear is whether these occupational guilds can be seen as fulfilling the roles that NIE would like to assign to them.

Notes

1 Waltzing (1895–1900: 1:322): "Après une journée consacrée au travail, après une semaine passée dans un dur labeur, les ouvriers se réunissent dans leur maison commune où ils peuvent se délasser et se recontrer avec leurs confrères."
2 Finley (1985: 138). Finley (1965: 37 n. 1) thought that the word "guild" was misapplied to antiquity.
3 Wilken (1984: 34). Similarly Burford (1972), Garnsey and Saller (1987: 156–8), and others.
4 Kloppenborg (1996: 19). Similarly Jones (1974: 44), Ausbüttel (1982: 99), Carroll (2006: 48), and Ausbüttel (1982: 99).
5 See Mickwitz (1968: 166–82).
6 There are, famously, a few disruptions that have been labeled as strikes: Buckler (1923), MacMullen (1962–1963), and Baldwin (1964).
7 On IEph 215 and the "strike" of bakers, see Arnaoutoglou (2002: 27–44, esp. 39–42) and Perry (2015). On P.Bremen 63 and an alleged "strike" of woolworkers in Hermopolis, see Van Minnen (1987: 62), who shows that the reference is not to a strike or "a collective group of textile workers in action, but to a few men employed by Apollonius on his estate."
8 Van Nijf (1997: 13–14). "Unfortunately, we have no good ancient parallels for this text. The price declarations from fourth-century Oxyrhynchus are not strictly comparable with it" (14).
9 Perry (2010: 499–515, here 503).
10 IV BCE: Paris, Bibliothèque Nationale 241 (ed. De Cenival, 1988.) (IV BCE) [TM 46326]; IG II² 1361 = GRA I 4 (Piraeus, 330–324/323 BCE); III BCE: IG II² 1275 = GRA I 8 (Piraeus, 325–275 BCE) (fragmentary); Agora 16.161 = GRA I 14 (Athens, early III BCE); IG II² 1283 = GRA I 23 (Piraeus, 240/239 BCE); IG II² 1328 = GRA I 34 (Piraeus, 183/182, 175/174 BCE); II BCE: five Demotic regulations from the same association of the god Sobek, extending over thirty-three years: P.Mil.Vogl.dem. inv. 77–8 (178 BCE) [TM 47204–47205]; P.Cair. 30606 = P.Assoc. pp. 45–51, 218–19 (Tebtynis, 158/157 BCE) [TM 2775]; P.Hamb., Bibliothek dem. 1 = P.Assoc. pp. 59–61, 219–20 (Tebtynis, 151 BCE) [TM 3057]; P.Cair. 31179 = P.Assoc. pp. 63–8, 221–2 (Tebtynis, 147 BCE) [TM 3025]; P.Cair. 30605 = P.Assoc. pp. 73–8, 222–5 (Tebtynis, 145 BCE) [TM 2774]. Other Demotic associations: P.Bagnall 42 = P.Tebt. Suppl. 1578 (Tebtynis, 250–210 BCE) [TM 175279]; P.Würzb.dem. 10 = Würzburg, Akademie der Wissenschaften (Mainz) dem. 10 (Arsinoites, 245–243 BCE) [TM 133259]; P.LilleDem. 29 = P.Assoc. pp. 3–10 (Pisais [Arsinoites], 223 BCE) [TM 2784]; P.StanGreenDem 21 (Bakchias? 190–170 BCE); P.Cair. 31178 = P.Assoc. pp. 39–40, 215–18 (Tebtynis, 179 BCE) [TM 3055]; P.Cair. 30619 (Tebtynis, 137 BCE) = P.Assoc. pp. 93–7, 227–9 [TM 2776]; P.Prag.Satzung = P.Assoc. pp. 83–91, 225–7 (Tebtynis, 137 BCE) [TM 2928]; P.Berl.Spieg. 3115 = P.Assoc. pp. 103–31 (Memnoneia, Thebes west, 109–108 BCE) [TM 3058]; P.Cair. 30618 A – B (Tebtynis, II BCE) = P.Assoc. pp. 229–36 no. Cairo [TM 43286]; II/I BCE: TAM V 1539 = GRA II 117 (Philadelphia, Lydia, II/I BCE); I BCE: IG II² 1339 = GRA I 46 (Athens, 57/56 BCE); P.Lond. VII 2193 (Philadelphia, Fayûm, 69–58 BCE) [TM 2462]; I CE: LSAM 80 = GRA II 152 (Elaioussa Sebaste, Cilicia, 27 BCE–14 CE); P.Mich. V 243 (Tebtynis, 14–37 CE) [TM 12084]; P.Mich. V 244 (Tebtynis, 43 CE) [TM 12085]; P.Mich.

V 245 (Tebtynis, 47 CE) [TM 12086]; *AE* (1929) 161 (Trebula Mutuesca, 60 CE); BGU XIV 2371 (I CE) [TM 3991]; **II** CE: *IG* II² 1369 = *GRA* I 49 (Liopesi, Attica, II CE); *SEG* 31:122 = *GRA* I 50 (Liopesi, Attica, early II CE); *CIL* 6.33885 (Rome, 117–138 CE); *CIL* 14.2112 (Lanuvium, 136 CE); *AE* 2012, 312 (Ostia, II CE); *CIL* 6.10234 (Rome, 153 CE); *IG* II² 1368 = *GRA* I 51 (Athens, 164/165 CE); *IG* IX/1² 670 = *GRA* I 61 (Physkos, Locris, mid II CE); **II/III** CE: *IG* II² 1365–66 = *GRA* I 53 (Laurion, late II/early III CE). Two charters fall outside our chronological range: A fifth century BCE Demotic charter of a guild of funerary workers (P.Dem.Louvre E 7840 bis = P. LouvreEisenlohr 6 = de Cenival, 1986 [TM 46137]), and a sixth century CE set of bylaws of a guild of hunters (*SB* 3.6704l; Aphrodito, VI CE).

11 = P.Assoc. pp. 103–31 [TM 3058].

12 Dittmann-Schöne (2001), Zimmermann (2002), and Sommer (2006).

13 Liu (2009).

14 Van Nijf (1997: 13–16).

15 It is unlikely that Acts 19:23–28 reflects a historical event in the mid-first century CE. The Christ movement was far too small and insignificant to have any noticeable influence on the economics of the silver trade in Ephesus. It is not even clear that it was large enough to have any such effect in the early second century. But Luke *imagines* a more significant impact here and elsewhere in Acts. Hence, Acts 19 is important not as a historical report, but instead as an example of Luke's ability to imagine the economic impact of the Christ movement on the economy of a town.

16 Van Nijf (1997: 17).

17 Thrupp (1963: 246–65, here 263). See also Hawkins (2016: 72), who rightly observes that similarities with medieval guilds is a matter of degree: "[medieval] guilds generally enjoyed regulatory authority and nominal monopolies over the practice of their trades by virtue of municipal or royal concessions. They exercised this authority (with varying degrees of diligence and success) by promulgating and enforcing corporate statutes that were, in theory, binding not only upon their members but also upon all those who sought to practice trades that impinged on any given guild's privileges. Roman *collegia*, on the other hand, were typically unable to regulate economic life in the same way. Although some individual collegia may have purchased monopoly rights over narrow sectors of the economy in their cities from the civic authorities, such occasions seem to have been the exception rather than the rule."

18 Thrupp (1963: 264): "Medieval artisan apprenticeship was a product, not of gild monopoly, but of the family workshop. It was the simplest means by which small masters could find cheap help to supplement that of the family circle. Yet it had certain inconveniences. Under medieval conditions of life expectancy, the death rate among young apprentices was very high. Scarcity could often have been due to a neighbourhood epidemic."

19 Van Minnen (1987: 65) notes, however, that there is very little evidence that guilds had apprentices (against MacMullen, 1962–1963: 269): apprenticeship contracts are between a father or slave owner and a craftsman, not with a guild, although the reference to κατὰ τὸν νόμον in P.Oslo III 141.10–11 (Karanis, ca. 50 CE) and P.Mich. V 355 (Tebtynis) might suggest that a guild regulated apprenticeship relations.

20 E.g., Finley (1985: 136–8), referring to Dio's statement that the linen workers in Tarsos were so poor that they could not afford the five hundred drachmae cost to acquire local citizenship (34.21–23), and contrasting them with the wealthy textile guilds of Flanders (138).

21 *Dig.* 47.22.3.2 Marcianus 2 iudic. publ. *Servos quoque licet in collegio tenuiorum recipi volentibus dominis, ut curatores horum corporum sciant, ne invito aut ignorante domino in collegium tenuiorum reciperent, et in futurum poena teneantur in singulos homines aureorum centum,* "It is also lawful for slaves to be admitted to a collegium of the indigent with the permission of their owners; the *curators* of those societies must

know not to accept a slave into a collegium of the indigent without the invitation or knowledge of his owner; if they do, they will be liable to a fine of a hundred *aurei* for each slave admitted" (my translation).

22 Van Nijf (1997: 20), citing Quass (1993: 355–65).

23 Kolb (1990).

24 *SEG* 40.1063 (Sattai, second half of II – mid III CE):

    30.1 φ(υλῆς) Ἡρακ(ληίδος). φ(υλῆς)(?) – – –
    33.1 φ(υλῆς) Ἡρα(κληίδος). φ(υλῆς) [– – ίδ]ο[ς].
    34.1 φ(υλῆς) Ἡρα(κληίδος). φ(υλῆς) Λ[–]α[– ί]δος.
    35.1 φ(υλῆς) Ἡρακ(ληίδος). [– ? –]ευαρδοος ν(εωτέρου)(?).
    36.1 φυλ(ῆς) β' [λ]ινου[ργῶν(?)]
    37.1 [φ(υλῆς) λινου]ρ{α}γω[ν(?)] νε[ωτέρων(?)].
    38.1 [φυλ(ῆς) λινουρ]γῶν.
    39.1 [φυλ(ῆς) λινο]υ[ρ]γῶν.
    40.1 [φυλ(ῆς) λιν]ουργῶν.
    41.1 [φυλ(ῆς) λ]ινο[υργῶν].

    Kolb (1990: 117) and Dittmann-Schöne (2001: 198, no. III.3.11) reconstruct ll. 37–41 simply as [λινουρ]γῶν (etc.) but given the use of φ or φυλ as an abbreviation for φυλῆς in 36.1 and all the preceding lines, it is more likely that ll. 37–41 had either φ or φυλ, as space permits.

25 Dittmann-Schöne (2001: 199). However, she also opines that "Obgleich in Saittai eine und in Philadelphia zwei Phyle(n) nach Berufen bennant waren, ist eine politische Bedeutung aber nicht anzunehmen. . . . Daß die Phylen hier wohl nur den Stellenwert von Vereinen hatten, bestärkt auch die Tatsache daß diejenigen von Philadelphia selbst Beschlüsse geringerer Relevanz – wie die Aufstellung einer Ehrenstatue – der Bestätigung durch den Rat bzw. durch Rat und Volk unterwerfen mußten" (24). But see Pleket (2008: 536): "Denn *Phylen* wird nie in der Bedeutung von 'Verein' verwendet. Ich möchte den Tatbestand eher umdrehen: Vereine hatten hier den Stellenwert von politischen Unterabteilungen der Vollbürger als ein für die politische Struktur konstitutives Element."

26 IGLAM 648.26 = *IGRR* IV 1632 (Philadelphia, after 212 CE): ἡ ἱερὰ φυλὴ τῶν ἐριουργῶν; IGLAM 656.11 (Philadelphia): ἡ ἱερὰ φυλὴ τῶν σκυτέων.

27 Van Nijf (1997: 20).

28 Pleket (2008: 540).

29 Bagnall (2007: 184).

30 E.g., see the declarations of guilds in P.Mich. II 123.41 (Tebtynis, 45/46 CE): a guild *(plēthos)* of weavers; 6.25: wool-merchants; 8.26: *apolysimoi*; 14.37: fishermen; P.Mich. II 124.2.15 (Tebtynis, 45/46 CE): a guild *(plēthos)* of the wool-merchants; P.Oxy. VII 1029 (Oxyrhynchus, 107 CE): hieroglyphic carvers; P.Mich. IX 543 (Karanis, 135–6): a guild of camel keepers; P.Mich. II 1233.41 (Tebtynis, 45/46 CE): a guild *(plēthos)* of weavers; 6.25: wool-merchants; 8.26: *apolysimoi*; 14.37: fishermen. After Diocletian's price edict, declarations of maximum prices were required: e.g., P.Oxy. LIV 3734 (Oxyrhynchus, 312 CE): salt merchants; P.Oxy LIV 3740 (Oxyrhynchus, 312 CE): tavern keepers; and several other examples from P.Oxy. LIV. See also P.Sijpesteijn 30 (Hermopolis, II CE), a list of boat owners liable to pay a tax on fishing boats.

31 Similarly, P.Mich. V 243.2–3 (Tebtynis, time of Tiberius): κατὰ δὲ τοῦ ἀδωσιδικοῦντος ἐπὶ | τρύτων καὶ τῶν ἄλ[λω]ν ἐξέστω τῶι πρρστάτηι ἐνεχυράζειν, "It is permitted for the president to exact a pledge from one who fails to pay his dues in these or any other matters"; P.Mich. V 245.37–42 (Tebtynis, 47 CE): τὸν δὲ ἀδωσιδικοῦντα | [καὶ μ]ὴ [ἀ] γαπληρουντά τι τῶν δημοσίων ἢ καὶ τῶν | [προσε]νκληθησομένων αὐτοῖς ἐξεῖναι τῷ αὐτῷ Ἀπ||[ύνχι ἐνε]χυράζειν αὐτοὺς ἔν τε τῇ πλατείᾳ καὶ ἐν | [ταῖς οἰκί]αις καὶ ἐν τῷ ἀγρῶι καὶ παραδιδόναι αὐτοὺς | [καθὼς πρό]κιται, "If someone fails to pay and does

not pay any of the public charges or (fines?) laid against him, Apynchis (40) has the authority to arrest him, whether in the town square or in his house or in the field, and to hand him over as was indicated above."

32 See Zevi (2008).

33 Thus, Lewis (1983: 145): "In contrast with the medieval guilds, whose members banded together on their own initiative for the protection of their common interests, the guilds of Roman Egypt were created to serve the convenience of the provincial administration."

34 Gibbs (2011).

35 Thus, Van Minnen (1987: 53).

36 Cracco Ruggini (1976: 469, 485 n. 81): "Con una funzione quindi di mutua fiscale, la quale anticipa di circa tre secoli l'istituto tardoimperiale della corresponsabilità coatta, ma con il carattere di 'assicurazione volontaria,' spontaneamente scaturita dagli scopi assistenziali medesimi per cui le associazioni si erano costituite"; see also Van Minnen (1987: 53).

37 Guilds of bakers of fine bread, rush-sellers, wood-sellers, fruit-growers, olive-sellers, garland-plaiters, vegetable-sellers, crop-buyers, wool-merchants, grain-dealers, clothes-makers, shoemakers, shepherds, tinsmiths, butchers.

38 *SB* 16.12695.17–18 has a special category for "those private persons (?) who sell in the city."

39 P.Tebt. II 287 (Tebtynis, 161–169 CE).

40 BGU VII 1572 (Philadelphia, 139 CE).

41 Monson (2006).

42 Tilly (2005: 13).

43 Tilly (2005: 8), citing *(inter alii)* North (1990, 1997).

44 Monson (2006: 234).

45 Hawkins (2016: 71), citing Liu (2009: 115–22).

46 Brennan and Pettit (2004: 195–221).

47 Putnam (2000: 19, 21–2).

48 Venticinque (2016: 37–8).

49 Broekaert (2011: 227): "Members not only share membership in the network, but also the same religious belief, origin, social background, upbringing, cultural taste, etc. The more ties, the closer the connection between the members and the more likely they are to help and protect each other."

50 Hawkins (2016: 73–4): "Roman artisans may have been able to use the private regulatory functions of collegia to transform these organizations into governance structures with which they could coordinate the efforts of multiple specialists who had invested heavily in intensive human capital. By providing organized governance structures, both firms and networks permit entrepreneurs to circumvent problems that would make it difficult or undesirable for them to coordinate production were they to contract instead with specialists whenever necessary. Networks, however, can do so in ways that permit entrepreneurs to adapt more effectively to seasonal and uncertain demand than can firms." ("Firm" in the context refers to "an integrated and durable organization of people and other assets, acting tacitly or otherwise as a 'legal person,' set up for the purpose of producing goods or services, with the capacity to sell or hire them to customers, and with associated and recognized corporate legal entitlements and liabilities"; Hodgson [1999: 235–41, and esp. 238]).

51 Broekaert (2011).

52 Kloppenborg (2013).

53 Van Minnen (1987: 64–5), Van Nijf (1997: 13–14), Broekaert (2011: 246–7), Hawkins (2016: 73), and Venticinque (2016: passim).

54 Broekaert (2011: 230), citing *CIL* 13.8354: "The combination of closure and multiplex often implied that the feeling of solidarity and bonding among *collegiati* could be

rather intense. . . . Maybe this affectionate phrasing was used to denote his colleagues in an association of *negotiatores*, who to the deceased were no less than his real *fratres*. This psychological link to the strength of family ties implies that *collegiati* were supposed to be as reliable as the next of kin."

55 See in addition to *CIL* 13.8354, *CIL* 5.7487 (Monteu da Po, Regio IX: Liguria): fabri | fratres; AIJ 364 (Ptuj, Pannonia superior): collegium fabru]m tign[uariorum – – –] | [– – – quo]d frat[res – – –]; *CIL* 3.1553 (Apulum, Dacia): D(is) M(anibus) | Fabricius | Iucun[dus] | vixit an(nos) L[– – –] | Fab(ricius) I[u]c[und]|us her(es) et F[a]|[b]rici S[i]lv[an(us)] | et Licinia[n(us)] | fratres [cum] | collegio fa[b]|rorum tit(ulum) | [p] os(uerunt) fratri | pien(tissimo); *CIL* 6.7861 (Rome): L. Octavius L. l. Secundus | Maior mag(ister) quinq(uennalis) | co‹l›l(egii) cent(onariorum) lustri XI et | decurio | vixit ann(os) LV | L. Octavius Primigenius vixit ann(os) LVIII | L. Octavius Secundus vixit ann(os) | fratres viatores coll(egii) centonariorum; *CIL* 6.9411 (Roma): Vivit | C. Gavius C. l. Dardanus || vivit | C. ‹G›avius Spu(ri) f. Rufus || vivit | Gavia CC(aiorum) l(iberta) Asia || duo fratres fabr{e}i tign(uarii) | C. Gavius C. l. Salvius; *CIL* 6.9796 (Rome): C. Lucretius C. [– – –] | Pamphilus | fratres pigme[ntarii] | vici lorari A[– – –] | Poblicia lib(erta); *CIMRM* 2.1243 (Bingium, Germania superior): In h(onorem) d(omus) d(ivinae) | deo Invicto | M‹i›t‹hr›(a)e ara|m [[et templum]] «ex voto dei» | de suo impen|dio instituer(unt) | A. Gratius Ioven|is pater sacroru|m et A. Gratius Po|tens m(iles) l(egionis) XXII mat|rica[ri]us fratres | dedic[aver]unt co(n)s(ule) Afri(cano); and probably some of the other inscriptions that simply refer to *fratres* without mentioning other persons related by blood to the deceased.

56 Broekaert (2011: 236; italics added).

57 North and Thomas (1973: 1).

58 NIE distinguishes between institutions and organizations. "Institutional economists define institutions as essentially *sets of enforceable rules that constrain and guide human interaction*" (Acheson, 2002: 30, citing North, 1990: 3). Institutions lower uncertainty by constraining malfeasance, enforcing compliance with contracts, or simply facilitating transactions by some agreed-upon conventions (such as driving on one side of the road). Organizations, according to North, are groups that instantiate those rules and conventions (North, 1990: 45).

59 Acheson (2002: 28), argues that NIE assumes a "bounded rationality" in which information is expensive so that opportunism (malfeasance) is a ubiquitous danger.

60 North and Thomas (1973: 4); similarly Acheson (2002: 29).

61 Acheson (1994: 7).

62 North and Thomas (1973: 57–8).

63 North and Thomas (1973: 88, 127, 132).

64 Ogilvie (2004: passim and 319).

65 Ogilvie (2004: 330).

66 Ogilvie (2004: 329–30).

67 Arnaoutoglou (2016) notes only *IG* II² 2934 (Athens, mid IV ʙᴄᴇ), a group of twelve "washers" who make a dedication to the Nymphs: οἱ πλυνῆς Νύμφαις εὐξάμενοι ἀνέθεσαν καὶ θεοῖς πᾶσιν | Ζωαγόρας ‹Ζ›ωκύπρου Ζώκυπρος Ζωαγόρου Θάλλος Λεύκη | Σωκράτης Πολυκράτους Ἀπολλοφάνης Εὐπορίωνος Σωσίστρατος | Μάνης Μυρρίνη Σωσίας Σωσιγένης Μίδας. Slightly later is *IG* II² 2941 (Athens, 268/267 ʙᴄᴇ): ἐπὶ Φιλοκράτου ἄρχοντος [οἵδε ἀνέθεσαν στεφανωθέντες] | ὑπὸ τοῦ κοινοῦ τῶν ἐργαζ[ομένων – – –] | <col. i.3> ταμίαι | Ἡδύφιλος || Σώστρατος | Σάτυρος | <col. ii.3> γραμματεῖς | Ἐπίστρατος || Αἰσχυλίδης | ἐπιμεληταί | Φιλόμηλος | vac. | <col. iii.3> Δημ – – | Φα – – || Μο – – | Σ – –.

68 E.g., IBeroia 27 (Beroea, before 212 ᴄᴇ): thirty-seven members of an association dedicated to Theos Hypsistos, including craftsmen with several occupations, several slaves and several freeborn persons; IBulg. IV 1922 (Serdica/Sophia, II/III ᴄᴇ): nine members of an association, probably cultic, of a variety of trades; *SEG* 46.864 (Pautalia,

150–200 CE): a list, probably a subscription list (ἐπίδοσις) of a cult association that includes several priests but also coppersmiths and fullers.
69 See also Poland (1909: 114), and Arnaoutoglou (2016: 4 n. 16) who comments "It is certainly appealing to assume that Rhodian traders found an outlet to satisfy their sociability in the numerous cult associations active in the island. But, as far as I know, there is no epigraphic testimony to link traders and members in cult associations. . . . It is one thing for members of cult associations to promote their financial, economic and trade interests and quite another to compose a group explicitly stating the prevalence of similar interests."
70 E.g., *OGIS* II 729.4–5 (Alexandria, 221–205 BCE): οἱ πρεσβύτεροι τῶν ὀλυροκό‖πων; P.Mich.Zen. I 57 (Philadelphia, 248 BCE): a litigation concerning a συνέργιον.
71 E.g., IDelos 1520 (Delos, 153/152 BCE): τὸ κοινὸν Βηρυτ[ί]‖ων Ποσειδωνιαστῶν ἐμπόρων καὶ ναυκλήρων καὶ ἐγδοχέων.
72 Thus, also Verboven (2015: 36).
73 Van Minnen (1987: 63–4).
74 *SB* 3:6704 (Aphrodito, 538 CE).
75 Van Minnen (1987: 65).
76 Lopez (1976: 126).
77 *CIL* 6.9034, 9415b; Liu (2017: 207).
78 Erdkamp (2014), online: https://oeconomia.revues.org/399.
79 Erdkamp (2014).

Bibliography

Acheson, James M. "Transaction Costs Economics: Accomplishments, Problems, and Possibilities." Pages 27–58 in *Theory in Economic Anthropology*. Edited by Jean Ensminger. Society for Economic Anthropology Monographs 18. Walnut Creek, CA: AltaMira Press, 2002.

———. "Welcome to Nobel Country: An Overview of Institutional Economics." Pages 3–41 in *Anthropology and Institutional Economics*. Edited by James M. Acheson. Monographs in Economic Anthropology 12. Lanham, Md.: University Press of America, 1994.

Arnaoutoglou, Ilias. "Roman Law and *Collegia* in Asia Minor." *Revue internationale des droits de l'antiquité* 49 (2002): 27–44.

———. "Were There Craftsmen Associations in the Hellenistic World?" Paper presented at the colloquium "Status personnels et main-d'oeuvre en Méditerranée hellénistique, mars 17–18, 2016." Clermont-Ferrand, 2016.

Ausbüttel, Frank M. *Untersuchungen zu den Vereinen im Westen des römischen Reiches*. Frankfurter Althistorische Studien 11. Kallmünz: Verlag Michael Laßleben, 1982. (*AE* 1983, 181).

Bagnall, Roger S. "Family and Society in Roman Oxyrhynchus." Pages 182–93 in *Oxyrhynchus: A City and Its Texts*. Edited by Alan K. Bowman, R.A. Coles, Nicholas Gonis, Dirk Obbink, and Peter J. Parson. London: Egypt Exploration Society, 2007.

Baldwin, Barry H. "Strikes in the Roman Empire." *Classical Journal* 59.1 (1964): 75–76.

Brennan, Geoffrey, and Philip Pettit. *The Economy of Esteem: An Essay on Civil and Political Society*. Oxford: Oxford University Press, 2004.

Bresson, Alain. *The Making of the Ancient Greek Economy: Institutions, Markets, and the Growth in the City-States*. Translated by Steven Rendall. Princeton and Oxford: Princeton University Press, 2016.

Broekaert, Wim. "Partners in Business: Roman Merchants and the Potential Advantages of Being a *Collegiatus*." *Ancient Society* 41 (2011): 221–56.

Buckler, William H. "Labour Disputes in the Province of Asia." Pages 27–50 in *Anatolian Studies, Presented to Sir William Mitchell Ramsay*. Edited by William H. Buckler and William M. Calder. Manchester: Manchester University Press, 1923.

Burford, Alison. *Craftsmen in Greek and Roman Society*. Aspects of Greek and Roman Life. London: Thames & Hudson; Ithaca: Cornell University Press, 1972.

Carroll, Maureen. *Spirits of the Dead: Roman Funerary Commemoration in Western Europe*. Oxford Studies in Ancient Documents. Oxford and New York: Oxford University Press, 2006.

Cracco Ruggini, Lellia. "La vita associativa nelle città dell'Oriente greco: tradizioni locali e influenze romane." Pages 463–92 in *Assimilation et résistance à la culture gréco-romaine dans le monde ancien: Travaux du VIe Congrès international d'Etudes classiques*. Paris: Société d'Edition "Les belles lettres," 1976.

De Cenival, Françoise. "Comptes d'une association religieuse Thébaine datant des années 29 à 33 du roi Amasis (P. Démot. Louvre E 7840 Bis)." *Revue d'Égyptologie* 37 (1986): 13–29.

———. "Papyrus Seymour de Ricci: Le plus ancien des règlements d'association religieuse (4ème siècle av. J.-C.) (Pap. Bibl. Nationale E 241)." *Revue d'Égyptologie* 39 (1988): 37–46.

Dittmann-Schöne, Imogen. *Die Berufsvereine in den Städten des kaiserzeitlichen Kleinasiens*. Theorie und Forschung 690. Geschichte 10. Regensburg: S. Roderer, 2001.

Erdkamp, Paul. "How Modern Was the Market Economy of the Roman World?" *Oeconomia* 4.2 (2014): 225–35.

Finley, Moses I. *The Ancient Economy*. 2nd ed. Sather Classical Lectures 43. Berkeley: University of California Press, 1985.

———. "Technological Innovations and Economic Progress in the Ancient World." *Economic History Review* 18 (2nd series) (1965): 29–45.

Garnsey, Peter, and Richard Saller. *The Roman Empire: Economy, Society and Culture*. London: Duckworth; Berkeley: University of California Press, 1987.

Gibbs, Matthew. "Trade Associations in Roman Egypt: Their Raison d'Être." *Ancient Society* 41 (2011): 291–315.

Hawkins, Cameron. *Roman Artisans and the Urban Economy*. Cambridge: Cambridge University Press, 2016.

Hodgson, Geoffrey M. *Evolution and Institutions: On Evolutionary Economics and the Evolution of Economics*. Cheltenham: Elgar, 1999.

Jones, A.H.M. *The Roman Economy: Studies in Ancient Economic and Administrative History*. Oxford: Basil Blackwell, 1974.

Kloppenborg, John S. "Collegia and *Thiasoi*: Issues in Function, Taxonomy and Membership." Pages 16–30 in *Voluntary Associations in the Graeco-Roman World*. Edited by John S. Kloppenborg and Stephen G. Wilson. London: Routledge, 1996.

———. "The Moralizing of Discourse in Greco-Roman Associations." Pages 215–28 in *"The One Who Sows Bountifully": Essays in Honor of Stanley K. Stowers*. Edited by Caroline Johnson Hodge, Saul M. Olyan, Daniel Ullucci, and Emma Wasserman. Brown Judaic Studies 256. Providence: Brown Judaic Studies, 2013.

Kolb, Frank. "Sitzstufeninschriften aus dem Stadion von Saittai (Lydien)." *Epigraphica Anatolica* 15.1 (1990): 107–19.

Lewis, Naphtali. *Life in Egypt Under Roman Rule*. Oxford: Clarendon Press, 1983.

Liu, Jinyu. *Collegia Centonariorum: The Guilds of Textile Dealers in the Roman West*. Columbia Studies in the Classical Tradition 34. Leiden: Brill, 2009.

———. "Group Membership, Trust Networks, and Social Capital: A Critical Analysis." Pages 203–26 in *Work, Labour, and Professions in the Roman World*. Edited by Koenraad Verboven and Christian Laes. Impact of Empire 23. Leiden: Brill, 2017.

Lopez, Robert S. *The Commercial Revolution of the Middle Ages, 950–1350*. Cambridge: Cambridge University Press, 1976.

MacMullen, Ramsay. "A Note on Roman Strikes." *Classical Journal* 48 (1962–1963): 269–71.

———. *Roman Social Relations, 50 B.C. to A.D. 284*. New Haven: Yale University Press, 1974.

Mickwitz, Gunnar. *Die Kartellfunktionen der Zünfte und ihre Bedeutung bei der Entstehung des Zunftwesens: Eine Studie in spätantiker und mittelalterlicher Wirtschaftsgeschichte*. Societas Scientiarum Fennica. Commentationes Humanarum Litterarum 8.3. Amsterdam: Hakkert, 1968.

Monson, Andrew. "The Ethics and Economics of Ptolemaic Religious Associations." *Ancient Society* 36 (2006): 221–38.

North, Douglass C. *Institutions, Institutional Change, and Economic Performance*. Political Economy of Institutions and Decisions. Cambridge and New York: Cambridge University Press, 1990.

———. "Institutions." *Journal of Economic Perspectives* 5.1 (1991): 97–112.

———. "Understanding Economic Change." Pages 13–18 in *Transforming Post-Communist Political Economies*. Edited by Joan Nelson, Charles Tilly, and Lee Walker. Washington: National Academy Press, 1997.

North, Douglass C., and Robert Paul Thomas. *The Rise of the Western World: A New Economic History*. Cambridge: Cambridge University Press, 1973.

Ogilvie, Sheilagh. "Guilds, Efficiency, and Social Capital: Evidence from German Proto-Industry." *The Economic History Review* 57.2 (2004): 286–333.

Perry, Jonathan S. "'L'État intervint peu à peu': State Intervention in the Ephesian 'Bakers' Strike.'" Pages 183–205 in *Private Associations and the Public Sphere: Proceedings of a Symposium Held at the Royal Danish Academy of Sciences and Letters, 9–11 September 2010*. Edited by Vincent Gabrielsen and Christian A. Thomsen. Scientia Danica. Series H, Humanistic, 8 9. Copenhagen: Royal Danish Academy of Sciences and Letters, 2015.

———. "Organized Societies: *Collegia*." Pages 499–515 in *The Oxford Handbook of Social Relations in the Roman World*. Edited by Michael Peachin. Oxford Handbooks. Oxford: Oxford University Press, 2010.

Pleket, H.W. "Berufsvereine im kaiserzeitlichen Kleinasien: Geselligkeit oder Zünfte?" Pages 533–44 in *Antike Lebenswelten: Konstanz – Wandel – Wirkungsmacht: Festschrift für Ingomar Weiler zum 70. Geburtstag*. Edited by Christoph Ulf. Philippika: Marburger altertumskundliche Abhandlungen 25. Wiesbaden: Harrassowitz, 2008.

Poland, Franz. *Geschichte des griechischen Vereinswesens*. Leipzig: Teubner, 1909.

Putnam, Robert D. *Bowling Alone: The Collapse and Revival of American Community*. New York: Simon & Schuster, 2000.

Quass, Friedemann. *Die Honoratiorenschicht in den Städten des griechischen Ostens: Untersuchungen zur politischen und sozialen Entwicklung in hellenistischer und römischer Zeit*. Stuttgart: Steiner, 1993.

Sommer, Stefan. *Rom und die Vereinigungen im südwestlichen Kleinasien (133 v. Chr. – 284 n. Chr.)*. Pietas 1. Hennef: Clauss, 2006.

Temin, Peter. *The Roman Market Economy*. Princeton Economic History of the Western World. Princeton: Princeton University Press, 2013.

Thrupp, Sylvia L. "The Gilds." Pages 230–80, 624–34, in *Economic Organization and Policies in the Middle Ages*. Vol. 3 of *The Cambridge Economic History of Europe*. Edited by M.M. Postan, E.E. Rich, and E. Miller. Cambridge: Cambridge University Press, 1963.

Tilly, Charles. *Trust and Rule*. Cambridge Studies in Comparative Politics. Cambridge and New York: Cambridge University Press, 2005.

Van Minnen, Peter. "Urban Craftsmen in Roman Egypt." *Münstersche Beiträge zur antiken Handelsgeschichte* 6.1 (1987): 31–88.

Van Nijf, Onno. *The Civic World of Professional Associations in the Roman East.* Dutch Monographs on Ancient History and Archaeology 17. Amsterdam: Gieben, 1997.

Venticinque, Philip F. *Honor Among Thieves: Craftsmen, Merchants, and Associations in Roman and Late Roman Egypt.* New Texts from Ancient Cultures. Ann Arbor: University of Michigan Press, 2016.

Verboven, Koenraad. "The Knights Who Say NIE: Can Neo-Institutional Economics Live Up to Its Expectation in Ancient History Research?" Pages 33–57 in *Structure and Performance in the Roman Economy: Models, Methods and Case Studies.* Edited by Paul Erdkamp and Koenraad Verboven. Collection Latomus 350. Bruxelles: Editions Latomus, 2015.

Waltzing, Jean Pierre. *Étude historique sur les corporations professionnelles chez les Romains depuis les origines jusqu'à la chute de l'Empire d'Occident.* Louvain: Peeters, 1895–1900.

Wilken, Robert Louis. *The Christians as the Romans Saw Them.* New Haven: Yale University Press, 1984.

Williamson, Oliver E. "The Economics of Organization: The Transaction Cost Approach." *American Journal of Sociology* 87.3 (1981): 548–77.

Zevi, Fausto. "I collegi di Ostia e le loro sedi associative tra Antonini e Severi." Pages 477–505 in *Le quotidien municipal dans l'Occident romain.* Edited by Clara Berrendonner, Lamoine Mireille Cébeillac-Gervasoni, and Laurent Lamoine. Collection "Histoires Croisées." Clermont-Ferrand: Presses universitaires Blaise-Pascal, 2008.

Zimmermann, Carola. *Handwerkervereine im griechischen Osten des Imperium Romanum.* Monographien, Römisch-Germanisches Zentralmuseum Mainz. Forschungsinstitut für Vor- und Frühgeschichte 57. Mainz: Rudolf Habelt, 2002. (*SEG* 52:1895).

7   The Economics of solidarity

Mutual aid and reciprocal services between workers in Roman cities

Nicolas Tran

Proposing a chapter on skilled workers, in a book on the extramercantile economy, might seem a little paradoxical. Indeed, these Romans chose to introduce themselves, especially on stone inscriptions, as craftsmen, shopkeepers, or merchants. They produced objects for sale or bought goods for resale, and these mercantile activities defined their social identities. Their skills defined them as *artifices*, and this social status was a source of pride.[1] Nevertheless, they were not only artisans or traders, all day long and in every aspect of their life. They had multiple identities due to their involvement in various relations of kinship, friendship, patronage, or citizenship.

Those interpersonal links created more or less formalized networks, out of which professional *collegia* stood among the most structured ones.[2] In comparison with more informal circles of friendship, networks based on associations recognized by public authorities were more stable and more precisely defined. All of these social relations developed by craftsmen and shopkeepers had powerful economic implications. Some of them were clearly aside from work and from any market activities. Yet some others did impact work, even if they were tied to extramercantile sociability and values. As a result, we shall not limit the coming pages to extramercantile activities, but also explore the margins and the porosity between mercantile and extramercantile fields.

Professional *collegia* are the most visible groups that companionship between Roman workers created, during the late republic and the early empire. They gathered individuals who practiced the same trade, or a trade belonging to the same economic sector. In small or average cities, associations gathered quite diverse professionals: all the local artisans could form a single *collegium fabrum*, for instance. Conversely, in great economic centers, they were more numerous, and their recruitment was based on more advanced occupational specializations. Associations contributed to structure a lot of urban societies, especially in Rome and other great towns of the Roman West. Often called *collegia* or *corpora*, these communities corresponded to voluntary associations and, above all, developed convivial activities.[3] From this point of view, professional *collegia* did not differ from other associations, in particular from religious groups of *cultores*. As other associations, they were modeled on civic institutions. Decrees voted by the general assembly ruled common life. Ordinary members formed a *plebs* and elected magistrates, who conceived their function as a prestigious honor. Patrons did not usually belong to *collegia*.[4] Most of the time, associations chose these official protectors and benefactors from the upper classes, in the local or even imperial elites. Only a minority, in major commercial cities, were businessmen. Most association members were freemen (and not slaves) and modest plebeians (but distinct from the needy).[5] Only a few members, who monopolized magistracies, were wealthier. Despite their hierarchical organization, members in professional *collegia* had a very strong feeling of community. Communal worship fostered this cohesion, especially through sacrifices offered to the *genius collegii*: the main protective deity created by the group itself. This sense of belonging and a shared access to collective resources created a spirit of solidarity. This was favorable to the development of reciprocal exchanges of services, which could be considered in an economic perspective.

The sharing of common resources

One of the main functions of professional *collegia* was to provide goods that their members could not afford alone. Convivial meetings took place in buildings occupied by associations.[6] Meeting rooms themselves were often called *scholae*. Not all the associations acquired their common houses under the same conditions.[7] Yet they were often the legal owners of these places, sometimes after benefiting from a generous gift. A few documents show that the city council sometimes authorized the construction of a common building or helped it by the gift of a public plot. For example, the *fabri tignuarii* (i.e., carpenters) from Tolentinum, in central Italy, built their *schola Augusta* from its foundations, at their own expense, and on a plot given by a private benefactor.[8] In Ostia, the seaport of Rome, some public spaces had a very specific status. Hence, between 101 and 103 CE, the *corpus lenuncu-lariorum traiectus Luculli*, a local association of boatmen, needed a permission granted by the *curator* of the banks of the Tiber, to embellish and consolidate its meeting place.[9] This common building was probably located in the immediate vicinity of the river and, to achieve its restoration, the association spent its own funds *(sua pecunia)*. Explicit evidence demonstrates that the *lenuncularii traiectus Luculli* and the *corporati qui pecuniam ad ampliandum templum contulerunt*, who had the same magistrates and patrons at the beginning of the early second century CE, formed a single community.[10] Therefore, the *corpus* met in a temple built with a great care *(opere firmiori et cultiori)* that the *corporati* could not have afforded without a special fundraising.

Associations seem to have almost always arranged their *scholae* freely. For this reason, the expression *l(ocus) d(atus) d(ecreto) collegii* – which means "place given by a decree of the association" – appears at the end of a few inscriptions, for instance on a statue base discovered in Comum.[11] C. Plinius Philocalus dedicated this monument to his friend C. Coesidius Euzelus, in the clubhouse of the local *collegium fabrum*. Moreover, Euzelus gave two thousand sesterces to these craftsmen, for the monument's maintenance. Both gifts indicate how *collegia* could fund the decoration of their meeting place, without resorting to contributions of their members. The relation between the donors and the *collegium* from Comum is unclear. Philocalus and Euzelus might have belonged to it, but there would have been no need to refer to their membership in a place where everyone knew them. The inscription only mentions C. Coesidius Euzelus's title of *seuir*, which Roman cities gave most of the time to wealthy freedmen. Anyway, the town council of Comum acknowledged him as a respectable citizen.[12] In sum, membership in a professional association enables plebeians to become real estate owners. Their property was collective and often related to wealth transfers (i.e., euergetic donations) that did not belong to the mercantile economy, in the strict sense.

The opportunity to convene in a collective building had great consequences on the social life of association members, in particular for the most humble ones. Indeed, common places were decorated with great care, so that skilled workers could meet in luxurious environments. "Luxury" is not too strong a word to describe the best-preserved *scholae*. Archaeological remains discovered in Nîmes (in Southern France) fall into this category.[13] A fragmentary inscription reveals that they belonged to a building occupied by a *collegium utriculariorum* during the second century.[14] This professional association gathered transporters, whose occupational name referred to the use of animal skins *(utres)*, maybe as liquid containers. Their common house consisted in two spacious rooms. Marble was very present, as shown not only by engraved plaques, but also by fragments of marble plating. The floor was entirely paved with beautiful mosaics, and statues completed this elegant décor. One of them must be identified as the *genius collegii*.

So the *utricularii* met in a sumptuous place, but this luxury was not a simple reflection of their wealth. It emphasized much more the support provided by rich notables to the *collegium*. Indeed, inscriptions tend to indicate that gifts funded the whole décor.[15] No *utricularius* could have offered such a nice home to his family, and the *collegium* itself could not have afforded it without benefactors belonging to the social elite. It was not always the case, since a significant number of associations also benefited from the generosity of their richest members. For instance, in Rome, L. Sextilius Seleucus was in charge of a subdivision of an association of textile workers. As a *decurio*, he gave to this *collegium centonariorum* a rich furniture composed of a statue, its base, and a pair of bronze candelabra. The effigy of Cupid holding a basket carved on them was probably elegant.[16] Whether benefactors belonged to the association or not, the possession of common goods resulted from wealth transfers from individuals to the group.

Members in *collegia* took advantage of shared resources. On the one hand, they enjoyed a collective life, which included banquets, afternoons spent at baths or attendance at public spectacles, in seats reserved for the *collegium*. On the other hand, each member received goods individually. Hence, dedications of monuments gave rise to distributions of money, with or without food. These *sportulae* were sometimes shared only once, on the occasion of a specific event. For example, in the Adriatic port of Aquileia, the *collegium incrementorum cultorum Mineruae* paid tribute to L. Domitius Epaphroditus and M. Livius Tertius, two officials *(decuriones)* of the local association of craftsmen.[17] *Incrementum* means "growth," and Minerva was the artisans' tutelary goddess. So the *collegium incrementorum cultorum Mineruae* might be the youth organization of the *collegium fabrum*. Anyway, the *decuriones* gave to the *collegium* a silver statuette (certainly of Minerva), and Epaphroditus seems to have invited everybody to a picnic at the beach. On this occasion, each member received bread, wine, ham, and two sesterces to buy other food. Actually, participants had a nice day, but received quite modest gifts. Other benefactors could behave more generously. Hence, during the late second century CE, L. Apuleius Brasidas made a good living as a businessman involved in commerce between the Adriatic and the Danube.[18] The *collegium fabrum* of the seaport of Pisaurum chose him as president and patron, before erecting a statue in his honor. Then, Brasidas expressed his gratitude by distributing fifty sesterces (besides bread and wine) to each *faber*. Many unskilled workers earned less in two or three weeks.

Other benefactors set up perpetual endowments, which provided for annual distributions of *sportulae*. For instance, in 149 CE, the *collegium fabrum* of Narbonne erected a statue to its patron, Sex. Fadius Secundus Musa. In his letter, engraved on one side of the base, this notable promised to pay sixteen thousand sesterces to the association treasury.[19] The annual interest on this donation, which – at a rate of 12.5% – amounted to two thousand sesterces, would pay for a birthday banquet and a distribution of money. Such *sportulae* were probably too small to have significantly increased members' incomes. Nevertheless, association life cost money too. It required the payment of entrance fees, regular dues, and exceptional subscriptions. Thus, members probably appreciated getting some money back. Roman *collegia* did not provide goods of vital importance, because their members did not need them. They were not poor people struggling for their subsistence. Nevertheless, gifts and access to common resources did matter, because they contributed to distinguish associations' members from the poorest.

This brief overview might suggest that professional associations' activities represented the extramercantile part of members' social lives. These people devoted most of their existence to work and business: to *negotium*. Contrariwise, *collegia* gave opportunities to cultivate *otium*. In other words, associations provided access to leisure; that is, to unnecessary but pleasant goods. This ability to enjoy *otium* that associations offered had great implications. Indeed, most of the time, *otium* was a privilege of notables and aristocrats, who were rich enough to live without working. Again, *collegia* fostered social distinction, through resources that association members acquired by means distinct from the market economy. Consequently, does it mean that craftsmen and merchants built an absolute separation between their work and their social activities? If this separation did exist, does it symbolize a gap between mercantile and extramercantile economies? Epigraphic evidence may create this perception, because it focuses on ceremonies, feasts, dedications of monuments, association structures, and decision-making processes. Yet we should not answer these questions too quickly. Of course, it is absurd to assume that historical reality is to be found beyond or even against available evidence. Nonetheless, friendship experienced in *collegia* seems to have impacted economic solidarity among workers.

Financial solidarity

The spirit of solidarity among workers, in general, and among associations' members, in particular, could have financial implications. Of course, not all the support obtained by Roman workers consisted in mutual and extramercantile aid. On the one hand, access to credit through the market did exist and played an important part in the economy of Roman craftsmanship. For instance, as known by a wax tablet, C. Sulpicius Faustus, a Roman financier from Pozzuoli, lent three thousand sesterces to a producer of copper rust *(aerugo)*, to develop his dyeing workshop.[20] Their relationship was obviously a mercantile one. On the other hand, as a social group, Roman skilled workers often benefited from external financial support. Patrons, who belonged to the upper classes, lent money to their freedmen and clients, who needed these loans to run their businesses. Such credit relations reflected social solidarity, since patrons had to get involved in it, as a social duty. Yet when lenders belonged to the elite, it was not mutual aid between workers at all. Lenders were not craftsmen or traders, even if they funded craftsmanship or commerce.

At a lower social level, well-to-do professionals granted credit to humble – and quite often itinerant – merchants. Roman jurists defined their agreements as contracts of *aestimatum*.[21] The former could provide merchandise to the latter, after an estimation of its value. The wealthier artisan or trader remained the owner of this good. But, after its sale, he became the creditor of the petty merchant, who owed the estimated amount. In other words, the richest workers advanced money to the poorest, who could not afford initial investments required by their trade. Yet these hierarchical relationships can hardly be interpreted as mutual aid, despite their helpfulness for modest workers.

Romans could also obtain credit without professional bankers or patrons, and among peers, in a quite informal manner. Potential lenders and borrowers just met, often in the forum. "*Eamus in forum et pecunias mutuemur*," says Trimalchio in Petronius's *Satyricon*.[22] Unfortunately, we lack very explicit evidence that craftsmen and traders were involved together in such credit relations. Yet consistent clues are preserved, and it is noticeable that they are often tied to moral values. As a short manual on wisdom and morality, which might have been written before the end of the second century CE, the *dicta Catonis* enjoined readers to lend money. The imperative sentence "*mutuum da!*" prescribes a correct moral behavior that entailed avoiding being considered a miser.[23] Thus, loans were partly a matter of solidarity between members of the same community.

Moreover, some epitaphs of merchants insist on the *fides* of the deceased. For instance, L. Statius Onesimus worked for a long time on the *uia Appia* as a businessman *(negotians)*.[24] When he died, probably during the second century, his wife paid tribute to a *homo super omnes fidelissimus, cuius fama in aeterno nota est*. Such homages emphasized a general quality of honest and loyal professionals, but *fides* could also be related to confidence and trust, in the context of credit.[25] Indeed, in a technical sense, the Latin expression "*fidem habere*" defines the ability to borrow money. The *amicitia* between workers was a business friendship, which implied trust in each other and the willingness to provide mutual aid. If this conclusion is valid, in general, it deserves to be taken into account when we consider professional *collegia*.

Roman *collegia* were, by definition, private and voluntary associations based on diverse forms of conviviality. These communities did not aim at organizing economic activities. Somehow, they were extramercantile institutions, insofar as their members met outside of work, apart from their mercantile activities. Nevertheless, *collegia* had an indirect but considerable impact on the economy, because each *collegium* corresponded to a network of friendship. It connected professionals whose economic interest and cultural values encouraged helping each other, in particular by moneylending.[26] During the last decade, historians have often highlighted *collegia* as economic networks.[27] Yet we should wonder if *collegia* did more and, especially, if *collegia* themselves helped their members financially.

Associations possessed funds, which came not only from contributions of their members or from one-shot gifts, but also from perpetual endowments. Again, scholars have studied these foundations intensively, but Jinyu Liu published an original paper on this topic in 2008.[28] Indeed, she has focused much less on the benefactors' statuses than on the impact of endowments on association structures and on access to credit among the lower classes of Roman societies. A key issue is to determine if *collegia* lent money to their members. A definitive conclusion is unreachable, but some clues make the hypothesis quite plausible. *Collegia* often received amounts of money whose interests financed annual feasts. Unfortunately, epigraphic evidence about the financial arrangements of foundations is very scarce. A few inscriptions mention an interest rate, usually between 5% and 12%, but none indicates precisely how the money was invested.

In a very few cases, cities managed foundations set up for associations whose members were concerned only with the payment of interest.[29] But no trace of any bank placement is preserved. Contrariwise, epigraphic vocabulary suggests that most of the time, *collegia* received cash money and kept it in their treasury *(arca)*. L. Sextilius Seleucus, a benefactor already mentioned, not only offered nice furniture to the *collegium centonariorum* at Rome, but also paid to its treasury five thousand *denarii* (i.e., twenty thousand sesterces), which had to yield six hundred *denarii* per year, in order to fund an annual celebration of the *diuus Augustus*'s birthday. Seleucus gave his money to the *arka* and then the interest was paid out from the *arka – erogentur ex ark(a)*. Therefore, the *collegium centonariorum* seems to act autonomously, not only to keep its financial assets but also to make them productive. Moreover, the *fabri* and *centonarii* from Milan possessed an *arca Titiana*: a specific fund created when someone called *Titius* made a gift to their *collegium*.[30] These skilled workers took as a model cities that owned this specific kind of treasury. Public magistrates were in charge of it. Therefore, Jean Andreau has assumed that Roman cities must have lent money with interest.[31] Indeed, their funds had to yield enough profits to comply with the endowment clauses. In general, *collegia* imitated cities as much as they could: it was a matter of practical organization, but also a matter of prestige. Hence, it seems plausible that private associations lent money with interest too. Sometimes, associations of craftsmen did not receive money, but land whose income had to fund ceremonies. For example, smiths from Orange, in southern Gaul, benefited from the legacy of a *fundus*.[32] In return, they had to sacrifice each year in front of their benefactor's grave. In such circumstances, professional *collegia* must have leased their properties to farmers, just as cities did. So, in the context of endowments, moneylending seems as suitable as real estate leasing.

Who were the potential borrowers? Egyptian papyri provide parallels, but – given their geographic and chronological contexts – imperfect ones.[33] Nevertheless, from an economic perspective, the credit supply provided by *collegia* would have met the demand created by the professional needs of their members. Cultural values would have fostered this match between supply and demand.[34] Furthermore, through their magistrates, *collegia* could consider that lending money to members lowered financial risks. Indeed, in this situation, associations knew their debtors and had previously judged them trustworthy enough to be admitted as fellows. They could easily put pressure on them – through the threat of exclusion – to ensure repayments. Beyond financial issues, professional *collegia* might have encouraged also such a match between supply and demand of work.

Work solidarity

Informal discussions during association meetings must have led to agreements between members, regarding topics other than moneylending. Work itself and workforce management were probably a frequent topic of conversation. Associations' social recruitment and Roman enterprise organization strengthen this hypothesis. First, associations gathered mostly entrepreneurs, rather than all the individuals involved in a specific sector. Second, most of the time, these employers managed small firms, which had to collaborate to face demand. Roman *collegia* offered very good contexts to develop this collaboration.

The construction industry may illustrate this point.[35] It employed a significant part of the total population of Rome and Ostia during the second century and the early third century. In the capital and its seaport, public and private orders provided work to thousands of craftsmen. A lot of them called themselves *fabri tignuarii*. Nonetheless, this expression tended to encompass "*omnes qui aedificarent*": all the construction workers.[36] Therefore, the *collegia fabrum tignuariorum*, attested in about forty Roman cities, might have gathered workers who had different and complementary skills. Hence, they had a great interest in collaborating. In Ostia and Rome, these *collegia* had a large number of members. In 198 CE, the *fabri tignuarii Ostienses* erected a statue to Septimius Severus and engraved a complete register on its base.[37] This album lists more than three hundred and fifty members. There were no slaves, but a lot of freedmen, among them. Such a composition suggests that a large part of the workforce – the servile part – was not admitted to the association. Besides, the *collegium fabrum tignuariorum* of Rome was divided into sixty *decuriae*. As an inscription mentions the twenty-two members of the tenth *decuria*, the whole *collegium* might have gathered about thirteen hundred members.[38] It is an impressive number, compared with other associations, but it is not so much in a city of one million inhabitants. According to Janet DeLaine, at the end of the second century, the construction industry would have employed between 4% and 6% of the urban population.[39] The total of thirteen hundred *fabri tignuarii* amounts only to 0.13%. Again it is probable that only entrepreneurs, and not their manpower, belonged to the *collegium*.

These numerous *redemptores* were in charge of small firms. As a result, large or even average construction sites must have employed several units at the same time, which implied a sharing of work. It would have been organized either through several contracts of service or through subcontracting. Anyway, as networks, *collegia* supplied professionals with partners and opportunities to form what one calls consortiums of enterprises nowadays. Such practices had the advantage of flexible cooperation. Such consortiums could be adapted specifically to each building project, better than a single large firm. In a neoinstitutional perspective, we could say – after Cameron Hawkins – that networks made transaction costs lower, compared with integration costs incurred by the organization of great firms.[40]

Furthermore, the *fabri tignuarii* would have shared not only construction projects, but also the extra workforce required to achieve them on time. Some clues support this idea. Among the richest dignitaries of the *collegium fabrum tignuariorum Ostiensium*, a few individuals were involved in different activities, which had nothing in common but the employment of numerous unskilled slaves. For instance, M. Licinius Privatus was a wealthy freedman, since he gave fifty thousand sesterces to the *colonia* of Ostia.[41] The *fabri tignuarii*, in 200 CE, and the bakers *(pistores)* from Ostia and Portus appointed him as a president *(magister quinquennalis)*. Above all, the members of this kind of association probably owned slaves, either employed for their own activities or lent to other professionals. Indeed, the *locatio* of servile workers is well attested in Roman law.[42] So it seems plausible that lenders and borrowers of slaves met in professional *collegia*. They would have made deals regarding the supply with extra workers. So, even if they represented nonmercantile institutions, *collegia* would have contributed to the regulation of the job market.

We must admit that, fostered by association gatherings or not, exchanges of workforce between professionals often belonged to the mercantile economy. Indeed, they were based on *locationes operarum* ("employment contracts") or *locationes operis* ("contracts for services"). Yet this mercantile dimension was sometimes absent, because agreements were built on a principle of free services. The fragments of Roman jurisprudence compiled in Justinian's *Digest* provide a small sample of such practices. Once again, since we know it existed, it is plausible that professional associations' members behaved in the same way.

During the early third century, but with quotations of his predecessors, Ulpian studied the case of a loan of a servile worker, a roofer *(tector)* or a stonecutter *(lapidarius)*.[43] The scene is so vivid that it can hardly consist in a simple fiction, invented by a professor of law. The roofer had fallen from scaffolding and the issue of the borrower's liability arose. Was he compelled to compensate the lender or not? Ulpian answered that it was too simple to consider that the lender could not demand anything. If the agreement did not provide for work at height, or if the scaffolding was defective, the borrower was liable. This discussion suggests that the lending of slaves was not always tied to a financial agreement. Solidarity between masters sometimes resulted in loans of slaves, as free exchanges of services. However, owners were not disinterested. In the context of such an exchange, each "friend" cared a lot about the preservation of his property.

In Roman law, mandate implied free service, too, so that it was supposed to unite two friends by definition. In a fragment of the jurist Paul, apprenticeship as a craftsman is an important part of such a relationship.[44] A *faber* received a mandate to buy a slave. He trained him and then sold him back, although he had no right to do so. The slave appreciated in value, but, in the context of a mandate, one should not make profit at the expense of a friend. Usually, craftsmen were asked to train young workers under a contract of *locatio operarum*.[45] They had to pay remuneration to the master, father, or guardian of the apprentice, who contributed to the workshop's production. The use of a mandate would belong to another configuration, which would presume a balance between work and training.

Last, the free exchange of workforce was not only a matter of solidarity between peers on an equal footing. On the contrary, very unequal relationships appear through the working days that freedmen owed to their former master.[46] These *operae* were related to the respect *(obsequium)* due to a patron. When they were freed, slaves committed themselves, often by an oath, to provide more or less numerous *operae*. Then the only way to avoid them was to pay compensation, which enabled the former owner to hire a substitute. If the patron did not need labor, he could ask his freedman to serve another person. Thus, he could profit from the lease of *operae*. On the one hand, when they deal with this issue, Roman jurists sometimes refer to freed craftsmen. On the other hand, epigraphy demonstrates how frequent it was that freedmen and patrons practiced the same trade. Beside funerary inscriptions, the registers engraved by professional *collegia* in Ostia shed light on this phenomenon.[47] As a result, *operae* must have greatly impacted work relations, which therefore were not limited to a job market organized by supply and demand. Concretely, the wealthiest professionals were the patrons of many freedmen and *operae* helped them to respond to manpower needs in a costless and efficient way.

Because of their very hierarchical context, *operae* might seem totally extraneous to solidarity and mutual aid. Yet a look at only one part of the social reality would be misleading. Indeed, patrons had also a moral duty to provide material and financial assistance to their dependents.[48] Thus, *operae* belonged to relations based on reciprocity. Some freedmen expressed their fidelity and gratitude to their patrons. For instance, Faustianus, Epictetus, and Eufrosynus paid tribute to their *patronus indulgentissimus* P. Aufidius Fortis.[49] This wheat merchant *(mercator frumentarius)* and president of a wheat merchants association became an important notable of Ostia in the mid-second century CE.[50] Yet another inscription shows that P. Aufidius Faustianus and P. Aufidius Epictetus were also dignitaries of the *corpus mercatorum frumentariorum Ostiensium*.[51] So they certainly took advantage of their dependence on their patron, even if they had to serve him partly for free. In *collegia*, family groups constituted networks within the network. Cooperation through *collegia* was a matter of cooperation between hierarchical networks or a matter of individual affiliation with one of them.

What kind of solidarity?

In conclusion, evidence reveals links of solidarity between Roman craftsmen and traders, in the performance of their work and beyond. Nevertheless, we should not misunderstand the nature and the different aspects of this solidarity. Roman workers were united by a business friendship. The convivial atmosphere offered by *collegia* reinforced trust among them. Yet it would be naïve to limit ourselves to such an idyllic description.[52] Indeed, solidarity between workers was not only horizontal, but also vertical, because it was very often made of hierarchical relationships. The richest professionals ran *collegia* as magistrates, and they probably used these associations to strengthen their superiority. Dignitaries probably tended to control admissions, so that they controlled an economic network. Outsiders were probably not able to work, even in the absence of a legal monopoly.

Did this solidarity belong to the mercantile or extramercantile economy? Of course, it belonged to both. Sometimes, as historians, we have the feeling of walking on or near a ridgeline. Sometimes, it seems that we are in the middle of a swamp, whose waters mix. Anyway, the distinction between extra and intramercantile might help to qualify the traditional theory of an embeddedness of ancient economies, immersed in social relations. Social relations were part of the Roman economy too; they were embedded in it. Beyond the distinction between sociability and economy, diverse economies did exist and were more or less interconnected.

Notes

1 Tran (2017).
2 It would not be useful to mention a large list of references here. Besides classics such as Waltzing (1895–1900) and De Robertis (1955), see, for instance, the general bibliography of Dondin-Payre and Tran (2012) or Perry (2006) for a historiographical approach.
3 *Collegia* were voluntary associations in the sense that one should personally apply to join a *collegium*, which was free to accept or reject this application. On the concept of voluntary association in the Graeco-Roman world, see Wilson (1996).
4 Clemente (1972).
5 Tran (2006).
6 On associations' meeting places: Bollmann (1998), Agusta-Boularot and Rosso (2014), Rodríguez, Tran, and Soler (2016).
7 Tran (2013: 144–8).
8 *CIL* 9.5568: *Ex s(enatus) c(onsulto), / schola Aug(usta) colleg(ii) fabror(um) / tignuar (iorum), impendis ipsorum ab in/choato exstructa, solo dato ab T(ito) Fu/rio Primigenio, qui et dedic(atione) eius HS X(milia) n(ummum) ded(it), / ex cuius summ(ae) redit(u) omnib(us) annis XII K(alendas) August(as), / die natalis sui, epulentur.* ["Following a decree of the Senate, the Augustan hall of the association of carpenters was built at their own expense from the foundations up, after Titus Furius Primigenius had donated a plot of land. At the hall's dedication, he also gave ten thousand sesterces, so

that from the interest of which every year on the 21st of July, his birthday, (the members) might have a banquet."] See Fagan (2015: 497).

9   *CIL* 14.5320: *[N]umini domus Aug(ustae), / [co]rpus lenunclariorum / traiectus Luculli pecunia sua / firmiori et cultiori opere / fecerunt, / [per]missu Ti(beri) Iuli Ferocis, curatoris aluei / Tiberis et riparum.* ["To the divine power of the House of Augustus. The association of the boatmen of Lucullus' dock made (this building) stronger and more elegant at his own expense, with the permission of Tiberius Iulius Ferox, *curator* of the bed and banks of the Tiber."]

10 Tran (2012: 327–30). On the "association members who collected money to enlarge a temple," see *CIL* 14.246 and 5374.

11 *CIL* 5.5287: *C(aio) Coesidio / Euzelo, / (se)uiro, / C(aius) Plinius / Philocalus, / amico optim(o). / In cuius tutel(am) / Coesidius / Euzelus / colleg(io) fabr(um) / dedit (sestertium) II (milia), / l(oco) d(ato) d(ecreto) colleg(ii).* ["To Caius Coesidius Euzelus, *seuir*, Caius Plinius Philocalus, for the best friend ever. For the preservation (of this monument), Coesidius Euzelus gave two thousand sesterces to the craftsmen's association, the place being given by a decree of the association."] See Reali (1998: 96, no. 104c).

12 The Greek *cognomina* of Philocalus and Euzelus indicate that they were probably former slaves. The *praenomen* and *nomen* Caius Plinius suggest a connection with Pliny the Younger, who was also from *Comum*.

13 Christol and Darde (2014).

14 Christol and Darde (2014: 55–56, no. 3) (*AE* 2014, 853): *[--- Au]g(ust-) sacrum, coll(egii) u[tri]c(lariorum) / [--- T(itus) Iulius T(iti) f(ilius) Vo]l(tinia tribu) Dolabell [a – / – cum? ---]ma [u]xor[e – / ------.*

15 See also *AE* 2014, 851.

16 *CIL* 6.9254: *Collegio / centonariorum / [---] / cum basi marmorea et ceriolarib(us) / duobus aereis habentibus effigi/em Cupidinis tenentis calathos, / L(ucius) Sextilius Seleucus, decurio, d(onum) d(edit); / hoc amplius ark(ae) rei p(ublicae) collegii s(upra) s(cripti) / donum dedit (denarios) V (millia), ut ex usuris / centesimis eius quantitatis / quae efficit annuos (denarios) DC, die / VIIII kal(endas) octobr(es), natali diui / Augusti, erogentur ex ark(a).* See Liu (2009: 342, no. 41): "Lucius Sextilius Seleucus, *decurio*, gave to the *collegium centonariorum* . . . with a marble base and two bronze candlesticks bearing an effigy of Cupid holding baskets. In addition, he gave five thousand *denarii* to the treasury of the above-mentioned *collegium*, the interest of which (at a rate of 12%) – six hundred *denarii* – is to be paid out from the treasury every year on September 23, the birthday of the deified Augustus."

17 *AE* 1995, 573: (a) *L(ucio) Domitio Epaphrod[ito] / et M(arco) Liuio Terti[o], / dec(urionibus) in colleg(io) fab[r(um), / co]lleg(ium) incrementoru[m / c]ultorum Minerua[e] / ex aere conlato meren[t(ibus)], / l(oco) d(ato) d(ecreto) d(ecurionum).* (b) *L(ucius) Domitius Epaphroditus, decurio in col[leg(io) fabr(um)]. / Is anno primo magisteri sui imaginem ar[genteam] / cum base et hasta pro parte dimidia coll(egio) fa[br(um) dedit]. / Isdem pridie Nonas Iulias ad mare euntibus p[an(em) et uin(um) et?] / pernas IX et cibaris aeris octonos d[edit].* [(a) "To the deserving Lucius Domitius Epaphroditus and Marcus Livius Tertius, *decuriones* in the craftsmen's association, the association of the young worshippers of Minerva (made this monument) by subscription, the place being given by a decree of the city councilors." (b) "Lucius Domitius Epaphroditus, *decurio* in the craftsmen's association. During the first year of his charge, he gave a half of a silver image, with its base and its spear. On July 6, he also gave to people going to the sea bread, wine, nine hams and eight *asses* each."]

18 *CIL* 11.6358: *L(ucio) Apuleio / Brasidae, / habenti IIII lib(erorum) ius, / dat(um) ab Imp(eratore) M(arco) [[Aurelio / Commodo]] Aug(usto), / VIuir(o) Aug(ustali), / ornament(is) / decurional(ibus) honor(ato) / et Aug(ustali) mun(icipi) Ael(i) Karn(unti) / colleg(ium) fabr(um) / patrono et quinq(uennali), / ob eximiam eius erga / se liberalitatem, / cuius dedicatione cum / collega singulis (sestertios) n(ummos) L, /*

adiecto pane et uin(o), ded(it), / l(oco) d(ato) d(ecreto) d(ecurionum). ["To Lucius Apuleius Brasidas, having the right of the four children, given by the Emperor Marcus Aurelius Commodus Augustus, *seuir Augustalis*, adorned with the insignia of city councilor and *Augustalis* in the *municipium Aelium* of *Carnuntum*, the craftsmen's association (erected this statue) for its patron and president, because of his amazing generosity. At the dedication, he gave with his colleague fifty sesterces to each, plus bread and wine, the place being given by a decree of the city councilors."] In Pompeii, the daily wage of an unskilled laborer was between one and a quarter and four sesterces.

19 *CIL* 12.4393b, l. 8–10: . . . *[seste]rtia sedecem millia nummum, V K(alendas) Maias primas, die natali meo, / [ar]cae uestrae inferam eaque die usuras totius anni computatas / [ass]e octono pernumerabo* . . . ["On April 28, my birthday, I will pay sixteen thousand sesterces to your treasury and, on the same day, I will count the interests of an whole year out, at a rate of one for eight *denarii*."]

20 *TPSulp*. 66, revised by *AE* 2000, 330.

21 Tran (2013: 295–6, 310–11), about *Dig*. 19.3.1 pr-1, 19.5.13 pr., 17.2.44, 19.5.17.1.

22 Petr. 58.11.

23 *Dicta Catonis* 15.

24 *CIL* 6.9663: *D(is) M(anibus). / In hoc tumulo iacet corpus exanimis / cuius spiritus inter deos receptus est. / Sic enim meruit L(ucius) Statius Onesimus, / uiae Appiae multorum annorum negotia(n)s, / homo super omnes fidelissimus, / cuius fama in aeterno nota est, / qui uixit sine macula an(nos) p(lus) m(inus) LXVIII. / Statia Crescentina co(n)iux / marito dignissimo et merito, / cum quo uixit cum bona concordia, / sine alteritrum animi lesionem, / bene merenti fecit.* ["To the gods *Manes*. In this tomb lies a lifeless body, whose spirit has been received amongst gods. Indeed he deserves so, Lucius Statius Onesimus, businessman on the via Appia for many years, the most loyal of all men, whose reputation is known eternally, who lived more or less sixty-eight years without stain. Statia Crescentina, his wife, to the worthiest and most deserving husband, with whom she lived in good harmony, without hurting each other's feelings, made (this monument)."]

25 Veyne (2000: 1187).

26 *Amicitia* and *fides* were based on reciprocity, a traditional value amongst "cultural beliefs" which (as shown by Verboven, 2012) impacted greatly the Roman economy.

27 For example, Bang (2008: 249–62) and Broekaert (2011).

28 Liu (2008).

29 See *e.g.*, *AE* 1998, 282 (benefaction to the *collegium dendrophorum* at *Lauinium*).

30 *CIL* 5.5869: *Innocenti cum Encratio uiuas. / Gen(io) et Hon(ori) / Magi Germani Statori / Marsiani, eq(uitis) R(omani) eq(uo) p(ublico), dec(urionis) dec(uriae) V, / ex (centuria) IIII coll(egi) fabr(um) et centon(ariorum),/ curat(oris) ark(ae) Titianae coll(egi) s(upra) s(cripti) / anni CLI, colon(iae) G(allienianae) A(ugustae) F(elicis) Med(iolani), / et Iunoni / Cissoniae Aphrodite eius, / (centuriae) XII ex coll(egio) s(upra) s(cripto) patronis/ plura merentibus. / Innocenti qui sic agis bene uiuas.* ["To Innocens, may you live with Encratius! To the Genius and Honor of Magius Germanus Stator Marsianus, Roman knight, *decurio* of the fifth *decuria*, member of the fourth *centuria* of the craftsmen's and textile workers' association, *curator* of the *arca Titiana* of this above-mentioned association, during the 151st year (of the association), in the *colonia Gallieniana Augusta Felix* of Milan, and to the Juno of his wife Cissonia Aphrodite, the twelve *decuriae* of the association mentioned above to their very deserving patrons. To Innocens, who behaves so, may you live well!"] See Scuderi (2007: 733 n. 67).

31 Andreau (2012).

32 *AE* 2009, 828: *L(uci) Veturi L(uci) fil(i) Quirina [---] / leg(ionis) XX V(aleriae) V(ictricis), qui sibi uiuu[s –]/iae uxori suae fecit e[t legauit] / collegio fabrorum f[errariorum] / Araus(iensium) fundum Domit[ianum], / ut ex reditu eius om[nibus*

annis per ui]/ces ab eis parentar[etur]. ["Of Lucius Veturius (. . .), son of Lucius, from the tribe *Quirina*, (. . .) of the twentieth legion *Valeria Victrix*. He made (this monument) in his lifetime for himself and (. . .)ia, his wife, and he bequeathed to the smiths' association from Orange the estate of Domitius, so that from its return they sacrifice each year alternately for them."]

33 Fikhman (1994: 37) and Liu (2008: 245); about P. Strasb. IV, 287.

34 Broekaert and Zuiderhoek (2015: 152–6).

35 Tran (2017).

36 *Dig.* 50.16.235.1: *"Fabros tignarios" dicimus non eos dumtaxat, qui tigna dolarent, sed omnes qui aedificarent.* ["We do not describe as 'carpenters' only those who cut wood but every one who is a builder."]

37 *CIL* 14.4569.

38 Compare *CIL* 6.33856 and 33858 to 9405.

39 DeLaine (1997: 201, 2000: 231).

40 Hawkins (2013: 176–8, 2016: 74–9).

41 *CIL* 14.374: *Marco Licinio / Priuato, / decurionatus ornamentis honorato et / biselliario, in primis constituto / inlatis rei publicae sestertis / quinquaginta milibus n(ummum), // quaestori et q(uin)q(uennali) corporis pistorum Ostiens(ium) et Port(ensium), // magistro quinquennal(i) collegi(i) / fabrum tignuariorum lustri XXVIIII et decurioni eiusdem / numeri decur(iae) XVI, decuriali scrib(ae) // patri et auo decurionum // librario, tribuli tribus Claudiae// patri equitum Romanorum // patruum et liberorum clientium, / uniuersus numerus / caligatorum / collegi(i) fabrum tignuariorum Ostiens(ium) / magistro optimo, ob amorem et merita eius, / l(oco) d(ato) d(ecreto) d(ecurionum) p(ublice).* ["To Marcus Licinius Privatus, honored with the insignia of city councilor and a seat of honor, mainly because he gave fifty thousand sesterces to the public treasury, treasurer and president of the bakers' association of Ostia and Portus, president of the carpenters' association for the twenty-eighth *lustrum* and *decurio* of the sixteenth *decuria* of the same unit, member in the *decuria* of record-clerks, father and grandfather of city councilors, member in the tribe *Claudia* of the fathers and free clients, father of Roman knights, the whole soldier unit of the carpenters' association of Ostia to the best president ever, because of his love and merits, the place being given publicly by a decree of the city councilors."] See Caldelli and Gregori (2010: 137–41, no. 3).

42 Thomas (2004).

43 *Dig.* 13.6.5.7 (translated by A. Watson): *Nam et si seruum tibi tectorem commodauero et de machina ceciderit, periculum meum esse Namusa ait. Sed ego ita hoc uerum puto, si tibi commodaui, ut et in machina operaretur: ceterum si ut de plano opus faceret, tu eum imposuisti in machina, aut si machinae culpa factum minus diligenter non ab ipso ligatae uel funium perticarumque uetustate, dico periculum, quod culpa contigit rogantis commodatum, ipsum praestare debere. Nam et Mela scripsit, si seruus lapidario commodatus sub machina perierit, teneri fabrum commodati, qui neglegentius machinam colligauit.* ["Clearly, if I lend you a slave who is a builder and he falls from the scaffolding, Namusa holds the risk to be mine. But I think it is right only if I lent him to work on scaffolding. But if the loan was for him to work on the ground and you sent him up scaffolding, or else if the disaster happened because the scaffolding was defective having been lashed together, not by him, with too little care or with old ropes or poles, then I maintain that the risk which materializes from the fault of the borrower must be made good by him. In fact, it is also held in Mela's writings that if a borrowed slave stonemason dies in a collapse of scaffolding, the builder is liable in action on loan for use for too negligently putting together the scaffolding."]

44 *Dig.* 17.1.26.8 (translated by A. Watson): *Faber mandatu amici sui emit seruum decem, et fabricam docuit : deinde uendidit eum uiginti, quos mandati iudicio coactus est soluere.* ["On the mandate of his friend, a smith bought a slave for ten and taught him smithing; then he sold him for twenty which he was compelled to pay over in an action on mandate."]

45 Tran (2013: 159–75).
46 Tran (2006: 501–7).
47 Tran (2006: 409–49).
48 Mouritsen (2011).
49 *CIL* 14.4621: *P(ublio) Aufidio / P(ubli) fil(io) Quir(ina) / Forti, / [II]uir(o), q(uaestori) aer(arii) Ost(iensis) V, / p(atrono) c(oloniae),/ [Fa]ustianus, Epictetus, / [Eu]frosynus, Ianuarius / patrono / indulgentissimo.* ["To Publius Aufidius Fortis, son of Publius, from the tribe *Quirina, duumuir, quaestor* of the treasury of Ostia five times, patron of the colony, Faustianus, Epictetus, Eufrosynus and Ianuarius, to the most benevolent patron."]
50 *CIL* 14.303: *P(ublio) Aufidio P(ubli) f(ilio) Quirina / Forti / [d(ecurionum) d(ecreto)? decu]rioni adlecto, IIuiro, /[quaesto]ri aerari Ostiensium IIII, / [praefe]cto fabrum/ [tignuariorum] Ostis, patrono / corporum mensorum / frumentariorum / et urinatorum, decurioni adlecto / Africae Hippone Regio,/ corpus mercatorum / frumentariorum/ q(uin)q(uennali) perpetuo.* ["To Publius Aufidius Fortis, son of Publius, from the tribe *Quirina*, elected city councilor by a decree of the city councilors, *duumuir, quaestor* of the treasury of Ostia four times, prefect of the carpenters at Ostia, patron of the associations of the wheat measurers and of the divers, elected city councilor of *Hippo Regius* in Africa, the association of the wheat merchants to their perpetual president."]
51 *CIL* 14.161: *Q(uinto) Calpurnio C(ai) f(ilio)/ Quir(ina) Modesto, / proc(uratori) Alpium, proc(uratori) Ostiae / ad annon(am), proc(uratori) Lucaniae, / corpus mercatorum/ frumentariorum, per / M(arcum) Aemilium Saturum / et P(ublium) Aufidium Faustian(um), / q(uin)q(uennales), ex decreto corporat(orum), / q(uaestoribus) M(arco) Licinio Victore et/ P(ublio) Aufidio Epicteto, / l(oco) d(ato) d(ecreto) d(ecurionum) p(ublice).* ["To Quintus Calpurnius Modestus, son of Caius, from the tribe *Quirina, procurator* of the Alps, *procurator* of Ostia for the grain supply, *procurator* of Lucania, the association of the wheat merchants, through Marcus Aemilius Saturus and Publius Aufidius Faustianus, its presidents, by a decree of the association members, Marcus Licinius Victor and Publius Aufidius Epictetus being treasurers, the place being given publicly by a decree of the city councilors."]
52 Liu (2017).

Bibliography

Agusta-Boularot, Sandrine, and Emmanuelle Rosso, eds. *Corpora et scholae: Lieux, pratiques et commémoration de la sociabilité en Gaule méridionale et dans les régions voisines.* Vol. 2 of *Signa et tituli.* Nîmes: École antique de Nîmes, 2014.

Andreau, Jean. "Les cités prêtaient-elles de l'argent à intérêt?" Pages 191–9 in *Gérer les territoires, les patrimoines et les crises: Le quotidien municipal II.* Edited by Laurent Lamoine, Clara Berrendonner, and Mireille Cébeillac-Gervasoni. Clermont-Ferrand: Presses Universitaires Blaise-Pascal, 2012.

Bang, Peter F. *The Roman Bazaar: A Comparative Study of Trade and Markets in a Tributary Empire.* Cambridge: Cambridge University Press, 2008.

Bollmann, Beate. *Römische Vereinshäuser: Untersuchungen zu den Scholae der römischen Berufs-, Kult- und Augustalen-Kollegien in Italien.* Mainz: von Zabern, 1998.

Broekaert, Wim. "Partners in Business: Roman Merchants and the Potential Advantages of Being a *Collegiatus.*" *Ancient Society* 41 (2011): 221–56.

Broekaert, Wim, and Arjan Zuiderhoek. "Society, the Market, or Actually Both? Networks and Allocation of Credit and Capital Goods in the Roman Economy." *Cahiers du Centre Gustave-Glotz* 26 (2015): 141–90.

Caldelli, Maria Letizia, and Gian Luca Gregori. "Sulle ripartizioni interne alle tribù urbane e rustiche." Pages 133–47 in *Le tribù romane: Atti della XVIe Rencontre sur l'épigraphie*. Edited by Maria Silvestrini. Bari: Edipuglia, 2010.

Christol, Michel, and Dominique Darde. "Le site des AGF à Nîmes: Archéologie, décor, inscriptions." Pages 47–64 in *Corpora et scholae: Lieux, pratiques et commémoration de la sociabilité en Gaule méridionale et dans les régions voisines*. Vol. 2 of *Signa et tituli*. Edited by Sandrine Agusta-Boularot and Emmanuelle Rosso. Nîmes: École antique de Nîmes, 2014.

Clemente, Guido. "Il patronato nei collegia dell'impero romano." *Studi Classici e Orientali* 21 (1972): 160–213.

DeLaine, Janet. *The Baths of Caracalla: A Study in the Design, Construction, and Economics of Large-Scale Building Projects in Imperial Rome*. Portsmouth, RI: Journal of Roman Archaeology, 1997.

———. "Bricks and Mortar: Exploring the Economics of Building Techniques at Rome and Ostia." Pages 230–68 in *Economies beyond Agriculture in the Classical World*. Edited by David J. Mattingly and John Salmon. London: Routledge, 2000.

De Robertis, Francesco Maria. *Il fenomeno associative nel mondo romano: dai collegi della Repubblica alle corporazioni del Basso Impero*. Napoli: Liberia scientifica editrice, 1955.

Dondin-Payre, Monique, and Nicolas Tran, eds. *Collegia. Le phénomène associatif dans l'Occident romain*. Bordeaux: Ausonius éditions, 2012.

Fagan, Garrett G. "Social Life in Town and Country." Pages 495–514 in *The Oxford Handbook of Roman Epigraphy*. Edited by Christer Bruun and Jonathan Edmonson. Oxford: Oxford University Press, 2015.

Fikhman, Itzhak F. "Sur quelques aspects socio-économiques de l'activité des corporations professionnelles de l'Égypte byzantine." *Zeitschrift für Papyrologie und Epigraphik* 103 (1994): 19–40.

Hawkins, Cameron. "Manufacturing." Pages 175–94 in *The Cambridge Companion to the Roman Economy*. Edited by Walter Scheidel. Cambridge: Cambridge University Press, 2013.

———. *Roman Artisans and the Urban Economy*. Cambridge: Cambridge University Press, 2016.

Liu, Jinyu. *Collegia Centonariorum: The Guilds of Textile Dealers in the Roman West*. Leiden: Brill, 2009.

———. "The Economy of Endowments: The Case of Roman Associations." Pages 231–56 in *Pistoi dia tèn technèn: Bankers, Loans and Archives in the Ancient World; Studies in Honour of Raymond Bogaert*. Edited by Koenraad Verboven, Katelijn Vandorpe, and Véronique Chankowski. Leuven: Peeters, 2008.

———. "Group Membership, Trust Networks, and Social Capital: A Critical Analysis." Pages 203–26 in *Works, Labor and Professions in the Roman World*. Edited by Christian Laes and Koenraad Verboven. Leiden: Brill, 2017.

Mouritsen, Henrik. *The Freedman in the Roman World*. Cambridge: Cambridge University Press, 2011.

Perry, Johnatan S. *The Roman "Collegia": The Modern Evolution of an Ancient Concept*. Leiden: Brill, 2006.

Reali, Mauro. *Il contributo dell'epigrafia latina allo studio dell'amicitia: Il caso della Cisalpina*. Firenze: La Nuova Italia, 1998.

Rodríguez, Oliva, Nicolas Tran, and Begoña Soler, eds. *Los espacios de reunión de las asociaciones romanas: Diálogos desde la arqueología y la historia, en homenaje a Bertrand Goffaux*. Sevilla: Editorial Universidad de Sevilla, 2016.

Scuderi, Rita. "Donne di rilievo nell'epigrafia della Transpadana." *Athenaeum* 95.2 (2007): 725–36.

Thomas, Yan. "Le droit comme matrice des catégories économiques à Rome." Pages 201–25 in *Mentalités et choix économiques des Romains*. Edited by Jean Andreau, Jérôme France, and Sylvie Pittia. Bordeaux: Ausonius éditions, 2004.

Tran, Nicolas. "Ars et Doctrina: The Socioeconomic Identity of Roman Skilled Workers (First Century BC–Third Century AD)." Pages 246–61 in *Works, Labor and Professions in the Roman World*. Edited by Christian Laes and Koenraad Verboven. Leiden: Brill, 2017.

———. "Les collèges dans les espaces civiques de l'Occident romain: Diverses formes de dialogue entre sphère publique et sphère privée." Pages 143–59 in *Interactions entre sphère publique et sphère privée dans l'espace de la cité romaine: Agents, vecteurs, signification*. Edited by Alexandra Dardenay and Emmanuelle Rosso. Bordeaux: Ausonius, 2013.

———. *Dominus tabernae: Le statut de travail des artisans et des commerçants de l'Occident romain (Ier siècle av. J.-C.-IIIe siècle ap. J.-C.)*. Rome: École Française de Rome, 2013.

———. "Entreprises de construction, vie associative et organisation du travail dans la Rome impériale et à Ostie." *L'Antiquité Classique* 86 (2017): 115–27.

———. *Les membres des associations romaines: Le rang social des collegiati en Italie et en Gaule sous le Haut-Empire*. Rome: École Française de Rome, 2006.

———. "Un Picton à Ostie: M. Sedatius Severianus et les corps de lénunculaires sous le principat d'Antonin le Pieux." *Revue des Études Anciennes* 114.2 (2012): 323–44.

Verboven, Koenraad. "Cité et réciprocité: Le rôle des croyances culturelles dans l'économie romaine." *Annales: Histoire, Sciences Sociales* 67.4 (2012): 913–42.

Veyne, Paul. "La 'plèbe moyenne' sous le Haut-Empire." *Annales: Histoire, Sciences Sociales* 55.6 (2000): 1169–99.

Waltzing, Jean-Pierre. *Étude historique sur les corporations professionnelles chez les Romains*. Leuven: Peeters, 1895–1900.

Wilson, Stephen G. "Voluntary Associations: An Overview." Pages 1–16 in *Voluntary Associations in the Graeco-Roman World*. Edited by John S. Kloppenborg and Stephen G. Wilson. London: Routledge, 1996.

Epilogue

David B. Hollander and Thomas R. Blanton IV

In September of 2018, Jeff Bezos, founder of Amazon, announced the Bezos Day One Fund and a pledge of two billion dollars to help homeless families and create a network of preschools in "underserved communities."[1] While many praised this act of philanthropy, others expressed concern over an unelected private individual relegating to himself such a major role in determining how children are educated. Some suggested that this large gift would not have been necessary if Amazon were taxed properly and noted that Bezos, whose company had recently lobbied against taxes that would have accomplished some of the same ends, was receiving good publicity at an opportune moment. This sort of debate must have been quite familiar to inhabitants of the Greco-Roman world since euergetism by the wealthy was a regular feature of urban life for much of classical antiquity, as the chapters of Marc Domingo Gygax, Rachel Meyers, and Arjan Zuiderhoek all show. A prominent form of extramercantile wealth transfer, benefaction has been a major focus of this volume, but we need to remain aware of the sometimes-fuzzy boundary between the mercantile and extramercantile as well as their shared features. Domingo Gygax, for example, notes that euergetism involved an exchange of donations and honors, and it was important the honors granted to the benefactor be proportional to the gift, not unlike a market transaction. As Zuiderhoek puts it, "The exchange of gifts for honors . . . often require[d] a lot of institutionalized (and partly ritualized) bargaining." He also points out that euergetism interacted at least indirectly with the market economy in a variety of ways (the lending of foundation capital, the renting of foundation real estate, etc.). Along the same lines, Meyers observes that the buildings and banquets provided by benefactors in Hispania Tarraconensis often required considerable amounts of labor and material, presumably supplied by market transactions. The same remains true today. Bezos himself nicely (if curiously) illustrated how the market insinuates itself into acts of benefaction by declaring of his preschools that "the child will be the customer." All three of our chapters that discuss benefaction make clear, however, that the dynamics of this sort of extramercantile exchange are complicated. The motivations behind acts of euergetism were liable to be a combination of political, social (e.g., elite competition), and economic considerations. Moreover, John T. Fitzgerald's chapter demonstrates that writers such as Xenophon and Philodemus understand *oikonomia* to be a branch of ethics, as the well-being of members of household and community are fundamental considerations in financial planning, both at the level of the household and the polis. Ethics, with all the political considerations that it entails, as well as intra-elite competition for prestige, the operation of markets, and the provisioning and defense of household and polis numbered among the factors that shaped the ancient economy in complex interaction.

Another major focus of this volume has been associations, whose role in the ancient economy has long been the subject of lively debate. Here, again, it is difficult to distinguish the boundary between the mercantile and the extramercantile; Nicolas Tran notes the "porosity" between them. While granting that occupational guilds probably created trust networks, John Kloppenborg observes that it is uncertain to what extent members actively exploited the economic opportunities created by such networks. Tran also notes the networks created by associations and enumerates the potential economic benefits to members of *collegia*: access to nicely appointed meeting places, distributions of money or food, and perhaps easier access to loans of money or slaves. *Collegia* could generate solidarity among workers, and that could, in turn, yield economic advantages; but, Tran cautions, there was also vertical, hierarchical solidarity, and we should not underestimate the extent to which the richest members used associations for their own ends.

In devoting this volume to the extramercantile economy, we are not trying to deny the importance of markets in the Greco-Roman world but to work toward rectifying an imbalance of attention. Even if, as Temin argues, market exchange was the "modal form of economic integration,"[2] there is ample evidence for non-market transfers of wealth ranging from small private gifts to the wholesale confiscation of cities, lands, and their people. The essays presented in this volume focus on only a few aspects of the extramercantile economy (see the Introduction for a planned follow-up publication examining taxation and the fiscal effects of imperialism) but prompt two preliminary observations. First, as already noted, the mercantile and extramercantile are often intimately connected. Some acts of euergetism were large enough to have a substantial impact at least on a local economy, and associations could certainly enhance their members' economic well-being. That said, these institutions were not invariably positive forces. Large gifts could disrupt established markets. Competition among elite benefactors could be financially ruinous, and associations could stifle innovation or artificially inflate prices to the detriment of consumers. Second, the New Institutional Economics is not as helpful a framework for understanding the ancient economy as it initially seemed. Kloppenborg questions its usefulness with respect to occupational guilds, while Thomas Blanton and David Hollander observe that NIE tends to privilege the construct of the market. Future economic histories of the ancient world must pay more attention to developments beyond the market and engage in the "methodological pluralism" recommended by David Lewis (2018: 21–2). Given the vast literatures involved, this is an incredibly difficult task, but the results should be fascinating.

Although the essays represented in this volume concern benefaction, euergetism, and *collegia* in ancient Greece, Rome, and Spain, and do not touch per se on early Christian or Judaic literature, the issues examined are relevant not only to classicists, but also to scholars of early Christianity and Judaism in the Greco-Roman period as well. There are two main reasons for this. The first and most obvious reason is that scholars in the areas of early Christianity and early Judaism have already shown an interest in patronage networks, with studies either affirming or denying that patronage was a salient aspect of early Judaic and Christian assemblies or, in a more nuanced approach, showing that while some aspects of patronage systems were adopted in a fairly straightforward manner, other aspects were significantly modified and adapted (e.g., Schwartz, 2009; Joubert, 2000; Chow, 1993; Clarke, 1993; Friesen, 2010; Crook, 2004, 2017; Neyrey, 2005). Inseparable from issues of patronage and euergetism are broader questions of gift exchange, as Domingo Gygax and Zuiderhoek make clear in their contributions in this volume. The question of gift exchange in early Christian assemblies has likewise received attention in recent studies of the epistles of Paul of Tarsus (Briones, 2013; Barclay, 2015; Blanton, 2017). The studies presented in this volume thus not only provide additional data on issues already recognized as important in the fields of early Judaic and early Christian studies, but also present cogent arguments to show that issues of gift exchange, patronage, and euergetism themselves must be understood as significant aspects of "the ancient economy," which cannot be reduced to discussions of market exchange.

Beyond the obvious relevance of the essays presented in this volume to the issues of patronage and gift exchange, there is another issue that is both less obvious and arguably more important. Generally speaking, scholars of early Judaism and early Christianity are trained in philology, textual criticism, and hermeneutical approaches to the Bible as a foundational element in the construction of contemporary Judaic and Christian identities and practices. Although this type of training facilitates studies that have yielded impressive results concerning the history of the transmission, interpretation, and reception of biblical texts, it leaves scholars at a disadvantage when questions of economic organization arise. In what may attempt to pass for an "economic" analysis of a given text, scholars often merely apply one traditional tool of their trade, that is, textual analysis; but the result amounts to nothing more than a repetition of what a text has to say, for example, about wealth, poverty, or charitable donations.

What is missing in such textually oriented approaches is any attempt (1) to reflect seriously on the methods that historians use to analyze ancient economies (issues addressed by Blanton and Hollander and Kloppenborg in this volume); (2) to reconstruct broad networks of economic activity, on the macrolevel of the Roman Empire and the microlevel of particular local communities in the provinces (Meyers's essay in this volume offers an example of how the latter topic might be approached); and (3) to place particular Judaic or early Christian communities, associations, and agents (i.e., named individuals and/or the authors of particular texts) within those networks of economic activity. If we are to make any progress in our understanding of broadly "economic" issues in early Judaism and early Christianity, specific texts and artifacts need to be placed within the macro- and microlevels of economic activity of Hellenistic and Roman Empires, as various provinces did not function in an economic vacuum, but participated, willingly or unwillingly, in the economic activities of imperial powers (e.g., patronage, predation, plunder, taxation, tribute, trade, enslavement, and property destruction).

In order to remedy these methodological shortcomings in studies of early Christianity and early Judaism, more sustained interaction with the work of classicists, economic historians, and archaeologists will be required. Granted, this is no small task, but it is one that will be necessary if scholars are to move beyond approaches that simply recapitulate what particular texts have to say, for example, about wealth, poverty, and charitable giving, in attempts to understand and reconstruct the broad systems that regulated economic production and distribution. Thus, if it wishes to provide anything that might be termed an "economic analysis," exegesis must move beyond the scrutiny both of the plaintive cries of the exploited and of the impassioned pleas to wealthy exploiters to amass credit with God (see Eubank, 2013) and community by donating lavishly; it must certainly also consider the ways in which those utterances make manifest different positions within the sociopolitical systems that regulated the production and distribution of goods and currency in antiquity.

As noted in the introduction, the "economic history" of early Christianity has yet to be written. By offering an overview and criticisms of some of the methods (particularly NIE) being used by classicists and economic historians in attempts to understand the "ancient economy," and by showing that the economy must be understood holistically, incorporating both its mercantile and extramercantile aspects, the present volume hopes to provide some of the tools that will be necessary when attempts are made to write such an economic history. Moreover, the studies in this volume indicate important avenues of research for classicists interested in economic history and for scholars in Judaic studies who are interested in the economic analysis of ancient texts.

Notes

1 Jeff Bezos, "Day One Fund," Twitter, https://twitter.com/JeffBezos/status/1040253 796293795842.
2 Temin (2001: 181).

Bibliography

Barclay, John M.G. *Paul and the Gift*. Grand Rapids and Cambridge: Eerdmans, 2015.

Blanton, Thomas R., IV. *A Spiritual Economy: Gift Exchange in the Letters of Paul of Tarsus*. Synkrisis: Comparative Approaches to Early Christianity in Greco-Roman Context. New Haven: Yale University Press, 2017.

Briones, David. *Paul's Financial Policy: A Socio-Theological Approach*. LNTS 494. London: Bloomsbury T&T Clark, 2013.

Chow, John K. *Patronage and Power: A Study of Social Networks in Corinth*. JSNTSup 75. Sheffield: JSOT Press, 1993.

Clarke, Andrew D. *Secular and Christian Leadership in Corinth: A Socio-Historical and Exegetical Study of 1 Corinthians 1–6*. AGJU 18. Leiden: Brill, 1993.

Crook, Zeba A. "Economic Location of Benefactors in Pauline Communities." Pages 183–204 in *Paul and Economics: A Handbook*. Edited by Thomas R. Blanton IV and Raymond Pickett. Minneapolis: Fortress, 2017.

———. *Reconceptualising Conversion: Patronage, Loyalty, and Conversion in the Religions of the Ancient Mediterranean*. BZNW 130. Berlin: de Gruyter, 2004.

Eubank, Nathan. *Wages of Cross-Bearing and Debt of Sin: The Economy of Heaven in Matthew's Gospel*. BZNW 196. Berlin: De Gruyter, 2013.

Friesen, Stephen J. "Paul and Economics: The Jerusalem Collection as an Alternative to Patronage." Pages 27–54 in *Paul Unbound: Other Perspectives on the Apostle*. Edited by Mark D. Given. Peabody, MA: Hendrickson, 2010.

Joubert, Stephan. *Paul as Benefactor: Reciprocity, Strategy and Theological Reflection in Paul's Collection*. WUNT 2/124. Tübingen: Mohr Siebeck, 2000.

Lewis, David. "Behavioural Economics and Economic Behaviour in Classical Athens." Pages 15–46 in *Ancient Greek History and Contemporary Social Science*. Edited by M. Canevaro, Andrew Erskine, B. Gray, and J. Ober. Edinburgh: Edinburgh University Press, 2018.

Neyrey, Jerome H. "God, Benefactor and Patron: The Major Cultural Model for Interpreting the Deity in Greco-Roman Antiquity." *Journal for the Study of the New Testament* 27.4 (2005): 465–92.

Schwartz, Seth. *Were the Jews a Mediterranean Society? Reciprocity and Solidarity in Ancient Judaism*. Princeton: Princeton University Press, 2009.

Temin, Peter. "A Market Economy in the Early Roman Empire." *Journal of Roman Studies* 91 (2001): 169–81.

Index

Achilles 32
aestimatum 134
Africa Proconsularis 92
Agamemnon 31
Aglietta, Michel 20
agriculture 16, 32–3, 54
Agrippa II 2–3
Albernus Major 120
Alcibiades 73
alimenta 57, 86
alimentary programs *see alimenta*
altruism 18, 69
amicitia 116, 134; *see also* friendship
amphitheaters 97–9
Andreau, Jean 15, 135
antidosis 72, 74
Antisthenes 32–3
Antoninus Pius 98, 101
aqueducts 52, 54, 86–9
Aristogiton 75
Aristotle 34, 37, 41–2, 69–71
Arnaoutoglou, Ilias 118, 126n69
artisans 110, 114, 130, 133, 134
Arucci 88
Asmis, Elizabeth 39, 41
associations: cultic 109–10, 113–16, 118, 120; voluntary 114, 130, 135
Athens 32–7, 68, 70–9, 118
Augustales 89, 94
Augustus 83, 96, 135

Badian, Ernst 34
Baetica 85, 88, 96, 98
Bagnall, Roger 111, 113
bakers 109, 110, 137
Bang, Peter 16, 17, 52
banquets 52, 84, 86, 100–1, 109, 132–3
Barcino 83, 90, 92–6
barter 43, 53
baths 52, 86–7, 94–5, 98–9, 132

behavioral economics 18
belt-makers 110
benefaction 17, 52–4, 63–4, 74, 77–9, 83–101, 146–7
Bezos, Jeff 146
Bithynia 56
Blaug, Mark 10–11
Boer, Roland 1, 20, 22
Boulanger, André 63
Braudel, Fernand 51
bridges 86–9
bronze smiths 110
Bryson 42–6
Bücher, Karl 14
bullion 91
bylaws 108–9, 122

Calpurnius Bibulus, M. 90, 102n15
Cambridge Economic History of the Greco-Roman World 8, 13, 17, 18, 21n1
capital, social 114, 117, 120–1
capitalism 52, 68, 119
Carandini, Andrea 15–16
Cartagena 90–1
cartels 110, 117
Carthaginians 17, 83, 90, 92
Carthago Nova 90–4
Cartledge, Paul 36, 68
Castulo 90, 96–9
Cato the Elder 18
centonarii 109, 114, 132, 135
Christianity 3–5, 17, 20, 148–9
Cicero 33, 101, 110
Cimon 70, 72–3
Claudius 96–7, 99
Coase, Ronald 12–13, 52
cobblers 39, 110
collegia 107–10, 114–16, 130–3, 135–7, 139, 147
Collegia centonariorum 109, 132, 135

Printed in the United States
by Baker & Taylor Publisher Services